From

The Women's Press Ltd
34 Great Sutton Street, London EC1V 0DX

Lesley Saunders is a writer, mother, teacher and researcher. She is a classicist by education and disposition. Her poems have appeared in *One Foot on the Mountain, Why Children?, Bread and Roses* and a variety of magazines. She performs with three other poets, The Bloody Poets, whose aim is to 'put politics and poetry firmly together'. She is a contributor to *Sex and Love,* and is co-author of *Intercontinental Ballistic Poems* and *Room to Write.*

Lesley Saunders lives in Slough and is currently working on a book about miscarriage, *Hidden Loss,* to be published by The Women's Press in 1988.

LESLEY SAUNDERS
Editor

Glancing Fires

An Investigation into Women's Creativity

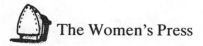 The Women's Press

First published by The Women's Press Ltd 1987
A member of the Namara Group
34 Great Sutton Street, London EC1V 0DX

British Library Cataloguing in Publication Data

Glancing Fires: an investigation into women's creativity.
  1. Creative ability   2. Women – Psychology
  I. Saunders, Lesley
  153.3'5   BF411

  ISBN 0-7043-4061-5

Typeset by Reprotype, Peterborough
Reproduced, printed and bound in Great Britain by
Hazell, Watson and Viney Ltd,
Aylesbury, Bucks

For Arvati

Energy has been liberated, but into what forms is it to
flow? To try the accepted forms, to discard the unfit, to
create others which are more fitting, is a task that must
be accomplished before there is freedom or
achievement.

Virginia Woolf, *Books and Portraits*

We the women making
something from this
ache-and-pain-a-me
back-o-hardness

Grace Nichols, *A Dangerous Knowing*

Landscape consists in the multiple, overlapping
intricacies and forms that exist in a given space at a
moment in time. Landscape is the texture of intricacy.

Annie Dillard, *Pilgrim at Tinker Creek*

A thousand thousand glancing fires
Seemed kindling in the air;
A thousand thousand silvery lyres
Resounded far and near:

Methought the very breath I breathed
Was full of sparks divine,
And all my heather-couch was wreathed
By that celestial shine.

From A Daydream by Emily Brontë

in *The Complete Poems of Emily Brontë*
ed. C. W. Hatfield, Columbia University Press 1941

Contents

Hollering for the Earth: Form

Introduction

I am paralysed with fear; I stare at the blank paper. Nothing comes.

I am walking down the street. An idea falls out of the sky into my mind. It explodes with life and meaning. I rush to get home and, in my room, to give ordered form to this glowing amoeba.

When I read what I have written, I am disappointed and ashamed. Is this what I thought would illumine the world, or at least my own consciousness of it?

I am with a group of women; we talk animatedly about the reasons why it's so difficult to write or paint, how bad we are at organising our time, how dreadful those moments before the first word is written, the first image attempted; how much worse knowing our skill in avoiding the desk or the easel altogether. When I get home, I remember one woman's poem: I cannot imagine writing anything as candid and beautiful.

I fall asleep and in the moments as consciousness melts, I compose and immediately forget a poem at once delicate, erotic and politically articulate.

What is it, to *create?*

And today the sun makes deep shadows on the uncut grass, yellow roses relax and open, small green knobs among the apple leaves show where the fruit will come; a child smiles herself awake; two engineers from the Chernobyl nuclear plant are said to be on the run, not seen or heard of since the explosion which also blew a hole in Nato governments' 'safeguards' against radiation; Margaret Thatcher persists in vetoing trade stoppages against the Botha government in South Africa; obituary notices of Simone de Beauvoir and Dora Russell appear in the papers. One woman in this book is harassed by immigration controls, another is leaving Britain because she can't earn a living here. Monica Sjöö writes of the death of a son, Gabriela Müller connects her painting to her childhood knowledge of Nazi Germany. By the time this is in print, other public outrages and personal sorrows will have succeeded, though not replaced, these.

These disparate elements are not simply a transient background to what the 20 women describe and examine in the following pages: one of the paradoxes of creative work is its dual role, celebratory and confrontational, its location at the heart of both stillness and struggle. The politics of the state and of social relationships, the visitations of death and loss, the renewals of pleasure and hope, have materialised in our lives and in this book in far from easy coexistence. Each writer tries to make sense of their interaction as best she can, provisionally or provocatively, in order to create answers to the question these events pose: Where do we go from here?

When someone asked me how I drew up this list of contributors, another woman replied, We're all names in Lesley's address book . . . Well, it wasn't quite the rabbit's friends and relations charabanc that implies; on the other hand, knowing many of the contributors personally meant I already knew and respected their work. From the beginning, I didn't want this book to try to establish its credentials on the basis of being 'representative', artistically or politically, all things to all women. I thought it ought, more usefully and realistically, to illuminate various corners of current activity. A few contributors have made a name for themselves and are making a living at their work; others normally identify themselves in quite other ways than by what appears here. Several of the women come from other countries, but all of them have experience of living and working in Britain in the 1980s. The cast-list, as an entity, is random but not arbitrary.

Nor is there any overall ideological coherence, though initially I wistfully imagined there might be. The experiences and issues that inhabit these pages would not be coerced under any but the most general programme, the name of which is feminism. And the only point of the name is to suggest a starting-point, not a termination. Feminism is about politics, its impetus is to change the existing balance of power. Having said that, the ensuing questions about how it is changed, by whom and for what end, and whether it is safe to assume that all women can make common cause, with a common agenda, are implied, tested, dismissed, reflected on. Without being unduly apologetic, I did not think it would be useful to suppose that the editor's view, in this case, was anything other than white, heterosexual, middle class, and could not therefore enjoy the fiction of perfect vision. Unabashedly, I have left ends loose and contradictions jostling.

I mention the politics before the art not because I think politics is more real, less frivolous, but because I don't want to lose sight of the commonplace that all art is made in a political environment. I don't hold the view that any art women make is somehow feminist underneath because it is made by a female; feminism is rational, not biological. I don't hold the view, either, that self-expression, *tout court*, constitutes art: art is also work with a relationship to a tradition, not simply a private therapy or secret indulgence. Explorations of that relationship, which for feminists is inevitably a problematic one, were what many contributors were impelled to make, directly or obliquely. For most women, this involved asking questions like, To what processes and products do I want to apply the word *creative?* What can be taken for granted and what has to be scrutinised under the eye of the reader?

Self-revelation, therapy, indulgence too, make their necessary interventions. It seems to me – given that our common environment is an increasingly incapacitating one – that first-hand accounts of the processes of creating, those material and mental struggles, these idiosyncratic decisions and inspirations, are important. In particular, what makes women want to, able to, write, sing, paint, dance, *now?* How do different women relate their biology and their politics to their work? To what extent is this an intrinsic or a tangential connection? What inhibits or bends a woman's work? How and why does change in her work come about? These are questions about personal values, subjectivities: anecdotal, circumstantial, practical.

In asking women if they would like to write for the book, I also left them to decide what they would write and how, in the hope that my editorial preconceptions might be as minor an influence on their contributions as possible. Autobiographical candour has become almost a hallmark of feminist writing; without elevating it into a priority, there are insights it can uniquely afford and some women chose to reveal profound vulnerabilities. In doing so they expose areas of more general contention.

While there is no overall 'truth' to be glimpsed, no propositions made that cannot be contradicted with equally good evidence and strong conviction, it does matter, I believe, what we make of the situation when conflict is painful and agreement lacks integrity. Feminists need to have some elbow room for their arguments – they are usually important ones – as well as to extend the collective space women may inhabit. An overriding demand for unanimity, an axiomatic appeal to sisterhood, narrows our space to the width of a tightrope. The gaps between these articles are as instructive as their overlaps.

What is common, I think, to these practices of making, connecting and risking is that they enlarge our conception of what is possible. They show us ways from what we are supposed to be towards what we, pluralistically, could be. The women here are making a space to go on exploring both immediate and long-standing meanings of creativity: what we express, how we express it and how we get access to our ability and confidence. Taking this space is in itself an act of resistance in a climate increasingly hostile to women's liberation from oppressive structures and to ordinary people's control over their own lives. But artistic expression can be more explicitly political than that; what forms and what issues can we constructively explore in our work and to whom do we want to direct our work? What do we call what we are doing? The point of identification, the touchstone, is different for black women and white, for heterosexual women and lesbians, for working-class women and middle-class ones. The possibility, the necessity, of moving outwards from our own centres of experience is fearful, exciting.

Arranging the articles was therefore a question of noting relative emphases: certain theoretical themes are developed in and through the individual pieces so that the presiding, though not exclusive, preoccupations of the three sections – the hinterland of the articles, so to speak – are respectively femaleness, politics and form; and these in wide rather than precise formulations. Of them, the first section bears, between the texts, the greatest theoretical burden; the second, by contrast, presents key political formulations without much editorial elaboration; while the third attempts to elucidate some general trends and tendencies, a sifting of straws in the wind beyond my competence but not beyond my responsibility.

A parallel but submerged theme in the book is that of 'space', 'territory'. Internal landscapes reflect and shape external territories in such a way that demarcations had better be signposts not fences and so, again, this theme is intended as a suggestive, not a definitive, one. Landscape is both an emblem of corporeal reality and symbolic of certain values, a site of moral debate: the ground on which I stand; the space we take; the territory we struggle over or attempt to reclaim; the earth from which each takes sustenance and to which each returns. Of course there is a danger of over-applying metaphors taken from nature – linking Woman to Nature encourages people to think sentimentally or deterministic-ally about both women and the physical world. Women are constantly at risk of having no meanings other than the culturally assigned ones*. Here, however, women are articulating 'space' in ways which construe their freedoms and confinements intelligibly. That exploration is done head-on in Ange Grunsell's writing, for instance, but emerges in the concerns and the language of many others. A major placing of the contradictions is in the experience of motherhood; on the other hand, a major source of political impetus is a concern for the literal survival of the known world.

The political rendering of personal space – deconstructing female body-images, legitimising women's needs for independent space, examining how differential power relations operate on the physical plane, teasing out the implications of locating women's space within or beyond the margins of male territory; the fact that we are occupiers of land, in and of the landscape, as well as shapers of spaces, makers of paths, vicarious but literal destroyers and builders of new geographies – all this means that the lexicon of landscape is both familiar and appropriately problematic.

In common with most editors, I suppose, I have had much joy and some anxiety compiling this collection; found new affections as well as confirming old ones; been challenged on my politics, on my style of editing, on my own creativity; demonstrated to my satisfaction the immense pleasures for head and heart in working, through thick and thin, with other feminist women. The ideas proposed in the editorial interludes are not wholly or even mainly my own – how could they be? – but the use to which they have been put is. Special thanks, for the quality both of their support and their criticism, go to Shirley Barrie, Catherine Itzin and Helen

*I thank Rachel May for her unpublished paper 'For modern women writers, what significance does the relationship between women and the natural world hold?'

McNeil of The Mothers, our own writers' group; to Gabriel Chanan, Brian Edgar and Penny Henrion, who with myself make up The Bloody Poets and who have nurtured my ideas, poetry and confidence; to Malcolm Rigg and Geoff Carr, to whose sure love, intellectual comradeship, word processor and fish soup these pages are in a material sense a testimonial; to Frances Glowing Moonwoman, a constant source of inspiration to me since we were both young and crazy, who has shared the sources and splendours of her creativity generously; to my children, Laura and Leon, for living these years with me and never once asking, Why do you have to be writing that book again, Mummy?; to Sarah Lefanu at The Women's Press for her professional, always gentle, guidance. Last, and most importantly, to each of the contributors, who responded, in their words and their commitment, beyond the demands made on them, extending the scope not only of what was planned but of what had been possible.

There was a princess locked in a tower. She let down a fine filament of hair; tied a thread on the end of that; then a string; and finally a rope, by which she escaped to the ground. She came down to earth; she grounded herself. It is on the earth – through our creative work – that our fantasies have their value, if value they have. These are our ropes translating us from tower to ground.

Acknowledgements are due to the author's estate and The Hogarth Press for permission to quote from Virginia Woolf's *Books and Portraits;* to the author and Jonathan Cape Ltd. for the quote from Annie Dillard's *Pilgrim at Tinker Creek;* to the author and Sheba Feminist Publishers for their kind permission to reprint the verse from one of Grace Nichols' poems in *A Dangerous Knowing: Four Black Women Poets*, Barbara Burford et al; to The Women's Press for the extract from Frankie Finn's *Out On The Plain;* the lines from 'A Litany for Survival', from *The Black Unicorn* by Audre Lorde, are used by permission of the publisher, W. W. Norton and Company, Inc. (Copyright © 1978 by Audre Lorde.)

Lesley Saunders

MAPPING INTERNAL LANDSCAPES: FEMALENESS

intolerable drain on my resources. Now I have time off and space to work with it but I continue to wrestle; this time with my own feelings of failure, inadequacy and guilt at not wanting to give and give and give. I run the gauntlet through echo upon echo of whispering ghosts; admonishing, vociferous women – mother, grandmother, back and on through all the years, through all the hands which have so lovingly prepared for me subjugation and martyrdom.

I murmur my rebellion.

I continue to do what I want . . . and shiver.
Those primeval rumblings . . . ?
Are my mountains moving?
Or are the gods indeed displeased?

I have found, and still find a great deal of pain in this process of adjustment. While still in the throes of it, I find it almost impossible to say what's wrong, but something is, and that sense of wrongness pervades my being and perfectly stifles creative impulse on all levels. Perhaps women will read this and wonder at my ignorant fumblings for truth. Perhaps they will then reach out a hand to me, help me lift myself up to their vision.

Afterthought: there are times when being with Rosie puts me spontaneously in touch with my inner, creative child, but these are moments which I rarely have the peace of spirit to gather and deepen.

The thought comes to me that being with children is not intrinsically the soul-destroying task which has largely been my experience so far, but I don't see how to get back the balance. Our mothers are wild-eyed and tormented. Our children are beaten and bleeding.

No doubt this has the seeds of creativity in it. Death-rebirth; confrontation-growth; if it were but recognised by her and by her culture, that the mother-woman needs a loving place to come to terms with herself and her children; support to undergo this, her own painstaking metamorphosis. But without this space, the process is singularly destructive to this woman who daily has her self-image undermined, often totally disintegrated, in relationship with her child(ren). There is little consolation in the fact that those images were mere delusion from the start. There is nothing but darkness, a cold wind blowing, with nowhere to shelter, to rest, to gather strength even to see the way she is going.

Our vocabulary is loaded with analogies and allegories between birth and art – the conception, gestation and delivery of a novel, the fertility or barrenness of ideas. It's hard to imagine expunging those references from conversation, serious or idle, about almost any project. But what do they mean? In the following piece, Ruth Noble develops a sense of the womb as matrix, simultaneously a physical place and an ontological space in which aspects of the self become manifest. I think there is an ambiguity about how far this is a resonant analogy and how far it is a literal description; the ambiguity arises from the way modern language and thought patterns are allocated to mind or body, unseen or visible, emotional or physical, with only the most tenuous of links spanning the resultant void between. Some women are attempting the difficult work of reorientating language so that it integrates experience more fully; the way Ruth's piece is written is central to its meaning. It is clear from other essays in this collection – Monica Sjöö's, Ange Grunsell's, Catherine Itzin's, for example – that the writers find uncomfortable a style which proposes a unified, controlling, detached strategy by the ego/author. Deliberately or not, the writer is bending and pulling at the language to make it accommodate her sense of ambivalence, non-exclusiveness – she cannot or will not compartmentalise, she uses three adjectives to describe something instead of one, she gives alternative meanings to what she has just written. This is not undisciplined prolixity; to do otherwise offends her defiant sense of fluidity, her grasp of the anarchy of primary experience.

The site of this kind of awareness is more than likely to have been her own body self. It is a commonplace that women's bodies have become alienated ground – neither fully human, when 'human' is made identical with male; nor yet 'natural', lacking in self-consciousness, capable of participating in life without a responsibility or a need to change how life and its meanings are constructed. Inhabiting her own body can feel to a woman like squatting invaded territory, having to boot out the colonisers and bivouackers, starting out with just a water-bucket and a rough shelter. (And how are we to build cities anew?)

Her femaleness, the source of the 'trouble', is the obvious and in some ways inevitable point of beginning the decolonisation. Here, under my fingers, is my gateway into myself. I carry new beginnings here inside me; I bleed and my blood gives me colour with which to paint myself, I begin to remake my image before my eyes – I reconstruct myself from the inside outwards. In this mode of creating, there is little or no space between the woman and her art: what she patterns – and liberates – in painting, dancing, writing, is herself.

Beginning to move, she creates a space that fits and flows with her; the space she creates with her own body is, look, human in scale, local in influence. She is 'touching the corporeal ground of our intelligence' (the poet Adrienne Rich in Of Woman Born. *See Bibliography).*

Ruth's work unites therapy and performance: here is the self as resource, unscripted and undirected in a formal sense but rendered conscious and contained – and therefore communicable.

Womban

Ruth Noble

*'The words came out of my body
with no ambivalence and no questions.'*

Woman felt sad and angry, empty inside she smelt the wood and
felt excited – the smells stirred a dim memory inside her – of
what? She needed more of the wood, so taking off her man-made
shirt she held the wood against her bare breasts; so cold and damp
from lying months on the open moor, the wood felt real, not
enough, she wanted more. Letting the wood slip between her legs
to the floor, she fondled the broken tip of the branch where it had
once been part of the tree. It reminded her of a penis; anger welled
up in her. 'You fuckers,' she roared and wept for her lost self,
raising her voice to the heavens, protesting to the Gods, 'How dare
you do this to me!', holding the cold damp wood close to her body,
smelling and remembering – what?

More, she wants, demands, more, her slumbering self reaches
out through the ages, her voice becoming stronger and more
insistent, yes, yes – she strips away the last of her man-made
clothes and draws the wood close to her awakening body – dare
she, can she – take inside herself this life – taking in the power,
owning her affinity with – ?

Stirrings in her mind, she knows what she must do – and
yet, what's the use, centuries of abuse and pretence, too much
time gone by. She is controlled and tamed, tears of frustration
and rage, primitive, primal rage, her birth-right torn away from
her centuries ago. Collapse. Smell the wood again – excitement, feeling it, her hands and body, rubbing it against herself,
taste it, see it, touching, feeling, smell, see, her breath
stronger now – her passion coming through – yes, yes, yes, she
does remember, they haven't destroyed it – her knowing. Feel
the wood, covering her body with the earthy dampness, oh so

good, more, more, coming alive again – remembering.

Standing up slowly, woman feels the earth under her feet, her feet that are so white and soft, how could they ever serve her well? More confident now, her body knows; she tests out her feet on the log, balancing, yes, this feels familiar, her body learning new/old ways of balancing – pleased now and proud too of her strong belly and hips; here high up in the trees her body serves her well, balancing, safe from the dangers below.

As her confidence grows, she looks out through the centuries and says her name – Womban.

When my children were small I started a school for them and eight other under-fives to provide a material environment in which they could explore. What they did excited and challenged me, and I had no authority breathing down my neck telling me what couldn't be done. The children and I learned to explore the limits of the possible through their curiosity, their trust, their bodies and the world around them. A seed was sown in me though I didn't know so at the time. Why had my own childhood been so impoverished? Well, at least I could give to my children what I had never had nor felt I ever would have.

Years later, I discovered it wasn't too late for me either. I learnt to dance, sing, write and draw just as those infants had done in my front room; testing out my body in movement, finding my voice and my words – giving birth to the seed of myself – exciting and exhilarating times. I learnt again to enjoy the movements of my body, to remember my first movements, the movements I made as a baby; to become engrossed in the tiny movements of my hand and experience the richness of that sensing; to touch my skin and be surprised and shocked at the intensity of that experience – a new experience or a remembered one? – to trick my body out of its adult stance into movements that were pleasurable and exciting. Learning to trust my body and my movements, learning to play again.

For years my feet had been the only part of me that had any familiarity with the ground, apart from when I lay like a landed whale on hot sand, soaking up the sun in an attempt to improve my image. Now I learnt to roll, jump, run and crawl, to play like a young puppy with other adults; to trust the ground to hold me, and to develop a dynamic relationship with it. My chronological age was between 37 and 39, but I was a very young child during this time, learning through exploring.

As I learnt to trust my movements so I began to give life to my words, my feelings and my images; to open the Pandora's box of my being; to find out that I am more than I thought I was; that I am in the process of becoming.

The heady times of those first awakenings are long past and the hardest thing for me to remember now is that once having said yes to myself I need continually to renew that pledge or I begin to die within myself again. Also to remember that there is a time for everything, including gestation, and that gestation by its nature is hidden from view and in those places I give way to fear and doubt, of myself and others. I am sometimes silenced by a terror of words.

Slowly, painfully I fumble for my words, my voice, my movement, my images;
For that flame inside that nourishes and excites me,
I can hardly imagine it now, there is but a faint glimmer at the
back of my mind.

Where do the dreams of young mothers go? a woman friend asked.

I am no longer a young mother, yet am a mother still. *Womban* came out of a time when I was researching through movement and images the experience of woman; my experience of being raised a female child in a patriarchal society; the his/herstory I carry in me; the remembering I can awaken in me through the process of going into an empty room and taking the risk of trusting my movement and images. *Womban* came out of the living experience of my body. She is only just upright, primitive woman. I carry the memory of her in me. She is also my child who takes her first uncertain steps away from mother out towards – ? What risks dare she take, will the world welcome or reject her? What has already been taught her about what to expect out there, of herself and others?

If I say yes and my body grows strong and powerful,
If I open my mouth and howl at the moon,
If I find my terror and my rage,
If I look in your eyes and see disgust and fear,
If I come to my senses –
Who will want me then?
Safer to stay home and cook the dinner.

My society, the culture I have learned, tells me that Art is something special, separate, something only the few can participate in while the rest stand by and watch; it does not carry the life of the people. So – why not stay home and cook dinner?

Our creativity is the means by which we name ourselves, individually and collectively. In the process of creating we are bringing aspects of the human condition to consciousness and some of what we bring is the dark side of being human. Nowadays individual artists carry that uncomfortable aspect of humanity for the rest of us, who can stay at home, feeling vaguely dissatisfied with life and label them crazy. But I believe we can no longer go on entrusting creativity to the few: we no longer know what it means to be fully human, we have lost our collective connections. It seems that women are at the leading edge in the search to re-establish that link; reaching into ourselves to find and bring alive our personal and collective stories, or names, roots and myths; giving ourselves the ground on which to stand and from which to move.

I feel gratitude to those who have stood beside me and privileged to witness the steps of others. I find my work exciting, frustrating, tedious, terrifying; but satisfying above all, saying yes wholeheartedly to what is asking to be expressed, what is demanding to be given birth to, what is thrusting through fear to life.

There are elements in Ruth's essay that resemble a poetics/politics of the feminine: turning on its head the traditional notion that having babies, or just possessing the capacity to do so, inhibits women from being artistically creative. This point of view, when developed – as in Monica Sjöö's work – offers women an immediate affirmation of their creative potential. Far from being biologically disadvantaged, women are naturally privileged; their procreativity is both prototype and archetype, the psycho-physical ground for all creativity. In her sexuality – orgasm, menstruation, birth, menopause – a woman possesses the key to an understanding of herself as Self and not Other, and simultaneously to a subversion of all that is oppressive, hierarchical, rigid in her environment. This puts woman, not man, at the centre, but with the significant difference that it is not her mentality, her rational ideas (which are anyway seen to be characteristic of men) with which she occupies this position, but her body and her subjectivities. *This amounts to a sort of democratisation of creativity – any woman can! – a powerful incentive which counters the fear and envy she may have learnt to feel towards 'artists'. She does not have to win men's approval by competing on their terms.*

But as soon as pen touches paper, she confronts a dilemma of some proportions. It is true that half the world, half of life has been suppressed from art: the subjectivity of being a woman. The thrill of recognition when we first read another woman's revelatory account, the cat-out-of-the-bag of sex, love, children, the dailiness and touchability and embodiedness of life. What could be more necessary, richer, than to document this private, silent, subtle, fluid, fascinating experience that is, joy of joys, common to others? But to do so, to take this as her sphere of consciousness and competence, could easily confine her – this time by her own hand – to her given place, the private and biological reality she was awarded for losing the public and human space. Even granting the project of 'writing

*Writing 'from the body' as a kind of collective source was not discovered/invented by modern feminists, of course. See, for instance, the poet Garcia Lorca's essay on the duende, *which has to do with 'blood . . . ancient culture . . . creative action . . . the spirit of the earth'. Or D. H. Lawrence's contentious 'blood-consciousness', whose most developed exposition is to be found in his essay 'Fantasia of the Unconscious'. Or compare 'I rarely draw what I see – I draw what I feel in my body', quoted of the sculptor Barbara Hepworth, in* Women Artists. *(See Bibliography.)*

the body' to be possible — and French feminist writers have shown this to be far from an intellectually unmediated activity — even so, celebrating the everyday, recording the shifts and minutiae of domestic and emotional life, affirms their importance to her, not to the rest of the world. Unless you decide to take to some extent on trust the intrinsic subversiveness of women's experience (as distinct from women's deliberate actions, say), there is no obvious momentum for social change. You may in effect end up sanctioning women's oppression. That is why, though we may affirm the validity of making a legitimate place in art for the articulation of female experience, it seems preferable to term this a feminine rather than a feminist poetics.

Or put it this way: in attempting to voice her emotions, her sexuality, her instincts, her body, what shall a woman do with her intellect, her effectiveness, her ambition? Or rather and first, what value should she assign to them? Is it true that what is most wrong in our society is its over-intellectualism? One way of compartmentalising creativity has been to oppose it to what is analytical or analysable: the following essay is a refutation of that polarisation.

Though Diana Scott, like Ruth, begins her description of inspiration in a rural setting, she ends in the city. All through her piece sparkles the evocation of a literature which similarly found in that relationship a symbol for competing attractions and aspirations.

What Emily Means to Me

Diana Scott

> A thousand thousand glancing fires
> Seemed kindling in the air;
> A thousand thousand silvery lyres
> Resounded far and near:
>
> Methought the very breath I breathed
> Was full of sparks divine,
> And all my heather couch was wreathed
> By that celestial shine.

It is March 1844; Emily Brontë's remembered early summer afternoon on the moors was being transformed with divine fire; for she was not afraid to live vividly in a world viewed from the intense, oblique standpoint of a visionary.

It is that summer of 1985 when it never stopped raining. On a July day, cold and misty as October, we drive out on to the high moors that separate this part of North Yorkshire from Lancashire. Once, on an exceptionally bright clear spring day, I had run along this road and as I climbed higher and higher and I saw farther and farther, the Three Peaks and behind them more and more hills whose names I did not know and then the blue hills and waters of Cumbria had unfolded to my dazzled vision. Today, mist hems in the road, and the far hills lurk behind it like shadows.

I have to write a poem and I don't know where to begin. The thought sits on the back of my neck like a heavy collar. Somebody I was once close to is getting married in a month's time and I am to write a poem to be read as part of the marriage service. The possible unfairness of the situation disappears into larger considerations. I understand perfectly the vision of mutual love and support that has brought my friends to marriage; or rather I don't, because irrespective of any political reservations I might have about marriage, my own relationship is currently on the rocks and from where in my experience can I find the fairness and generosity to let that incongruous vision in?

At the road's highest point we park and get out. The road drops steeply down the rocky side of the fell into Lancashire. All there is is silence and rain and the hills furred green and brown with bracken and moss and turf, tender as flesh over their hard unyielding bones. I look down the road towards that narrow unknown valley opening into fields bordered with dry grey stone walls, already darkening at three in the afternoon. I am a poet who hasn't written a poem or published a book in years.

Of course the mind never stops and the way of perceiving reality does not go away. A diary, letters, conversation, dreams, fragments and plans of a novel testify to the fact that the creative process cannot be stopped. But the feeling of being incomplete, the constant low-level sadness, the deadening sense of silence surrounding part of myself . . . can I call myself a writer without producing one completed thing, however small? And now a small completed thing is what I must produce, whether I like it or not.

I say to my friend, 'If you were in the middle of your own wedding and you'd just said "I do", what would you like the poem to say that you'd spend the first couple of minutes of your married life listening to?' He says, 'I'd like it to say that I was doing what the whole of creation was doing, life perpetuating itself, the seasons turning round, the crops growing, animals and people being born . . .' I look at the wet green hills where none of this appears to be happening. In the silence and the space and the fragrant rain something opens in my mind. I say aloud, 'The hills marry the quiet green earth.'

How it used to be was that the first line would come into my mind as if from nowhere and then I would draw the rest of the poem after it. I remember the old days, pacing around muttering 'I promised wrong when I promised to come' or 'And the people all around are looking' under my breath at work until I could get home and discover what the rest of the poem had to say.

Back home with our North Yorkshire friends where the very pages of the books are soft and damp to the touch, I explain that the poem seems to be on its way. 'So if you could sum up what this poem had to say in the smallest possible number of words, what would they be?' 'Well, er, jolly well done, I suppose,' I say, barely meaning it. 'And if you were the greatest poet in the world, what would you say in it?' 'Well, I'd say that this was just one of millions of marriages that have happened this year, people and cows and beetles, you know, and that this marriage celebrates life, as all other marriages have done.' I am surprised at myself. Where did all that come from? Is that what I really believe?

Thus, the poem.

And so, am I now a poet again?

Marriage Poem

The hills marry the quiet green earth;
Beneath the lake the water people feast:
The air is scented with peat and the cliffs fall to the sea.
This year, all kinds of living beings
Birds, beasts and people
Have married, in their proper season,
And their children are lovely and fitting.

This marriage celebrates life,
Here in this gathering of friends.
This marriage is a gift to us all;
We are all part of this wedding.
At its centre are the bride and groom
And their conscious loving commitment.
This is only the beginning of this celebration, this inspiration.
Let their joy be unbounded.

The poem is a small moment when all dissatisfaction disappears and life seems perfect and complete. And then, for me, the conflicts begin.

I want to be an ordinary person, intent upon the ordinariness, not the mystery, of life. I want to develop myself, to have an interesting job, to strike a fulfilling balance between work, relaxation and creative leisure pursuits.

Actually I do that, quite well. Why isn't it enough? Why do I keep on after that invisible moment of knowing and the words that may make it real? Why don't I like Westerns instead? Going to pubs? Eating meat? Why am I afraid to go regularly to the dentist?

Why don't I go on a diet? Wear contact lenses?

I hold strange views and see things that some other people don't see are there, so don't find interesting. But they would find them interesting if I could show them how truly interesting they are. I think I did that at the wedding. I don't know, I wasn't able to go. But it seems to have worked. My poem fitted into the charged atmosphere of the service between the vows and the reading of the Marriage at Cana. I hadn't found the words for all of what I saw but I found enough to feel satisfied. It didn't last though. Very quickly I found myself looking for that sense of completion again.

I look wise. Some of the time I act normal. I know how to cook, look nice, bring up a child, write a good business letter. I used to be very shy but now I'm a good conversationalist once I get going. In fact I can be very witty. I play the piano well too.

Not a lot of poetry to show for all that, though.

What do you mean? I had to go to work, and then there was the child and the shopping and I had to get some sleep.

Anyway, to get to the point – some years ago when I wasn't working a lot and before I learnt how to have my life more the way I wanted it, I edited a biggish anthology of nineteenth- and twentieth-century women's poetry, called *Bread and Roses,* on the theme of poetic inspiration. The process of putting a book together, of writing commentaries and biographical notes, showed me incidentally that I was as ignorant of professional publishing as I was, most of the time, of poetic inspiration. By the time the book was complete and published I knew rather more about both. Having a book published and marketed gave me modest opportunities to play the part of a literary woman and left me with the taste for more. I want to be prolific and famous and rich and wise and speak for my time, etc. Indeed I do.

But the question of where a poem comes from – for all the evidence I was able to present – is as elusive as ever.

Voices from the past:

Elizabeth Barrett Browning: Like to write? Of course, of course I do. I seem to live while I write – it is life for me.

Lavinia Dickinson (of her sister *Emily*): Emily had to think – that was what she had to do.

Emily Brontë: Thought followed thought, star followed star, through boundless regions on . . .

That sense of satisfaction, of feeling alive, of waking up after being asleep that came along with the completion of a poem – it became clear from the work of the full range of contributors to *Bread and Roses* that this was an experience many writers were familiar with. This sense of springing free in the process of artistic creation – even if it was a passing and irrational feeling – had obvious connotations for me as a feminist.

Poetry, or at least that poetry recognised as of enduring value, has traditionally and explicitly dealt with deep questions, life, death, meaning, truth, love. Much feminist literature, by contrast, insists on sharp observation of the day-to-day events of our lives. Is this reportage, born of contingency, material for our eternal truths? In compiling *Bread and Roses* I felt myself in an area of argument that I could perhaps only articulate using the words of others as well as my own. Some years later, the argument seems to have broadened, deepened. It's no longer a matter of whether visionary poetry is philosophical and realistic poetry political. The intense creative experience is common to painters, musicians, writers, revolutionaries, scientists, mathematicians, mystics.

At this point I find myself wishing I were a journalist or a political scientist or a historian, someone who could make professional sense of such phenomena. I wish I could even read the papers and remember what I read. I wish I was an active member of a political party, ambiguities successfully resolved. I wish I could work constructively at a chosen campaign, or two, or three.

What unkind fairy put me down instead in a dark wood, set my feet on a mysterious road?

Let us say, the creative vision is not a luxury but a necessity. It is not sought, it happens. Let us say, for those of us who write, it produces writing and along with that a sense of being fully and completely alive. But alive to what? and for what?

Sometimes I think of the world outside this room and I feel utter terror. Unemployment, poverty, famine, racism, war, nuclear missiles, star wars, and nuclear waste poisoning the earth itself – I must be crazy to want to be alive! Wouldn't it be more in the spirit of things just to give up and die now? Or anyway do the bare minimum for survival? Or just get drunk a lot?

If writing produces a sense of being fully and completely alive, it is an idea that asserts the vision – in spite of what we know is true – of a fuller and more benevolent humanity. Is this a) an irrelevant idiocy, b) a courageous defiance of the mood of the moment or c) an assertion of a truth that is obscured but not negated by the spectacle of mediocrity and death?

I beg your pardon?

I'm sticking my neck out. What connection can there be between grandiose visions of harmony and a poem?

More voices from the past: the words 'Bread and Roses' first appear in history as a slogan in a women textile workers' strike in New England, 1912. A contemporary socialist activist made it into a poem and other people of vision have been setting it to music and performing it ever since.

Not just bread, the song says, not just the necessities of life, but roses – art, beauty, vision, essential to life as bread.

As we go marching, marching, the future hears us call,
For the rising of the women means the rising of us all.
No more the drudge and idler, ten that toil where one reposes,
But a sharing of life's glories: give us bread but give us roses.

Or to put it another way. A transformative energy fills the writer – she writes a poem. That is to say, in her own mind she is productive, powerful and (almost always) *safe*. I know this – I've written many poems and read many, many more. You can see it clearly in the works of so many nineteenth-century women writers – really revolutionary ways of looking at the world in private that they'd never in a million years have been able to make public and put into practice.

This energy embodied in the poems of women is immensely powerful. If it were truly available everywhere in our lives and to all of us, mountains could be moved. And other things.

What am I doing, sitting here writing about being creative? What a joke. What are *you* doing, reading about being creative?

Terrible, the feeling of not being able to write. The ache of unfulfilment no lover, no jogging programme, no really good book can ever satisfy. The sense of a trust betrayed – yes, really – of a special job you have been given that only you can do – and you aren't doing it. Dissatisfaction with yourself; irritation with other people. Congestion in the body and the brain.

Rationalisations: writing is marginal. Starving people do not need poems. The unemployed need bread not circuses. You're just writing because you can't do anything really valuable in the real world. Who needs my work (if it's not published)? Who reads my work (if it is)? Am I a writer if I write very well sometimes and can't think of anything to say at the moment? Am I a writer if I write and no one wants to publish me, yet – or ever? Writing means being alone a lot. Living is a sociable activity. Physically producing a book means lots of time spent alone. I get lonely. I can't be a writer. I want to make my mark on life while I'm alive and if I put it all into poetry – if I'm lucky – they'll discover how good I was, after I'm dead. Writers can't make any money, serious ones that is. If I decide to be a serious writer, I'll probably be poor all my life. Is it worth it?

Emily Dickinson's sister Lavinia who survived her by many years was asked once how come she'd let Emily get away with just writing, while she herself had added to her own social duties those which would normally have been performed by her sister as an unmarried woman living at home. 'Emily had to *think*,' was her terse reply. 'That was what she had to do.'

Elizabeth Barrett Browning wrote in a letter, 'Like to write? Of course, of course I do. I seem to live while I write – it is life for me.' Most of the past comes to us as costume drama – two-dimensional records of acts, clothes, possessions, lacking depth. To know that a woman dead more than a century liked to write and felt in touch with life's essence when she was doing it brings her to life in a different way. Sometimes without any of the usual props I catch a sense of her being, just being who she was.

But – here's the catch – I think I want to do more with my life than just think; and I'm not convinced it's enough to say that writers write because they must, that communicating their vision is what makes life worth living for them. What is the point, for us, for me?

Emily Brontë is my hero. One day I am going to take a journey through her life viewed from inside her mind, I am going to write her writer's diary. I have been writing of my sense of the contradictions I feel in everyday life – wanting to be ordinary and conform and wanting to be extraordinary as well – the feeling of living uncomfortably in two worlds, which pose unanswerable questions to each other. Emily Brontë did live in two worlds, the everyday one and the one of visions, without apparent discomfort. She lived in a very practical way in the real world doing most of what was expected of a woman in her position at that time. But –

> But first a hush of peace, a soundless calm descends;
> The struggle of distress and fierce impatience ends;
> Mute music soothes my breast – unuttered harmony
> That I could never dream till earth was lost to me.

> Then dawns the Invisible, the Unseen its truth reveals;
> My outward sense is gone, my inward essence feels –
> Its wings are almost free, its home, its harbour found;
> Measuring the gulf it stoops and dares the final bound!

It was at two o'clock one morning that I started to think – feeling anxious and lonely and rather vulnerable about being awake and alone at that very quiet time – about how much Emily appears to have loved the night. The dark reminds me of insecurities and doubts I might repress by day; and I don't often, living in a large city (Leeds), make my way home alone without thinking I'm doing something rather risky. Emily, in perhaps no less danger than me, appears to have found the dark a private, protected space where she could do her best, her free-est thinking and dreaming. She loves the moon:

> How clear she shines! How quietly
> I lie beneath her silver light
> While heaven and earth are whispering me
> 'Tomorrow wake but dream tonight!'

At night the wind talks to her like a lover:

> Have we not been from childhood friends?
> Have I not loved thee long?
> As long as thou hast loved the night
> Whose silence wakes my song.

Perhaps this feels a little remote, a little romantic – but all of you who, like me, ever felt just a bit afraid of the dark, worried about going out at night or, anxious about being alone at home, have wanted to 'reclaim the night', might see, through her, a way to reclaim your own personal nights.

She took trouble to be good at what she did, from baking bread to playing the piano and learning French, to writing *Wuthering Heights*. She was a great walker, fit and energetic. In an early poem she describes herself as a 'mountaineer' and for much of her life she seems to have been something of an adventurer, ready to take on any challenge. Her best poetry is the product of thoughtful disciplined work, as well as of visionary inspiration. She was not especially academic to start with, she wasn't doing it to impress.

She made her own standards, and knew how to live up to them.

During her time at a Brussels girls' college, her French tutor, Constantin Heger, claimed, 'She should have been a man – a great navigator. Her powerful reason would have deduced new spheres of discovery from a knowledge of the old; and her strong imperious will would never have been daunted by opposition or difficulty; never given way but with life.' The Belgian professor could not perhaps have known to what extent the woman who voyaged in her thoughts, at night, through 'boundless regions' under the 'glorious eyes' of the stars, was indeed an explorer and a great navigator.

Emily Brontë had little paid-for education till she went to Belgium as an adult with her sister Charlotte. This did not prevent her from using to the full that unwomanly faculty, thought. Thought – and the heightened states of being and realisation that the awakened intellect can lead us into – emerges clearly as one of the central themes linking the poems I collected for *Bread and Roses*. The connection between intellect and education is not a necessary one. We may, with reason, distrust formal education. Education for what? For whom? Moreover, women now often experience education as divisive. But of course women's struggles of earlier generations focused on formal education as a symbol of liberation for women: for the reason that their 'unpaid-for education', which fitted the receivers of it so well for the unpaid profession of being a woman, consisted – as characterised by Virginia Woolf in *Three Guineas* – of 'poverty, chastity, derision, and freedom from unreal loyalties'.

We have wanted to pose more and other questions. I wrote a poem sequence nearly ten years ago called *Six Poems for Hospital Workers,* a series of vignettes of women doing domestic and catering jobs in a large London teaching hospital. Here's the sixth one.

> Here is a poem for
> the women who don't write poems
> who do the work because work is
> and do more work because work is
> who are: fast, kind, vacant, fat
> service and produce, produce and service
> There are no words to write this poem because
> they have no words

Who would do their jobs
if they had words. No more words. The poem's over.

I did know what some of the paradoxes were when I made this simple statement – I, as a woman making a statement apparently on behalf of women unable to speak out for themselves, using words themselves to say that some of us had no words to call our own; and at the end letting the poem disappear into the silence of all that those women can or will not say.

Now more questions. Is it really a straight choice between doing jobs and having words? Are the limits to our creative lives to be set by our paid or unpaid work, as they used to be by our paid-for or unpaid-for education? Is our main struggle, in the realm of creativity, with the contradictions between work and vision? What can we make (for ourselves and each other) of Emily's grand address to the stars?

> All through the night, your glorious eyes
> Were gazing down in mine . . .
>
> I was at peace, and drank your beams
> As they were life to me . . .
>
> *Thought followed thought – star followed star*
> *Through boundless regions on . . .*

What can I take from Emily for myself as a writer?

Both Ruth and Diana have enacted for the reader a particular creative process, the active reverie whose point of departure is the present moment. Since many people testify with alacrity to similar inner events, it would be easy to take visionary experience as unproblematical, self-explanatory; or else to lay a heavy verbal mesh over it so that only selected bits show through, as immobile definitions. Asking awkward questions is a more productive though tricky device, stylistically and psychologically; too much, and you risk collapse. One of the values of public self-doubting is its rejection of self-aggrandisement; such questions as Diana poses have the bite of real dilemmas, those not born of false modesty or private idiosyncrasy. Lisa Kopper, in the final section, takes forward this inquiry into the purposes and functions of artists.

Too often the heroic model of creativity presents the Artist with an identity in which 'he' is pictured as a protagonist in a great metaphysical battle; it isn't like that for most of us most of the time. It's the apparently trivial obstacles, whose size and shape Diana has sketched, that cause us to stumble. Tillie Olsen said in a press interview that what took the greater courage on her part was not being a writer but daily bringing up four children, getting them to school on time, seeing their clothes were reasonably clean, providing them with food; writing was a cinch compared with that. For mothers, what is arresting about the attempt to locate themselves as poets in an unbroken female line is the lack of female writers who were also mothers; we may suspect they knew by instinct or observation what they had to avoid in order to keep their vision safe from a major depredation.

What it is the business of the poet and the woman to do – who inhabit the same space but whose priorities and inhibitions may be very different – is an uneasy realm of inquiry, requiring introspection. Self-criticism is easily confused with self-censorship and acts of self-sabotage can prevent a project from reaching accomplishment: 'How can you call what you do art?' 'What makes you think anyone will want to see what you've done?' Catherine Itzin's essay in the next section looks deeply into this phenomenon. Here, Alix Pirani reveals the complex interaction between the development of her sexual awareness as a heterosexual woman and her writing of a particular poem as a practising poet. In following up suggestions from both literature and her own experience, she tries not to be drawn into censoring difficult messages, allowing instead oppositions and conjunctions to come into being transiently for the purpose of personal illumination more than programme. She shows how personal events were the 'ground' of her prize-winning poem; the stages in composing the poem, that work of reflection, revision, 'recycling'.

It is hard for feminist writers to find a selective approach to the main body of western literature: should they even seek to assimilate their work to a tradition which, by gender and class domination, has inhibited the majority of people from expressing and perceiving themselves through cultural production? (And which is demonstrated in many people's ambivalent attitude to 'culture'.) If they do and are successful, how do they prevent the ideological challenge their work contains from being incorporated, diluted into another commercial fad? But if feminists reject artistic tradition wholesale, must they not risk not only having to reinvent the wheel, so to say, in matters such as technique, but also denying themselves access to what can influence their own aspirations, both aesthetic and political? There is no such thing, actually and simplistically, as 'the mainstream': except in retrospect, most writers even of the dominant class, race or sex have an uncomfortable, needing-to-be-negotiated relationship with tradition. In Alix's essay there seems to reside an implicit plea that literary practice redeem its long-vaunted promissory note to humanise – that is, to express and transmit humane, humanitarian values.

In any case, can writing – the making of literate form – be simply self-referential, sufficient unto itself, speaking for itself? Is there not in what we write an ineradicable, if involuntary, connection with other literate forms ('intertextuality')?

Alix Pirani offers one convocation of these considerations; Anna Wilson's essay in the following section is premised on a more particular critique of the same dominances. By comparing in detail the differences and similarities between one woman's work and another – the ways in which experience, expression and tradition interact and get articulated – we can continue drawing the contours of women's art, which is a procedure of inclusion, not exclusion. (The question of whether and how we might distinguish between non-feminist and feminist art – compiling a checklist of ideological criteria, as distinct from using feminist theory to explore women's art – must rely heavily on the 'reading' of specific images as, for instance, emblems of resistance or collusion; and can therefore be a misleading one to ask.)

'The Song of Songs for 1984' (under the name of Alix Frank) was

awarded second prize in the 1985 Literature Festival Poetry Competition organised by the Buckinghamshire Arts Association.

The Song of Songs for 1984

Alix Pirani

My beloved is fat.
His shoulders are rounded and heavy like a washerwoman's
Bent over a desk for many seasons.
His legs are slender,
For the sap rises and does not return to the earth for sustenance.

His skin is uncertain to my touching:
It has shrunk from other women:
It has recoiled from the static of their synthetic loving.

How shall I know you, my love?
Your hot blood is familiar as a brother's.
Your locks are like a god's.
Your eyes look through your bearded face
Like a sad deer caught in a thicket.

I reach for your centre.
We are flushed with our meeting.

Now you are warm to my touch.
The iron-grey curled hair on your breasts
Is my forest: I am lost in your forest.
Your mouth is soft, tasting of tobacco.
You press into me, my love,
Eager and insistent,
Greedy for my comforts.
You drink from my cup.
You play on me: I am a thrice-plucked harp

Crying out. You master my art. You take me by storm:
I fight for my release.

We ride the angry waves of our passion.
Our passion is like the echoing of guns
In fertile valleys.

The storm has quietened.
The thunder has died behind the hill.
The guns are silent.
We are at peace, beloved.
Our fingers rove over their new-found territories.
We are without words.

★

My beloved's hands are a craftsman's:
He draws a finger down the lines of my body:
He seeks to define me.

I am become as a soft ripe peach
And my kernel is firm
With its knowledge.

My beloved is tender:
He is gentle as the crippled gardener
Who tends the gardens of green valleys,
The apple orchards of Kent.

I am tamed and warm in your arms, my love:
Like the young lamb in the arms of the farmer
In the spring-time of an ominous year.

★

I am dry, beloved.
Many men have drunk at the well
And the well is dry:
The earth is weary:
The well is polluted and the men abandon it.

There is a secret inside me:
A tomb and a sewer in my bowels:

The graves of my slaughtered aborted children.

Fathom the secret, my love, fathom the well.
Plunge into the dry earth, penetrate.
Rape me against your will.
Rape me till I yield my secrets:
Till the blood flows
And the stinking water flows from the well
And the wound weeps.

The acid rain falls:
The sky is angry.
The earth is ravaged.
The Bomb waits.

I pull you inside me.
Your taut and tentative cock
Unwilling, plays its role:
Sword into ploughshare.
Explode me then, love,
For we have waited so long, terrified,
For the end of our world.
Now is our second coming.
Ravaged.

★

I lie torn.
You have felt the horror of my passion
And are silent:
With the silence of the day after Hiroshima.
I weep, my love. My tears are hopeless
As you lie there smoking a cigarette, thinking.

How shall life return?
The birds have flown away from the places of destruction.
They have deserted the desolate waste that was Belsen.
The murderous land is infertile.

My beloved touches me.
Our skin is soft and living,
Ever newborn and innocent.

Perhaps the faithful earth will come to life
At length, after the scorched earth raiders
Have departed.

My love turns to me to comfort me
And I comfort him.
Our breasts, our hearts, are enfolded:
Our sad genitals touch each other.
We say nothing.

★

Sisters, tell me: where is my beloved?
He has gone from me:
I searched and could not find him.
He is at his desk. His secretary guards the way.
I have beaten at the door like a madwoman in labour,
Like a Greenham woman tearing her fingers on a barbed-wire
    barrier.

My body cried out
Do not deny me: do not starve me.
I cannot keep body and soul together.

He has not heard me.
My beloved has shrunk from me:
He has shrunk like a fruit that is dried and empty:
He is as the hard skin of a dried-out passion-fruit.

I went into the street with my sisters, mourning.
And I saw my beloved in the car showroom.
He has bought a Rover 2000.
I saw the men in their dark suits,
Handsome and upright.
Their hair is grey, iron grey:
Their eyes are deep and empty.

We watched him as he drove out on to the highway.

★

The earth is parched and cracked:
The land is dry and sullen.

My love's old Triumph lies rusted and rotting on a dump.
The nettles grow over it.
The dust blows and clings to it.

Come, sisters:
We will sit on the earth.
We will wait, weaving our figments, our mysteries.
Our breasts are proud and tender
And our eyes are fire.
We sit in a circle:
Our wounds are bleeding.

My beloved sits in his office.
He stands on his platform.
He sits in the serried chairs of his organisation.

Here is our little daughter.
What shall we do for our daughter
In the day of her awakening?
When her first blood drops from her
And her breasts ripen?
We have no man to bring her to.

My daughter is wide-eyed.
Look across the hills, my love, my daughter.
See where we bled the proud forest
And raped to the womb of the earth
And squandered the ripe harvest.

We have brewed poison
And we could not digest it.
We spat in the waters:
We were sick in the lakes.
We shat in the rivers:
The rivers stink.
What shall we do for our daughter
When she goes to the stream to drink?

They brought her to us,
Torn, raped and bleeding,
And we gathered her to us, into our circle of women.

We closed the circle.

My beloved has seen our daughter.
He has wept, he has hidden from me.
He has hidden his wrath from his brothers.
Where are you, my love?

He has taken the sun-dried corn
From the scorched earth,
And brewed alcohol, fire-water.
His eyes are angry and weeping.
He brings me raw spirit.
I will drink with my beloved, and dance.

How shall we dance, sisters, brothers,
In the time of our madness and our wildness?
A dance of hatred
A dance of death
A dance of ecstasy under the moon.
My body is alive: my womb sings. It remembers
The soft ripe fruit we ate in our passion,
The hard ripe apple we took in our teeth,
The juices running over.

But my beloved is stalled.
He stands rooted like a wounded tree:
He dances like a stricken stag:
Like an eagle soaring, not knowing where to perch.

How shall I be with him
In this time of our uncertainty?
Shall I lure him to my bed?
My breasts are proud and tender:
Can my womb bear a warrior?
There is fire in my belly, earth-fire,
And my beloved is afraid.

★

The wild dance is over.
My beloved's brows were knit.

My neck was stiff.
I have shut the door to him
And he has not knocked to enter.
He has returned to his office.

We have this peace.
We are exhausted with our struggle.

★

The moon recedes: the sun rises.
Come, my beloved.
We have slept. We have dreamed.
Let us rise, and go down to the field by the stream.
We shall sit on the grass, on the earth.
While the airplanes scream above us
And the blackbird sings in the tree.

Sit near me, beloved, in silence.
Let us wait.
We will listen for the hidden seed.
Our tears fall on it
As water from a deep well.

The tears of our grieving
Are purer and clearer
Than the angry rain that falls on the city.

The seed grows unknown under the dry earth.
We long for it, and for the joy of its emerging.

I've been studying creative process for years, but when I thought, what do I as a woman want to say right now about creativity, these words came: What I have wanted to be and what I am are not the same, ever.

I live daily with the pain of that, the constantly renewed shock, and the excitement. And I know that the more honestly I accept and express what I am, and put it into relation with what I supposed was intended for my life, the more creative I am. Thus fantasy and reality are continually being set against each other.

I think this may be particularly true for educated women of my generation. I grew up during the Second World War, and there was always a sense of promise to be fulfilled when it was over. Comfortably middle class, we were spoiled, not with material luxury (the war made sure of that) but with moral luxury. Good had triumphed over evil: there would be a future of unblemished happiness, deserved peace and prosperity, widening opportunities and freedoms for women.

That 'spoiledness' had to take severe blows. It is, after all, daughter being spoiled by father. And once I broke from father's rule, from patriarchal domination and values, and insisted on freedom without strings, I was up against some harsh realities. And also, of course, the exhilarating, joyful realities, finding new resources, powers, pleasures in myself and other people: making vital connections with others; because what I've had to do is repeatedly move on from the self-centredness that spoiling encourages.

For me, this kind of personal liberation didn't begin to happen fully until I was past 40, though I had always been heading towards it. Since it came so late it required a reassessment of all that had gone before – half my life – partly through psychotherapy, partly through writing. In my writing, using and reworking old forms was something I'd always been successful with: clearly the place where I match traditional expectation with present truth; what I have wanted to be, or supposed life would be for me, with what my life is; and in that reworking comes the transformation of myself.

'The Song of Songs for 1984' did that for me: it mingled expectation, idealism and painful reality; it belonged to many other people besides myself, as I shall show, and it marked an important stage in what has been a lifelong concern with the nature of love, sexuality and spiritual truth.

The *Song of Songs* – Solomon's Song – has long been known as the most erotically beautiful part of the Bible, appealing to readers through the exquisite direct imagery and intimacy of the lover, and through its allegorical significance, in which sexual union represents the union of humankind with God, or the union of body and soul. Whether or not one accepts religious interpretations, what's indisputable is that it somehow speaks directly to the sense we all have that personal love, and the physical consummation of love between two people, is also universal, devotional, spiritual, in a way which affects the universe. 'Make love not war' is the simplest expression of that feeling.

When love 'goes wrong' between men and women, the world seems out of joint; true creativity, fertility, are blocked, confounded. The tension, the war between the sexes, is at a critical stage just now, played out at every level, from the bedroom to the political actions and reactions around the women's movement.

From my own experience and that of the many people I've met in my roles as teacher and therapist I've been unceasingly aware of that crisis. I've also come to believe that the way out depends on women releasing and reclaiming their sexual-spiritual qualities, related to their menstrual selves: intuition, earth-and-moon-connectedness, heart feelings. Such qualities are vitally creative and have been too much suppressed in favour of their maternal and intellectual roles, which men can more easily handle and control.

Emerging from my own confinement in the maternal and intellectual, I decided at 54 to 'come out' as a writer – devote more time and commitment to it. I needed to come out with that sexual-spiritual quality, though I had only a dim idea of how that might happen. In the event, 'The Song of Songs for 1984' came from and generated sexual-spiritual energy. The pressure that produced it was a combination of personal joy and distress, and world pain, shared crisis.

'Working with people' had made me very sensitive to what is going on in the collective consciousness. 1984 meant something to everyone. I'd explored some of its personal and collective meanings in other writing but had still fallen short of expressing unashamedly the fully sensual erotic me, the immediacy of felt sensuousness in poetry that I'd long wanted to achieve. Much of my truth as a woman lies in body experience. Intense, numbed, ecstatic, agonising, aching – whatever it is, it has to be registered, recognised, because to suppress it is to suppress my life. And the suppression of life is what 1984 is about. I think the threat of 1984 was what made me speak out with a voice that had hitherto been very muted.

(Even as I write this now, I see how with every act of speaking or writing we push the frontiers further; with every honest confronting of experience we cross a boundary, tear back a veil, discover new power. I think I learned to have the courage for that from psychotherapy.)

I knew immediately, when I met the 'beloved' of the poem, whom I shall call C., early in 1984, that he was to be important in my life, though I didn't exactly know why or how. He was Jewish, as I am, of Mediterranean origin, with a hot-blooded violent temperament tamed and repressed by decades of life in Britain and marriage to an Englishwoman. He spoke of his desire for sexual passion and for sanctity. We met rarely: he was attempting ineffectually to separate from his wife: it soon became clear to me that little was likely to develop between us: that in itself gave a poignancy to our relationship. Sexually there was a depth of contact which touched and released so much that was stored in me: love, hatred, desire, anger, fear: the imprinted memories of a life's sexual, menstrual, maternal experience. It is all in my vagina and womb, which are my creative centre and engender passion: a passion for being alive and loving, and a passionate hatred for the corrupt world I live in and have borne children into.

About this time I came across an impressive article by D. M. Thomas on the power and quality of women's sexuality. I immediately responded to his statement that 'what happens in the vagina has more to do, in 1984, with H-bombs than with G-spots'. I'd been deeply affected and disturbed by *The White Hotel:* its impact had lasted. The *Song of Songs* was used there as a reference point in exploring women's sexuality and spirituality. I think now that my decision to use it was my way of reclaiming a birthright, for D M Thomas is neither Jewish nor a woman.

Another element at this stage was my interest in Zeus, that Jovial mixture of the randy and the divine, the sexual-spiritual patriarch. C. had an Olympian appearance and charisma: in the event he proved to be the inseminating father of the poem; like Zeus he didn't stick around for very long.

I wanted to celebrate this relationship and express its truth. The first four sections of the poem (as far as 'We say nothing') were written with a determination to focus on and register what I'd felt as faithfully as I could. The honesty, as I wrote, was a powerful validation of who I felt myself to be behind the woman usually visible to the world. Alongside that, I allowed whatever associations or images arose, however incongruous, to take their place in the poem: the symbolic mode and rhythm of the *Song of Songs,* which originated in a very small world, was able to accommodate a far-ranging set of twentieth-century images.

My active mind concerned itself with the problem of integrating

modern phrasing and language into the Hebraic form. There was
often a jarring, a shock I couldn't control, but I decided to let it be.
I think now it parallels the shock in the sexual encounter: both are
a violation one would be more comfortable without. But, as Susan
Sontag says, 'Real art has the capacity to make us nervous.' And
although the language deviated in places from the spare concrete-
ness of the *Song of Songs*, I felt that to allow modern expression
was in the spirit of the original, which has so strong a feeling of the
contemporary, the local.

One thing gave me particular satisfaction: that what I'd learned
about body-life and energy in therapy had not only become part of
my responsiveness but had an immediate symbolic life in the poetry
– the opening lines describing the lover's body, for instance.
Which is indeed about the sexual-spiritual, for the body is both a
symbol and an instrument of life's purpose. I knew that the rabbis
had said that the sexual union of the *Song of Songs* symbolised
spiritual union. I also knew from my studies of creative process and
of Jung that the balanced interaction of male-female, active-
passive (left brain/right brain, new brain/old brain) is vital to
creativity, as is the interaction of new expression with established,
even eternal, form, and that there must be a connection there with
the rabbinic view. I could already feel, in the act of writing, the
combination of 'masculine' and 'feminine' activity, and of new and
old expression. The shock I've mentioned reflects the quality of
their interaction, like the interaction of the lovers' bodies.

At the time I wrote this, C. was not as consciously aware as the
poem suggests of the power of my feelings. I was 'saying nothing'. I
was still idealising him as the visiting god of passion. But gradually,
as he withdrew, maintaining his patronage by solicitous phone calls
but rarely coming to be with me, I gave up hope, put the poem
away with my disillusionment, and decided to look for love
elsewhere.

And didn't find it. An abortive attempt at involvement with
another man, N., left me depressed and hopeless: it seemed that
my sexuality (and, as I well knew, many women's) couldn't be
matched by men at present. We women who'd freed ourselves
were too much for unliberated men: there were so many
unresolved emotional issues standing in the way of relationship.
My age, too, gave any man who was unsure of himself a stock
excuse to dismiss me. So here was an angry woman wondering
what the sexual-spiritual could mean in a desert of lovelessness –

and knowing, paradoxically, that somehow that was where the meaning was.

I forgot the poem, but 'creative rage' was undoubtedly building up in me. And it was 1984. The political climate was intensely oppressive. The miners' strike, with its violent passions, affected me deeply: in particular the heartless denial and rupture of their rootedness in community and tradition, of their earth-connectedness. The ever-present threat of nuclear and ecological annihilation was emphasised by the continuing protests of the women at Greenham and of Greenpeace, and the continuing militarism, fascism and terrorism everywhere else.

Two months after the first sections of the poem were written and put aside, I attended a four-day conference of some 300 European psychologists, called 'Transforming Crisis'. This title, and Britain, had been chosen because it was 1984. It took place on a university campus in green and pleasant countryside: the sun shone; there were many old friends there and much of the workshop activity revolved around issues of power, love, sexism, conflict, spirituality, body-life. The atmosphere was heartening. Though at times I felt vulnerable and lonely, I was accompanied and supported by a woman colleague for whom I have much love, who shares and understands many of my feelings. There were many women there concerned with feminism, and with the goddess, and one in particular made a strong impression on me. She'd recently spent time with an American Indian tribe and her presence had a strikingly beautiful quality of woman-related-to-earth. She had come to speak about 'eco-feminism' which explores the intricate links between what has happened to women and what has happened to the planet over the past centuries, and seeks to create an awareness that can promote change.

Of the men present there were several with whom I'd had professional or personal relationships, including N. I was looking forward to meeting R., whose theoretical work I knew and admired: we'd worked in similar areas and there was much that could be shared. He proved to be indeed highly perceptive, energetic, interesting – and totally dismissive of me: quite uninterested in my views and experiences and obviously wary of my feminine energy. He'd mounted a large complex display of material about the organisation he was running. I decided to attend the first of his seminars to see if I could then initiate some dialogue, but when I arrived to find him on a platform and myself in a chair behind a couple of hundred others in chairs I left, exasperated by his elevated distance. Most of the workshops were on a small scale and had offered warm, involving experiences.

The conference was due to end with a plenary session planned mostly by the women around the theme of eco-feminism, and I was invited to help or contribute: I had little idea of how I might do that. The night before it there was a disco-style dance in the university grand hall. Conferences are always highly charged with sexual expectation, fantasy, fulfilment, disappointment. My two hours of almost non-stop ecstatic and expressive dancing brought all that into sharp focus. N. was there and I couldn't go near him, but I could see him troubled and unable to approach other women. Another man to whom I was drawn turned away. There were past 'failures' there, too, and many people obviously as lonely as I was. R. sat it out and didn't dance; I felt very angry with him. And there was another man there, unexpectedly, for whom I felt an intense hatred, for some years back he'd brutally and viciously rejected me in a professional-personal situation in a way I could neither forget nor forgive. With some of the women I could be more at ease, light and playful, but there was a nagging frustration in that too, that sexual relating was possible but somehow never happened.

So, over-stimulated and frustrated, I went to bed in a state of irritable tension, and I woke in the morning with a frown and a feeling of tremendous pressure and discomfort. It's not easy to describe this pressure: something is weighing on you overpoweringly, but you don't know *where:* it's not embodied: it's nameless, unfamiliar and can't be located; not a tangible recognisable sensation or emotion, only a state in which you know something's got to happen next. Then it dawns on you suddenly that you have a poem waiting to be born. Enlightenment follows, in all senses of the word. You have very little to do once you've pen and paper: it all comes of itself – you are the vehicle, the channel, for what has to be expressed. And there seems to be a 'magical moment' of ripeness, when you catch what has come to fruition.

So I went down to the field and sat on the grass, by the stream, with the airplanes screaming and the blackbird singing. I could see the car-dump, an eyesore, in the distance, and I thought – ecology – and it immediately clicked that eco-feminism was in the same symbolic mode, had the same response to nature, as the *Song of Songs*. And that I had to continue on from the unresolved, unsatisfying experience with C. I wanted to write about myself and men and other women and the earth, about rape and neglect, and the bitterness and deathliness that was coming between men and women and how impossible it was in 1984 to achieve the union, the fertility, celebrated in the *Song of Songs*. I needed to register the bewilderment and grief that was around me in the conference community, as well as the hopes for transformation, the caring and love we shared and struggled with and hoped might bear fruit in the wider world.

I started with 'The earth is parched and cracked/The land is dry and sullen' – which was a description of how I was feeling – and what followed came mainly from the incidents, talk, feelings, of the previous three days, some of which I've mentioned here. The images of the 'stalled' lover were actual symbols chosen at random by men in a psychodrama session and mimed by them. The daughter was my woman friend's eleven-year-old of whom I'm very fond: she'd been phoning her at times over the weekend. The women had sat in a circle on the grass to talk about eco-feminism.

This writing, as I've said, came of itself, and was in its language more ready, more integrated, than the previous writing had been two months before, probably because of the white heat of its composition. And in that setting I was, as poet, more detached, more catalytic, in a medium role, already processing the emotions, ideas and associations I was picking up from the community. That I wasn't sexually active seems relevant also: the energy transferred itself to the writing. I now see that is how the transformation happens. The pressure I experienced was connected with body frustration, but the need was to find a meaning, to transform the pain of that frustration, and the poem does that: a spiritual act, an expression of the heart, beyond fleshly experiencing. The detachment involved a loss, a sacrifice of self that enabled inspiration to happen and a wider consciousness to enter; my hurt body became a significant symbol; the tension of suffering was eased, moving on into a more diffuse collective awareness. The poem, and the community it belonged to, that I belonged to, would receive, dissolve and heal the self-centred pain.

I read what I'd written that day at the final plenary session, conscious, as I stood by the microphone at floor-level, of the contrast with R.'s session two days before. I was very moved, and so were many of those listening, and I found I couldn't face them afterwards but had to go away, hide almost. There's a kind of awe in the impersonality of your position, the oracular quality of poetry, that has to be honoured and protected.

I left that evening for home, wondering what I might find on re-reading the poem I'd written two months before, of which I had scarcely any recollection. When I returned to it I was astonished at how the two made a progression, matching easily. Very little adaptation was needed to put them together. As I worked on it further I found the second writing giving new meanings to the first. Similarly, I was now seeing C. in a different way, essentially the same as those men who'd contributed to the second 'beloved', as much caught in the dynamic of fear and betrayal. He still kept in touch, but was now clearly avoiding the disturbing good and bad feelings aroused in him by our contact: later he would elect to return to his marriage and his workaholic existence. The bridging section of the poem – from 'Sisters, tell me . . .' which I now wrote – was prophetic.

At this point, in order to write that connecting piece, I went back to the Bible to refresh my connection, re-establish myself in the linguistic and emotional form, ground, of the *Song of Songs*. That language I could now appreciate for its fearlessness, its way of carrying intense feeling clear-eyed and without sentimentality ('We watched him as he drove out on to the highway.'); it provided the medium for the supportive sisterhood that sustains the speaker in the despair of her bereavement: 'I cannot keep body and soul together.' The language, the poem, keeps them together, turning the pain of body experience into a transcendent, patient acknowledgment of our powerlessness in time.

I'd gone instinctively to the Bible for its Hebraic parallelism, the bareness of statement that is profoundly accepting of the paradoxes of life: 'and . . . and' not 'either . . . or'. The English of the 1611 translation came, too, at a time when there still existed a wholeness of body-mind-spirit, a late medieval world-view which was soon to be lost. This language was still part of an oral, folk tradition, through pulpit preaching and popular ballad. We're now regaining something of that holistic view of life through our contact with Eastern and 'alternative' medical practice, and bioenergetic and other modes of understanding body-life. Thus the phrase 'My neck was stiff' was my physical reality, and it also carries a set of associations gathered since Anglo-Saxon times.

There's a theoretical connection emerging here now – and as I write I'm marvelling at the way the poem has constellated some ideas, thoughts and hypotheses that my head hasn't been able to sort out by theorising.

T. S. Eliot described what happened to language and literature from the seventeenth century onward with the term 'dissociation of sensibility': the wholeness was lost. This is the equivalent of what psycho-analysis calls the 'schizoid split'. It's precisely that split – a reaction to intolerable pain – that the 'hysterical' woman is afraid of: body and soul torn apart, mind and body split, male and female disconnected. In life, in therapy, we strive for reconciliation, healing the split. It was Eliot's aim to heal the dissociation in his poetry, and I see now that it was mine in this poem.

Reconciliation is of course hinted at in the last few lines of the poem. That brings me to what I subsequently realised was the 'hidden agenda' of my poem – that I'd gone to the Bible, where the Hebrew/Jewish and the English/Christian were so harmoniously related, because of the uneasy relationship between the Jewish and Anglo-Christian cultures I was raised in – which parallels the uneasy relationship between passionate self-liberating women and cool patriarchal men. Women of any oppressed ethnic minority have a doubly reinforced experience of victimhood and life-suppression.

So I recognised much later that the 'slaughtered aborted children' were, far more than I wanted to know, the millions who died in the concentration camps. I still can't come to terms with that in full consciousness. The wombs of Jewish women are full of that history, of intense buried unwanted feelings which the receiving and rejecting Christian environment sometimes helps to repress, sometimes to release and heal. Yes, we have the H-bomb in our vagina, and the Holocaust in our womb. It's vital that we free and voice our feelings about these atrocities of corrupt patriarchal power.

But that does mean admitting our collusive involvement as victims or destroyers. My own hatred and destructiveness invites, commits, rape and violation when I deny it instead of directing it creatively. The shock of fully realising 'the horror of my passion' came through the contact with C., who was himself much identified with the aggression and violence in the Middle East. The sexual encounter in the poem has disturbed many people. When I read it now it seems to me a manifestation of the goddess, who knows love and hatred, purity and corruption, light and dark, and who may well be angry enough with what men have done to our world to want to destroy it. They have suppressed her: she has been numb, untouched for centuries: perhaps only violence brings her to life.

'The Song of Songs for 1984' continues to reverberate and offer new meanings. Recently after a period of feeling much abused as a vulnerable woman, I realised I was also the innocent violated daughter in the poem. And I saw that though the women sought to keep her from harm to heal her, and closed the circle round her, ultimately she must be healed by a loving and self-forgiving father, who needs to be given access to her, lest she always be afraid of men. I think the implications of that, for the women's movement, for men, are considerable. And again it's about women's creativity: our capacity to go beyond the protective maternal role we've been stuck in – bitterly? self-righteously? – the closed circle; and gradually open the circle, inviting men to join us, and then move on to form ever widening circles, an expansion of love and creativity which may yet overcome the evil forces we are now confronting head on.

*When Alix sees her work in terms of 'opening the circle' to admit the
father with a healing gesture, she does so in the floodlight of a
specific historical drama, whose chief personage wields a heavy
hand in the lives of Jewish women. 'The father' is no pale shadow to
be huffed and puffed away: he is law-giving patriarch par excellence,
he is slaughtered god, not through the symbol of Christ but in the
actuality of the gas chambers. He exacts acknowledgement from his
daughters more severely than other less toughened idols. Alix's
reflections on cultural work and creative process are closer to sacred
than to secular concerns; her ambition to link sexuality and spirituality can be entertained only where there exist developed and
mutually comprehensible codes for both realms of experience.
Women whose own background does not offer this are turning
elsewhere – to European paganism or esoteric cults, to Oriental
philosophies, aboriginal religions or modern humanistic psycho-
therapies – for linguistic and symbolic resources which propose an
integration of conflict. This is an unwieldy recycled patchwork
whose overall pattern is yet unclear. But perhaps the whole point, to
shuffle metaphors, is that a generous cultural soup is brewing whose
constituents are digested more for their convertible food-value than
for their discrete flavours . . .*

*Helen McNeil's essay, like Alix's, charts a particular process, in
this case the story of its own writing. Her questions are secular ones,
however: the tradition she handles is the 'English' novel – a
tradition where women's contributions can hardly be overestimated
yet where women's achievements are variously patronised, problematised or reified. Novels tell stories and, though novelists continue to dissolve their consoling solidity, stories can be made to yield
evidence for contemporary social structures – not just manners and
mores, but the mediation of economic and ideological institutions.
But novels – those worth the effort of reading – are not of course
written as repositories; the narrative is always at a tangent to the
documentary impetus. That slippery inquiry into the relationship
between the life and the art, between biography and aesthetic, is
cajoled, in Helen's essay, into purposive musing about how the
convoluted social constitution of self for a woman writer informs –
or deforms – her creative output. Like Diana Scott, Helen sees both
instruction and disjunction in reading other, earlier women's work
– what, really, can we learn from other writers? From the apparent
circumstances of their lives, from their explicit aims, their unconscious choices, their partial satisfactions? Recognising the appeal of*

this line of inquiry, Helen unfolds her own experience into accessible material. To think clearly, as well as to feel strongly, about the occupational dilemmas of the 'woman writer' is to have a chance of undoing the mystification that the label seems to attract. Women are often recited for their emotional limpidity while finding it more difficult to acquire an unambiguous reputation for mental lucidity. Mostly this is a sympton of the selective failure of male critics to use their organs of discernment; but it is prudent of feminists to be wary of the self-contradicting manoeuvre that results in overvaluing and thereby dogmatising emotions.

Oh, No You Can't! Oh, Yes I Can!

Helen McNeil

We've just come back, it's late August, and it's time to write this piece. I've left writing it until the last possible minute so that it has to be done straight off, with no second thoughts. I know well why I left it so long. When Lesley invited me to write something about creativity, my first reaction was immense pleasure. Now, writing this at last, I feel that pleasure again. Lesley and I are in the same writing group, and over the past couple of years I've been impressed and moved, seeing Lesley's poetry develop and seeing her gradually work out a way of life which has space for creativity. When she told me about this project, and about how she wanted us to feel free to understand creativity in the widest possible sense, I thought it was a marvellous idea. Immediately I thought of part of what I wanted to write. Then the doubts started.

The doubts weren't about the project, and they weren't about creativity. They were about me. Am I creative? Who am I to write about creativity? Nine-tenths of what I've published has been criticism of one kind or another. My job as a university lecturer also centres on critical and analytical skills; increasingly, it's about administration as well. Shouldn't the invitation have gone to someone better than me? Or to some famous woman writer or creative person who could share with us an understanding of how she does it? Someone like that should do it. Not me. I shouldn't; I can't, really.

Whenever a newspaper or magazine prints a feature or does an interview with a woman writer or film-maker or artist of the moment, I read every word as if my life depended on it. I can't find out enough. I want to know how they do it, even when it is women whose work I find conventional (but they've done it, haven't they?). I must have read Penelope Mortimer's anecdote about how she advertised for room-and-board in order for her to go finish a novel a good half-a-dozen times, and each time it is almost as interesting as the time before. She had loads of replies and enacted her writerly solitude in the care of a very nice couple in the country.

I devour the habits and work of women whose accomplishment I find dazzling, life-changing: Margarethe von Trotta, Alice Walker. Or women who are less spectacular perhaps but honest and bold, sometimes neglected: Buchi Emecheta, Caryl Churchill, Anne Stevenson, Eva Figes. Nor do these women operate under some special cultural protection because they are known or their work has been published. A couple of months ago the reviewer in *The Times* called Figes' new novel, *The Seven Ages*, a history of the human race as seen from the perspective of the uterus. I could hardly credit my eyes when I read that, but it was almost culpably naïve of me to feel shocked. And to think that I had bought *The Times,* which I no longer read, because I thought they might have reviewed my own book, a feminist critical study of the poet Emily Dickinson. How nice, how appropriate, that it wasn't ever reviewed there. Even when our creativity speaks in dialects reasonably recognisable to our present culture, it can still be dangerous to the *status quo,* so it is best not considered, best derided, expelled where possible by innuendo. 'Demur – you're straightway dangerous/And handled with a chain', Dickinson wrote. She wrote from experience; of her almost 1800 poems, only about ten were published in her lifetime.

In the United States, where I grew up, there's long been a term for the wish to absorb something of those you admire by noting the details of their behaviour. This is the finding of 'role models'. These tend to be the first woman teacher or boss whom you respect on a personal as well as a professional level. Then (or at the same time) it's a series of very well-known women. In the US today, Jane Fonda and Alice Walker have their lives covered this way. As an actress, Fonda makes her living through self-representation; a public role for her creativity seems to have come as more of a surprise for Walker, though she has used these intrusions to great ideological effect. Walker herself quite consciously sought out role models or 'foremothers' to help her define herself as a creative black woman in the United States. She chose Coretta King, the civil rights activist who was the wife and then widow of Martin

Luther King, and Zora Neale Hurston, a black writer and anthro-
pologist who had died in poverty, her work virtually forgotten.

Yet the term 'role model' is insidiously, significantly, just off the
mark. If you model yourself on a role played by someone else, it is
just that – the role – that you have available for copying. You
may well emulate the externals while the core of that woman's
dynamism, the key to her creative practice, remains elusive,
hidden. It is, after all, *her* role in any case. And the part that is not
playing a role is precisely the part least visible in the hotel-room
interview of the book promotion tour.

Take writers: there's a great value in seeing how published
writers operate. You can feel that you're being let in on the witch's
secret recipe. Habit is obviously somewhere at the heart of it. But
because these women are by definition on the other side of the line
of public appreciation from most of us, the very existence of the
tell-all account can seem, ironically, only to confirm our distance.
It is often as if these are the problems and habits of other, superior
beings in some parallel world 'over there'. It is as if they are busy
telling us what it's like, but the declaration carries another, coded
message, there's a sub-text saying, 'I can reveal this because I'm
already there, whatever I say it won't make you like me, because
I'm different.'

I remember years ago in some series about parenthood,
Margaret Drabble wrote about how children were wonderful and
essential to her life, but you mustn't ever count on being able to
work after the children are asleep. When they're little, they do fall
asleep early, but you're too exhausted to budge. When they're
older, they never seem to go to bed. So, Drabble wrote, she went
to bed first, with her books and notebooks, and she let her children
look in from time to time to check that she was all right. How
interesting, I thought. How true. I see I must have memorised that
tale. But I couldn't make any connection between this instructive
anecdote and the way Drabble pushed out a new novel every 18
months. Nor, indeed, could I make a connection with the form of
her domestic realist novels. Did her assurances mean that the kind
of woman who makes them would write the kind of novels that
Drabble was writing in the seventies? What if that's not what you
want to write? Or was she saying something harder, clothing it in a
pleasant homily? Namely, don't expect to get ahead of your
situation in life. Don't think you can beat it on any regular basis. A
single parent mustn't expect the late night work-period available to

the childless. Accept, adjust. Was that it? It was all like the good cook who gives you her recipe, which then doesn't work out when you do it; she's left out some essential ingredient or process, maybe because she isn't conscious of it herself, maybe because she instinctively protects herself from being imitated. And without that element, what you produce is ordinary. It would be, of course, because even the perfect recipe is someone else's recipe. Only traditional recipes transfer, and then only to cooks who are in some way part of that tradition.

So there I was, glad to see Lesley's inclusiveness, glad to anticipate reading the other contributors' views of creativity, views which wouldn't be limited by definitions of success put out by a society which, among the groups it oppresses, oppresses women. I looked forward to this without applying my perception to myself. Lesley's being nice, I thought, she's asking me because she knows me, but I'm not really an appropriate choice. Not me.

I want to write some more about that 'not me'. It's a form of death, death by denial of being. It's like a worm that speaks up when you hesitate, and it always says No. No, you can't. Not me. When you show what you've written to friends and they say they like it, or when you look at what you've written a couple of days after, the worm lets you know that they were only being polite, saying that. And as for your own sense of satisfaction, how can your own impressions be accurate if your perceptions are banal to begin with?

What feeds this worm? What gives it voice? Where does it get its rigid notions of good and no good? There's a clue in the pronouns. The worm of negation appropriates the idea of self, the I or ego, as in 'I'm not good enough'. Sometimes it speaks as the internal representative of an outer judge. 'You're hopeless, really, when you think about it. Best not to keep making a fool of yourself.' It is articulating a notion of a discrete, limited and clearly defined 'me', then it proffers an image of that me, then it looks at that image from the perspective of those who form fixed images in our society. For whom is our creativity 'not good enough'? The professionals? Your former professor? ('Could do better.') Your father? God? Reviewers in *The Times* maybe?

Let me tell a story about someone who was eaten by the worm. A few years ago I went to a friend's house for lunch. A friend of his joined us, looking very distressed. The friend-of-a-friend – call him Edward – had just turned 40. After our not-very-funny commiserations, the tone of our lunch turned darker. Edward said that he now had to accept that he wasn't a creative person. He had written poetry for some years and, initially at least, some of it had been published. Later he had had less luck. Certain coteries at certain magazines had, he felt, taken against him. His success as an editor had made him enemies. But, Edward said, he had to admit that in recent years he had written less and less. Most recently, nothing at all. He had 'dried up'. He would have to face facts: he wasn't really creative.

Edward had a job that was involved with culture. He certainly made decisions about culture, about what would be published, and how. I had faintly envied him for having what seemed to be a creative job which was also pleasantly well paid. It was clear that Edward had great personal energy, he got things done, and he encouraged other people to express themselves. I didn't agree with his 'list', but I could see the point of it.

I couldn't believe that Edward was making such a mechanical distinction between creative and non-creative, and not seeing his own life, his daily being, as the source of creativity. I tried to tell him this, but it proved cold comfort. In the ensuing conversation he more than hinted that, while he appreciated my sympathy, etc., he considered my ideas of creativity to be rather diffuse . . . a bit naïve in a hard world . . . basically unprofessional, offering mere palliatives. The meal ended with all of us feeling worse than when we began. Since then, I've come across Edward only once or twice, at large gatherings where he has been working his way efficiently through the more eminent guests. So that's where his creative energy has gone.

Lesley is asking me to write about creativity. Before the worm raised its head, I thought, No problem. I know what I'll write about, I'll write about the most creative experience in my life. And I know what that experience was, it was the birth of my first child 14 years ago. In the month before her birth I had thought a lot about death. Since then I've learned that many women have these thoughts at that time. Your body is at an edge in late pregnancy, so burdened with about-to-be-life that it seems it might crack or burst carrying that life over into real being.

Liberty was born by natural childbirth, which was frowned upon then at the old St George's Hospital. I was the pushy American. Well, so be it. Since she was ten days late, although she was not showing signs of distress, my labour was induced as a matter of routine, at a tidy weekday nine a.m. The contractions started suddenly, violently, only three minutes apart. All round me the other five women who were also being induced were lying down, crying or groaning from the pain. One by one they were sedated or knocked out. Sooner or later their children were born. I was also offered sedation, but I didn't want the birth to be something that happened to an unconscious body, I wanted it to be all of me doing it, to be what I was doing. Right then, while I was panting and counting, one of the meanings of the connection between birth and death came to me. Whatever my opinions were about the matter, the birth was going ahead. The contractions weren't going to stop because I, Helen, didn't care for them to be happening then or would prefer them not to be quite so strong. They were going to go faster and stronger until I gave birth.

Birth shares this inexorability with death. When it is happening, it happens, then, there, that way. I had been trained, I had the biological luck to have an average female body, and I wanted with all my being to be fully there. When my daughter's head came out, I saw it. She had her thick brown hair even then. As I pushed, her shoulders appeared, and when I pushed again, she slid out, she almost flew out. I was able to hold her in my arms and kiss her and call her my darling. Her skin was purplish pink, she was curiously long and thin. She mewed. It amazed me that she didn't have sort-of-eyelashes or a general idea of hands. Every eyelash, every little moon in the cuticle of each fingernail was there, all finished. And hanging from her as she was pulled up into the air was the big purple snake of the umbilical cord, unearthly in appearance because it was the direct, absolute stuff of human creation. So she was born. Something had come from nothing. And my experience was nothing unusual. Lifemaking. Tens of thousands of women do it every day.

Over the next months, as I nursed my child and she grew and flourished, I kept thinking more and more clearly about that apparent paradox how there is a life where there had not been a life before. Something from nothing. If something comes from nothing, it is right that something goes to nothing too. I would die some day, we all would. And it wasn't just that our bodies would betray us, it was that we would run our course. We were our bodies. We bring forth and give way and we leave something. Or we can leave something. When I conceptualised these feelings, I realised why women have always been such poor advocates of the Western philosophy of Dualism, the soul in the body as the ghost in the machine. The idea took its modern form in Descartes' *Discourse on Method,* in the uncanny passage in which he is sitting at ease, dozing before the fire, only to be shot through with terror that he doesn't exist. How can he know for certain that he exists? And then he has it: *cogito ergo sum.* (He must have been thinking in Latin that evening.) I think therefore I am. Is that so? Is that how you know? (Checking with Descartes, I see I have over-dramatised the circumstances!) I first read that passage in an undergraduate philosophy seminar, but its chill will stay with me forever. The tutor, friendly and enthusiastic, explained how this short essay was in fact the seminal work of modern philosophical method. What was the matter with Descartes? How could he have been such a fool? And in retrospect, such a dangerous fool. But back then I only took my uneasy fear as a sign that I would be better off majoring in literature.

Having a child is only one instance, perhaps almost too literal an instance, of creativity. Not everyone wants or needs children. But birth serves as a model. The model is of making something. It is a creative act to live a just life. 'The best lack all conviction, while the worst/Are filled with passionate intensity', Yeats wrote. That state is the worm in its social manifestation, when you feel unable to act: someone else should do it, not me. Living a just life involves saying that it *is* you, what you do counts, simply do it. Sometimes there's a material result of creativity, sometimes there isn't. Unless its premises are utterly perverted, teaching is a creative act. Releasing other people into creativity, knowledge of themselves, command of skills for expression. A creative attitude can infuse everything we do with strength, value, freedom.

And yet . . . and yet . . . Isn't the everyday usually a lot less bright and pure, a lot more up and down? When you don't have any money, the need for money drives out the creative. Gas bills eat up energy. Or you have a job, but the job can yield only limited creative reward. Well, change the job or use it creatively. Yes, but most jobs are part of a hierarchy. The teacher can be promoted into administration, where the money and prestige are. Or she can continue to teach while others are promoted to administer her. Hierarchies reward those who think hierarchically. Some hierarchies can be 'turned'; others can't. Or you have those children, you wanted them, you love them, but when the baby naps, you collapse too; when children come home from school, they need real, direct attention. And your companion, your friends. Best to work with them, work together if you possibly can, shared energy multiplies. You do need friend-time, discourse, trust. You have a good bath, how long has the telly been on? And it's next day, next year.

I think hardly anyone lives a life without conflict of desires and demands. They can all be worthy. Then it's a question of calm and balance. Some can be killers – these are usually addictive, like the green sugar of money. Figure out slowly what it is you want, and figure out how to get it, slowly if need be. Lesley and Cathy and Shirley and I – our writing group – are all mothers. We're also all with someone, in a relationship. We're all involved with hierarchies, all uneasily. And we all write. The balance is constantly shifting. We must like it that way.

Once I was unwisely grousing about my children to an unmarried male friend. 'Oh,' he said, 'have you read Cyril Connolly's *Enemies of Promise?* You must read it. He says that the pram in the hall is the end of creativity.' I got off the phone wishing I had uttered the tirade of insults about his own rotten lifestyle that went through my head. But two wrongs don't make a right, as Granny used to say. He was wrong. Also wrong are the people who say that having children is the only real, the only true creativity. Such people often go on to remark that it's therefore natural that women are no good at other kinds of creativity such as art and music, they being so satisfied by their bellies.

If there's always going to be some balancing of forces, then clearing the space for the creative must become habitual. Only then can it hope to touch everything. Creativity is a habit and a skill. It needs the sun. Sometimes a student tells me that she just couldn't write this or that essay. Or he or she tried but just couldn't get into the story they had told me about, the one they so wanted to write. They were blocked somehow. The word 'inspiration' isn't used, but they have been waiting for lightning to strike, for something to happen that will make them write.

I do know one radical solution for writer's block, though it takes a while to set up. Have a couple of kids without having much money. Make arrangements for them to be taken care of, say, three mornings a week, maybe by exchanging time. Or they start school. Then you won't find yourself sitting at the typewriter unable to think of a thing. You'll be grateful for the time you have carved out and you'll use it. At least it was that way for me. The time when I began to write again coincided remarkably with my younger child starting school and my bad marriage breaking up, leaving me broke. Sometimes I think of Sylvia Plath, who had years of creative routine behind her when her marriage broke up. She awoke before dawn to write, hearing the chink of the milkman as she used the time before her children woke up.

Or I remember my friend the novelist Verity Bargate visiting me week-long in Norfolk, when the creative routine had decidedly more pleasure. Verity had two sons, I had a daughter and a son, and the children were all great friends, so while they played and explored round the cottage, Verity and I sat and gossiped. Then we got started on our never-to-be-perfected English tans and we cooked interesting messes with nettles and child-gathered fruit and we got stoned and listened to old records. We were total layabouts. We also read aloud what we were writing, and we each went off to a table and wrote – but, as I recall, not for all that long – every day. Later Verity credited that week as 'the week I finished my novel'. Or other times I took her sons at half-term to free her to write, because there was a play-scheme in Norwich and none in Greenwich. Filled with pride at earth-mothering four children, I phoned mid-week to report. The answering machine said they were out. Next night same thing. I began to wonder if I had been underwriting a binge. But when you do someone a favour, you don't also get to write the script of how that favour will be used, you just get not to do it again if you don't like it. End of the following week came the explanation. Yes, indeed she had spent the 'free' week going out a lot and sleeping late. There had also been experiments with bath oils and sparkly make-up, and she had only thought, almost only day-dreamed, about her writing. Then when the guilt had built up, both about me and about her own sloth, and Sam and Tom had come back and there was supposedly no free time at all, then she sat down and wrote like fury the whole week, ignoring all the obstacles. With that pattern of gathering-strength, using-strength, Verity figured out how to use virtually everything. When she got the cancer that finally killed her, she used that too, not as self-pity, rather as something changed round, made metaphorical.

Day in, day out I set myself rules so that the obligations which have timetables don't drive out the always-unscheduled writing time. Sometimes, as critic, I write in the abstract about literary form, but the conditions of writing are always concrete. I was not allowed to 'do a little shopping' on the way back from taking the kids to school. (I'd stagger in at eleven, completely zonked by the bright lights of Tesco's and the cheap thrills of comparison shopping.) No bill paying or admin – they set off the dread spiral of not enough money, not enough time. No washing up or cleaning. What did I want to remember about this period in my life, I asked myself, that I accomplished something or that even though no one knew and no one cared I had the house tidy every day, all day? It dawned on me at one point that I had been thinking of housework as a form of noble duty, that if a lightning bolt were to strike me while I was loading the wash, I would fly straight to heaven as a virtuous woman. What rubbish! And that attitude means drudgery is done in secret but then paraded like a cross one bears, annoying everyone else and serving to assert female guilt power. Meanwhile housework should be shared and seen for what it is, nothing special.

When I am writing, I allow myself small ritualised pleasures as breaks from the writing-pleasures. The cup of herb tea. Bright light. Luxury of the fan heater for half an hour. Tidying the workplace, because that's part of the work. A few minutes stretching or dancing, because the body is part of it. If it's not raining, I'll dig up weeds. Boring, eh? That's what they're meant to be.

And the other ways, the ordinary ways to get past blocks into the habit and time of creativity. Some can be communicated. Change the workplace to someplace neutral, like a small empty room or a desk in the physics section of the library. Work at the same time every day. Throw out the first page. Outline it spatially rather than linearly. Ease your way in by doing supporting work if you feel stale – retyping, doing the references if it's reference work. Think of it as dialogue, so you really argue. When you start for the day, only look back at the past page or two you've written, unless this is the moment for heavy revision; you can slip back further and further in endless reconsideration. And something that happens to me a lot: if another section of what I'm writing pops into my head, or if I think of something which is apparently not connected with the matter at hand, I try not to suppress it or postpone it, I try to write it out on another piece of paper, at least getting the key phrases. Almost always these 'orphans' turn out to be related to the 'main' work, and blocking them drains energy because part of you is still thinking about them. I choose what I'm working on for the given day or week. Can't start six things at once. Oddly enough, narrowing the drive to one main thing releases other thoughts, it's some principle of directed energy releasing other energy. And I try – though as you see I don't always succeed – not to think of myself as writing, me, the distinct and limited and vain and vulnerable person. I try to think about what is being written and its life. I suspect this last gets easier as one gets older.

Is what I have written a classic instance of teacherism, of 'Do as I say, not as I do'? I'm not content with the present balance of my life, and I feel doubt, sometimes paralysing doubt. Perhaps anyone who steps out of the system of institutional rewards has to reckon with the daily presence of the worm. When it says, 'Oh no you can't,' you can only reply, 'Oh yes I can,' and get on with it.

Last year at this time I was writing about Emily Dickinson. I would not want to have suffered her life, but she was a towering instance of a woman who figured out a way to keep writing and to write as she wanted to. I thought I had worked out my view of her poetry, and I was startled to find over the months that followed that my ideas changed radically under the pressure of being shaped into a book-length argument. My articles and reviews, even my thesis, hadn't prepared me for this. Nor had they prepared me for the satisfaction of feeling I had written something which served a purpose, something for which the effort had been worthwhile.

A couple of years ago I wrote the draft of a novel. I learned an immense amount about fiction from the inside while writing it. But it needed revision and meanwhile the time had come to finish the Dickinson. That fiction, and for that matter everything else up to the Dickinson revision, had been written out of a spirit of resistance, of awareness of the enemy. Kicking against the pricks. Recently, though, my life has been very happy and it has been a strange sensation for me to write out of happiness. The fiction bears a lot of negative emotion, though it is also meant to be cool and serene. I've been revising it, though uneasily. Last week, while I was working on it, another story interfered, a supernatural tale I'd had some vague notion of. Out came 20 pages. Maybe it's good, maybe it's the byproduct of my fear at revising the recalcitrant material of the first narrative. Or maybe it's both, or bad and a byproduct. I don't know yet. Maybe none of it is publishable. I'm deliberately writing about the embarrassing situation of unpublished fiction because I've already had a great creative benefit from writing it. It's a fake to feel you should hide writing away for fear of an abstract judge. I'd like to see it done, printed, public, but I've had a lot of the good of it already.

I'm just sending off this piece to Lesley. I want to try out my fiction with a more distanced perspective in the second half. I need to revise the article on the poet H. D. for Diana. There's a long review-article I've been reading for, on Nathaniel Hawthorne's letters. Now there was a truly creative person whom the worm silenced long before his death. Lib and Gabe come back next week, and my term starts in four weeks. I've got a huge teaching load, or to put it another way, I've decided to start several new seminars. Graham has just got a new studio. My Dickinson book comes out in the US next month, and I wonder what they'll think of it. When I'm back in Norfolk I want to look up supernatural beliefs there in the nineteenth century. Even though it's still August, it's raining and it's growing cold. We'll see.

Helen, like Liz, has intimated what a description of the connection between reproduction and writing might authentically be. This is one of the most difficult relationships from which to deliver a comprehensible body of thought, but it is likely to be the determining one for women artists. How does the writer-person do a deal with the mother-person, bargaining for minutes of free time? How does a woman evaluate her poetry and her babies on the same scale? How are we to relate the ecstasy of birth to the different ecstasy of composing art? Or, by contrast, how might we relate the notion of cultural production to the concept of motherhood as the reproduction of a replacement work-force?

Theoretical inquiries into these and related topics often remain dense and at a rather disheartening distance from most women's everyday lives and comprehension; much theory seems to spring out of a different source from the empiricism of women's liberation. The major appeal of feminism in Britain has been to appear pragmatic rather than abstract; also autonomous rather than Marxist, rhetorical rather than psychoanalytical. Despite the growth of academic feminism, the centre of gravity has up to now been to establish the means by which 'ordinary' women can think about, and think about changing, their lives. An impressive array of feminist insights has been gathered from workshops, refuges, conferences, pickets, festivals.

From them it has emerged that connections between creativity and procreativity are articulated all around us by all sorts of propositions, some plausible, some helpful, some degrading. There exist hundreds of accessible first-hand accounts by women of how, for instance, norms of reproduction – such as heterosexism or the expectation to have babies – can harm a woman's self-esteem whether she fails to achieve them or she consciously rejects them. We recognise that these messages indicate to a woman that she has, through some flaw in her own femaleness, failed to reproduce the behaviour appropriate to a female in this society.

Often such women, through a process of painstaking reclamation, manage to relocate their sense of creativity in their sexuality as they now begin to re-experience it. The rediscovery and enjoyment of their own sexuality, felt as a capacity for pleasure and regeneration, is intimately related to the disclosure of their desire to dance, sing, paint. The recurrence of womb-images and birth allegories in much feminist work points to a variety of readings of this relationship, often as a challenge to misogynist censorship or distortion of female sexuality. Undoing the disgust, opening Pandora's box, has been an energetic and energising enterprise.

Dinner Parties out of Giblets

Lesley Saunders

In September 1983 I had an abortion. The dedication at the front of the book is to the spirit of that flesh: nine months after conceiving, I was in The Women's Press office discussing the viability of a book about creativity. As I reach the final stages of editing this book, I feel nauseous, my breasts are tender, my stomach bloated but I am not pregnant. But nor is my subjective experience of writing a book at all like my subjective experience of having a baby. I cannot answer the questions these small facts pose.

This is a brief account of one writer's workshop I led; similar questions were posed for many of the participants. The women undertook an imaginary journey into their bodies: through their vulvas, into their wombs and as far as their ovaries. The purpose was two-fold: to enable women to have an 'inward' experience of their sexuality and to explore the significance of the images that came to them in the process. (The imagery I used as a guide owes a great deal to an excercise developed in workshops and courses by Jan Dungey.)

Some women were apprehensive when I announced the journey; they thought they might be overwhelmed by what they would find. One woman felt sick at the idea of entering her vagina, two women rebelled at the notion of creativity being linked with reproduction 'yet again'. Another woman, who was approaching menopause, wanted to journey into her brain which was where she felt the seat of her creativity now to be.

When it was over and they were talking, each woman without exception said she found the journey enjoyable and revealing, though each woman's experience seems to have been quite different from anyone else's. One woman said she felt more whole.

There were colours, light, brightness: one woman, who is a painter and going blind, said her ovary was so dazzling she could hardly look. One woman drank and swam in her menstrual blood, another went 'potholing', another felt playful as she bumped and slid down the ridges of her vagina. For a few, there was a sense of sanctity and peace – one woman found her womb was a temple with archaic inscriptions and her ovary a place 'of perfect purity and proportions'. In other words, the partriarchal womb – the one that caused women apprehension, the dark, devouring, smelly, messy womb-as-tomb – was not the one they discovered. They and I were moved by this shared revelation of the store of symbolic energy which is often inaccessible.

There were fearful aspects too – in particular one woman felt she was on the brink of reliving her birth and neither of us felt we could handle that; another woman felt claustrophobic at one point; the woman at menopause said she had to come to terms with her womb 'withering'. They were touching on charged material, areas of silence. Both the joyful and the sombre aspects of the workshop looked as if they would provide potent resources for creative work. We went on talking over tea and supper as well.

Envisaging a journey means agreeing to construe women's body-space as having, or being, an interiority. The women were encouraged to picture an architecture of the womb. Initially, this is no more than we are invited to do by convention, but with the difference that the women were asked to shape that space and inhabit it instead of complying with (or resisting) received images.

Menstruation, for instance, is perceived as a disturbed – and disturbing – time in our culture; by not agreeing to carry on as normal but by withdrawing a little into their interior chamber (a psychic menstrual hut?), women can behold the other face of 'the curse'. Several artists (among them Miriam Cahn, who appeared on Channel 4's *State of the Art*. See Bibliography.) are evolving ways of working directly with menstrual energy, giving themselves over to the different content and intensity of those days.

And at any time in their cycle, women can own something 'inside' them which is a source of inspiration: often depicted as somewhere dark, chaotic, primeval, vast, creative in a non-human mode (of which a graphic rendering is the mythic Magic Cauldron), the womb can instead be constructed as personal, differentiated, analysable, vivid and varied. It can be emblematic of that which is not in our control but in which we can discern a deeply meaningful pattern and to which therefore we can give our emotional and intellectual assent. This is an important change in the iconography of female creativeness, of which Judy Chicago's work is the famous and contentious example.

However, the apparent security of this relationship must be ruptured and the generality of its truth severely threatened; as the woman in the workshop knew. This is not to say that the relationship is unreal in the first place; but in some important way it cannot be taken for granted. The womb is not to be taken on trust. There are questions to be asked.

(See, for instance, an article by Mary Medicott (Guardian, *11 February 1987) in which she describes having undergone a hysterectomy, like a growing number of young women with invasive cervical cancer; and then wonders how she can 'feel creative without directly sharing these images [of blood and birth]' with which she grew up.)*

How and how far is it possible to turn what one is – a female – into what one does, to transform the passive and given into the active and chosen? Margaret Homans (see Bibliography) has provided a detailed argument to the effect that the Goddess, Mother Nature, the Womb, does not provide her daughters with an appropriate model for making the leap from what we are to what we want to become; powerful as she is, her powers are not the ones we need in order to write poetry, because she is herself not capable of self-representation. Might we not justly argue that the womb, like the phallus, is an organ not an emblem; is not the task to deconstruct rather than perpetuate its symbolism?

But the problem may take quite other forms. When Monica Sjöö's son died, she – the mother – outlived him, the child. That is a rift, a tear in the 'natural' fabric of procreation. Monica is, in one sense, the opposite of a deconstructionist, but she has found herself compelled to undertake an emotionally rigorous pursuit of meaning in her search for comfort and consolation. She tries, bitterly, to hear a response from the source of life and inspiration in her universe, whom she calls the Goddess. I have not encountered anything quite like this in feminist writing; though I can see resemblances to Christian struggles with God, in which, the universe seeming either overwhelmingly hostile or quite vacated, the believer strove to wring a communicable meaning from that suffering. But the Goddess is also the Womb, necessitating a specifically female theology. Giving oneself actively to Her in a trust that is also a conflict, wresting personal meanings from Her dark depths, asserting one's right to know as well as to be uncertain, demanding that what is silent should speak, locating the boundaries of self relative to Nature – in other words, ultimately subverting the naturalistic imagery on which this theology is based – all these have to be integrated into a feminist revaluation of spirituality.

Journey into Darkness

Monica Sjöö

Written at Full Moon, 26 January 1986

This is not the piece I first wrote for this book. I am writing now in the hope that in saying goodbye to all that was familiar and sustained me I will come through and decide to live again, but I do not know. *Mother, why have you forsaken me?*

We buried the ashes of my beautiful boy Leif, 15 years old, in the centre of the Medicine Wheel in the tipi village of South Wales. *Dark Mother, I screamed, it was I who was seeking you – why, oh why have you taken my son and not me? I hope you know what you are doing. Oh Mother, protect him!*

My son was run down and killed by a car in front of my eyes near Bayonne in the French Basque country on 26 August 1985. He'd run across the busy road without watching the traffic lights. On that day my life as I had known it stopped. Part of my soul went with him.

I feel chilled and disturbed by the circumstances that preceded his death, I cannot grasp the connections. Was it somehow fore-ordained? Did he himself have premonitions? He went through a profound change that summer, opened up, had strange dreams. How I wish I had talked more with him. I remember noticing many times that when he smiled his love at me there was a sadness in his eyes. He delicately tried out new emotions, new situations. How I wish I had told him more often how beautiful he was, how I love him.

I had always known that Leif was accident prone. I often feared for his life, particularly in connection with roads. Twice when he was little he had endured head injuries from accidents, had been taken to hospital. I lived with the fear that a third time would be fatal.

This Summer I relaxed a little. I had no sense of impending danger. My eyes did not tell me that it was my son being dragged along by the side of the car in front of us on the road before he went under the back wheel that fractured his skull. Would there have been time to catch him before he went under? Why did I not see clearly?

Leif and I had travelled south to get away from the rain that year. We were staying with my friend Musawa and her lover Nada on their farm in the Pyrenees. For a large part of the previous year, Leif and I had been quarrelling; he was full of anger. He resented our life in Wales and the man I was living with. His own father is a black American, an artist living in Sweden; Leif met racism at his secondary modern school in Fishguard as well as his step-father's lack of sympathy for his particular needs. Leif was explosive. He was extremely sensitive and intelligent and therefore even more prone to frustrations and paranoia. Often he was difficult to live with.

But this summer we were happy, at peace with each other. Leif was going through a great deal of creative changes. He learnt to play the drums, joyously, ecstatically. I said, *We are having a good time, aren't we?* He replied, *Yes, I am growing up, Monica, I am changing.* In France we enjoyed the sunshine, got healthy and brown. He learnt to ride the horses, helped with the harvest. There was a harvest feast – *I can see you now, Leif, grinning, pleased with yourself, joyously drunk, laughing, dancing faster and faster in the ring-dances that everyone joined in. You came up and danced – a young man, a near-adult – with me, for the first and only time. We were happy that night. I remember you in Tarbes when we went to market, wandered in the park and watched the birds together, you even holding my hand secretly but without awkwardness. The first time for years.*

How is it possible that only a little week later you are dead, my love, bleeding your life-blood away on that road outside Bayonne? How I grieve for your short life on this Earth-plane; how many times I ask your forgiveness for not having seen the danger, not seeing clearly your despair, not being able to protect you enough.

The weekend before Leif was killed we stayed with a group of women and children from England who were renting a rambling old village house. Leif was looking forward to it – and to being able to talk freely in English again. But he was six feet tall, smoked tobacco, was 15 years old. He was the enemy, man, to them as soon as we arrived and many of them rejected him, though a few were friendly and loving. The day before he died he told me he felt treated as a leper. This is a bitter memory for me.

My son was already dead when the ambulance arrived. The horror when I put my arm under his head and felt a hole behind his ear, saw blood on my clothes. For weeks the smell of his blood stayed in my hair from where I had rested my head against his during the hours in hospital, when Musawa and I stayed by his bed giving healing and love, trying to get through, hoping against hope that he would return out of his coma, that he would live. I had seen Leif lying on the road in pain, trying to lift his head, with unseeing eyes and blood in his mouth, crying out the once. *I was never able to say goodbye to you my child.* But when they turned him over and lifted him on to the stretcher the expression on his face was one of utter innocence, peace, nakedness, beauty. I thought, *You are innocent. Leif, you have done nothing wrong, you have nothing to fear.* Musawa said, *Sweet baby Leif.*

In hospital we saw how utterly beautiful he was, his body so finely formed and maturing, his arms and hands and legs and feet so like my own, so painful to see. We put little flowers in his red curly Afro hair, bleached by the sun, a flower in the middle of his forehead and leaves and bark on his chest. What I experienced in those hours of being in a hospital in a foreign country with only my one companion and in spite of the horror and remorse and dread was a sensation of light and flying, of freedom and peace, as I journeyed with him in my soul to the Spiritworld. I received images of him flying on great wings of pure light and the message clear beyond words that the only thing that matters is love; the absolutely only thing that matters.

Since this time, five months ago, he has returned in many of my dreams and in dreams of my friends, always carrying messages that he is fine and well. I feel as if I inhabit the space between different realities; I feel a great longing to fly with him into the infinite space of our Mother, the Spirit of the Universe, into the Summerlands, the Dreamtime, the Fairy realm, the Otherworld.

But now my oldest son Sean, 26, is ill. He needs my care and support, I cannot desert him. He has cancer of the lymph-glands, Hodgkins disease. I could have lost two sons in the space of two months. I know that Leif wants me to stay with him, and I am now back in Bristol. I am being stripped of everything, everything is being taken away from me, every day I prepare myself for my own death. It is as if I am made to undergo a psychic death and dismemberment like the ancient shamanesses throughout the world. I had a dream of the god Odin gaining knowledge and power undergoing a death and rebirth, hanging nine nights and nine days from Yggdrasil the Tree of Life. I suppose I am at the point when one can either swing into madness and dissolution or into wholeness and illumination. It is a fine edge indeed.

A thousand times I have relived my life and yours in minute detail, every memory flooding back . . . of you the day you were born, tiny with enormous black all-seeing eyes . . . a graceful vivacious child with a large voice and Afro hair, cherub and satyr, holding my hand . . . awkward schoolboy in your new uniform . . . everything I remember, everything. Every young boy and teenager reminds me of you, in every black person's face I see yours . . . always sorrow and remorse . . . unbearable to live with . . .

Leif's death happened in Basque country – home of many ancient traditions of the Craft. It was the time of the harvest festivals, a time of mourning as well as of celebration. A Welsh woman farmer said afterwards, *It's the time of year for it, isn't it?* Meaning that in this part of Wales for the last six or seven years teenage boys have been killed in some violent accident in late August. Is Leif one of the tender-faced and curly-haired sons of the Mother, whom she takes back to herself in the prime of their years?

I feel like a nun. It is as if because Leif was not able to experience sexual love in his life – and how he longed for this – neither am I. It is as if he is my son/lover waiting for me in the Otherworld. So much is left unfinished between us. Leif was always inordinately jealous of me.

I have always known that to lose a child is the most terrible thing that can happen in one's life. I have lost loved ones already, too many. My gentle and beautiful mother, a Swedish artist, whom I hadn't seen for six years because I was living in England, died unexpectedly from a stroke. She was only 53. Four years later, my father, helpless, shitting blood, unable to eat, died of cancer in a hospital bed. My Swedish lover, Charlotta Sandell, took an overdose. My ex-husband Andrew Jubb died, of alcoholism, at the age of 36. Both of them were talented and inspiring people, she a poet, he a musician-composer. It was very hard for Leif when Andy died. There had been a great and unconditional love between them, and Andy was the 'father' Leif knew and grew up with. I feared that he would want to pull Leif and me along with him into the Spiritworld. Although I hadn't lived with him for years there was a very close telepathic link between us and he has come back in my dreams from another reality . . .

Enough tragedies and deaths had happened in my life, I felt, but as long as my three sons lived and thrived I could face up to most things.

But Leif leaving me, the child born from my body, I the mother surviving my own child, that is unacceptable, impossible, an experience to shatter any notion of reality or sense I have ever had. I have never lived through such total despair and amputation of my being. My heart has been torn out; with Leif any sense of well being I had in the world, any sense of joy or hope or happiness, has vanished. I am a shadow-being. A great bitterness has filled me. Darkness settled over my mind at times. I could hardly see in the months after Leif's death and what I saw was ugliness all around me.

I was the one who used to talk of the indivisibility of spirit and matter and the sacredness of the living Earth, took pride in our woman's sexuality, our menstrual cycles, our flow of being – now I do not want to be in this body, life on the Earth-plane is but sorrow and pain, A prison of the soul. I fear my menstrual blood because every month when I bleed I can smell Leif's blood in my nostrils, blood of my blood, fruit of my body.

The thread of this time winds back to when I'd met Musawa on a walk from Silbury to Stonehenge on May Eve 1985. The full moon was eclipsed when we celebrated at Stonehenge after crossing the Salisbury Plain firing ranges; we had spent Beltane night on Silbury Mound. I had sensed changes beginning in my life. These powerful connections, inspired by Goddess energies, were what drew me to go and stay with Musawa in the summer. Never had I imagined changes in my life would be brought about through my son's death.

Silbury is the pregnant womb of the Earth, sacred site of the Goddess. There in the past I have had visionary, at times painful, experiences of transformative importance for my life. There I ate mushrooms and experienced the grief and sorrow through her Womb, through my own womb, at the destruction of her living body, the Earth. Parked in a layby on the autumn equinox in 1984 on my way to Greenham, I slept and dreamed a wonderful dream.

In my dream we were in the darkness at Silbury, waiting. Then we saw a vast luminous shape, a cloud of being which radiated bliss against the dark vastness of the mound. It was a great and healing blessing to have been allowed to witness this. This dream came to me during a difficult time. I had suffered mysterious pains in different parts of my body for some months and then had a continuous headache during the ten days at Greenham's Green Gate. Indeed I felt I was under psychic attack that autumn. I felt weaker, tired. Before then I always believed I was protected and that I have power to protect myself and my loved ones.

For I have long known that I am a target for men's hostile energies. Men who are involved in Earth Mysteries and occultism as well as male artists. They are locked into rigid mindsets and I am outspoken and public in both my paintings and my writings for Goddess vision, matriarchal women's wisdom and our original bisexual nature. I had lived through a childhood with first a father and then a step-father who were jealous of me, could barely tolerate my presence. I had survived; but I should have known better than to allow my son to live in the same situation. It turned out that my lover's love for Leif was not for the person he was, but for the boy he wanted him to be. Although claiming to be an 'antisexist' man, he projected his own guilt on to Leif and often behaved in a punitive way towards him. He often made my son's life a misery.

And now, with the feelings of guilt that every mother feels, I fear that my involvement in my work and exhibitions, my travelling in foreign countries, also damaged my son. Now that he is gone, I am living with my feelings of remorse and fear. *I pray that where you are now, in the Otherworld of the Mother, you are able to live your dreams without remorse of what you've lost. I always loved you intensely and I always will.*

I am angry, too. The women's movement has never faced up to what becomes of our sons, what happens to them as they grow up with a different consciousness, refusing to join the male gangs and therefore facing isolation. Leif was a true child of the women's movement: I was pregnant with him the summer we started the first women's group in Bristol; after he was born, he would lie gurgling and playing in the centre of a circle of women during innumerable meetings; when he was two weeks old I took him with me to the first women's conference at Ruskin College in 1970. Later I lived with two lesbians who were co-mothers with me. All my important work I have done since he was born. He watched my paintings come into being and discussed them with me as he grew older.

But, too often during the years of my sons' growing up, I also found them rejected by women because they were born male. Perhaps this was the reason why I found myself with a male lover after years of working in the lesbian movement. A woman lover (not a feminist) said to me when Leif was four years old, *Put him on the motorway.*

But I know it is not only our daughters but our sons also who are the victims of this violent society. Patriarchal technology killed my son. It kills physically, emotionally, psychically. This is how it turns our sons into killers, destroyers, rapists. They are not born that way.

The women in the house we visited on our last and fatal journey were not to know how he felt; but the fact remains that on the morning of the day he died there was an argument about whether we would be welcome to travel back to England with the women. Leif grew agitated; I do not know but I cannot help feeling that it all contributed to him rushing across the road without looking. It adds to my unease and despair. I wonder what I have been doing all these years, helping to create a movement that can engender such entrenched anti-life positions towards our male children.

Our culture has no common understanding of other realities. You are made to feel you're crazy if you talk of the Spiritworld and continuing life after bodily death.

But it is in Birth and Death that the pathways between this Earth realm and the Spiritworld are open and women are its mediators. The ancient religion was always about being able to cross the barriers between worlds and to gain knowledge, prophetic wisdom and healing powers. When I first looked into Leif's great dark eyes after his birth I felt that the newborn child is an ancient wise being. After the natural home-birth of my second son, Toivo, 25 years ago, I had an overwhelming experience of space, of darkness and blinding light, of great powers of my body and sexuality; it was then I first felt opened up to the knowledge of the Cosmic Mother. Now it is as if I have come full circle round, that with the birth of Leif back into the infinite space-womb of the Mother I have been given another overwhelming insight into light and space and love but also into almost unbearable pain and grief.

At the sacred places of the Goddess – Silbury, the mounds, the wells, the stone circles, the Fairy pathways – the cosmic realities emerge at certain times and seasons when the moon and the sun and the stars are in particular relationship to each other; then we are able to communicate with the Immortal Dead, the Blessed People, our Ancestors.

This is what I have talked and written and painted about for many years. But when I attempted to do some slide-showings in the autumn after Leif's death, I stopped in panic. I had to say that I no longer know what I am talking about.

What is the Mother trying to tell me? Perhaps, as mediums have told me, Leif is now to be my spirit guide and teacher. I have to hang on to the clear message from him that the only thing which matters is love. This is difficult to live up to . . . difficult not to feel negativity and bitterness. It feels to me as if the whole body of the Earth is suffering from cancer and I sense a madness and despair building up all around us. But I have received much love and healing from many women and some men – which gives me hope.

What will become of us all, oh Mother? These last years I have truly felt that I am entering into the realm of the powerful Dark Mother, the Wyrd, the Unknowable One. On Bride's Day (1 February) in 1985 I went with a group of women to visit the cave under Cerrig Cennen Castle near Carmarthen. Deep down in this cave under the mountain, there is a holy well. We sat in there with candles, singing and meditating. Suddenly as I turned my head the white and hooded face of the Dark Mother peered out at me from the rock face. The face is not carved but created by natural colouring and formation and can be seen only from a certain angle and in a certain light. The woman sitting next to me also saw Her. We each drew the face: it was the same one. Why was it on this day of the young Bride emerging from the earth to bring the first signs of spring and the warming of the waters that we should perceive not the young maiden but the crone?

I have lived longer than I ever expected to live and yet I have come to understand that I am not allowed to end my life deliberately. I have had to live through Yule and New Year and Leif's sixteenth birthday on 23 January, the night I had set for my own death. There seems to be no way out. I feel trapped between different realities. I now fear the coming of another summer, of beauty in nature and of the sun. The cold of winter, rain and darkness has been a relief. The grief for a child never lessens, gets worse as time goes; the loss is more and more real, the memories a thousand light-years away. Waking every morning not being able to understand where he is, why he isn't with me, every morning a renewal of pain. I long to be free and flying with Leif.

We had Leif's beautiful body cremated, the only way we could think of to bring him back home. We brought him back – the most hideous journey of my life – his ashes wrapped in his favourite T shirt and sewn into the little African drum he had been playing. In the tipi village, friends gathered from all over the country. I donned the White Winged bird headdress and became the Shamaness presiding over the ritual. We buried his ashes in the Medicine Wheel. We felt we honoured him truly, that he enjoyed what we were doing for him.

The night of Leif's birth, I and three other women went to Greenham and then on to Silbury, to be on the mound by ten o'clock, the hour of his birth. I shared my grief and thanked Leif for his life. I thanked the Mother for his life and asked her to help me understand why he had to leave so young and to allow me to be with him soon. I had not been here, on Her pregnant belly, since the walk when I met Musawa. Next morning I had a birth-dream of Leif and was given the image of him streaking through space like a proud and beautiful flame, red hair streaming.

New Year's Eve is my own birthday. I went with a dear friend to the tipi village so as to be able to communicate with Leif in the Medicine Wheel at midnight and at the dawn of the New Year. On our journey under the light of a huge orange moon we had been stopped by an owl sitting in the middle of the road staring at us in the car headlights. The owl is the bird of Hecate, guardian of the dead, She who is wise and sees in darkness. *What did she want to tell us? What does she want to tell us all?*

It seems to me that here is an explicit demand for art to carry the burden of cultural transformation: that out of personal extremity must come a public, not a private, set of connotations. These connotations carry universal moral imperatives. Most of us are used to an aesthetic programme which is much less ambitious. Many women certainly want their work to convey more than a mere record of sensation: they consciously relate what they do to an identifiable if marginalised tradition and there is sometimes a polemical thrust about their work: it is intended to change the world in some degree. What Monica exacts from her work is something beyond even this. The scope of her programme reflects the hugeness of the demands made on her, demands that have threatened to unseat her sense of sanity.

Fear of going mad, in some extremity or in a dislocated sense of daily life, is something not many of us escape. We fear madness because the penalties for non-conforming behaviour, for expressing violent emotion, for rejecting conventional roles, for hearing voices or seeing visions, are varied and effective. Feminist theory has provided the means to reappraise these different feelings, but not simply in order to elide madness with either creativeness or resistance. Telling the difficult story, if done scrupulously like Liz Hood's or Monica's, may inch a way out of a felt impossibility.

What, additionally, makes people psychically fragile is our permeability to the unreason, masquerading as social health, that governs the housing, employment, fiscal and welfare policies to which we are subject. Sympathy with the rural landscape, its rhythms and vistas, its capacity for regeneration, its birds and animals and flowers, offers the hope of spiritual salvation (as it has done for centuries) – that is where peace and creativity are to be found, where the heart will be at rest. The reality is, of course, other. Most people are visitors to the countryside rather than workers in it, earning their living in service to conurbations. When creativity is identified with the childlike free play of faculties and with a sense of unruptured oneness with 'nature' (urban middle-class notions in origin), it is likely to make women with part-time indoor jobs, dependent relatives and sparse leisure, feel cheated as well as exhausted. What are the alternatives to claiming 'nature' as creative source, the countryside as inspiration and the pastoral as exemplar of creative expression?

MAKING SPACE IN THE WORLD: POLITICS

The final achievement of a belligerent and repressive government is the occupation of your mind. Unemployment becomes a form of social control. The police have powers of attack and arrest for which there is no accountability. Trade union activities are proscribed. The national budget is grotesquely distorted by planning for the destruction of the world. In the name of national defence, civil liberties are curtailed. A whole range of activities – from striking in defence of jobs and working conditions, to celebrating at Stonehenge; from selling gay books or talking to school pupils about sex, to protesting against the threat from nuclear weapons or accident and against the harassment of black citizens by police – all these are named as perverted or subversive; attempts are made to structure them out of our lives by legislation. The government is intent on the cultural and ideological defeat of any opposition – and has already won several major skirmishes: persuading people to become shareholders of what the public already own; selling off council houses; dismantling the NHS, to name a few.

As the erosion of rights bites harder – rights which perhaps the older ones among us imagined secured, even while we campaigned for wider and deeper changes – we often find ourselves in retreat: we have to defend rather than innovate; preserve rather than pull down. To people who want change, who see that structures of class, race and gender still divide and oppress people, that feels very odd. Change, under such a regime, has become something to be feared rather than welcomed. It is not something you need in order to grow and develop, it signals advancing poverty and powerlessness. In the face of aggressive policy-making, it is the loose, uneasy alliance of socialists, feminists, 'greens' and others who must adopt conser-

vative strategies. No wonder you or I feel confused, demoralised, pulled in a dozen different directions.

Creativity, stepping outside the bounds of convention and dependence, is dangerous – it makes you visible. You have a job, a position, however tenuous, to protect; or maybe you have neither without much hope of either. Bills to pay and no safety net make you less inclined to take risks on your own. You blame yourself for playing safe or for sticking your neck out too far; you wonder where everyone has gone. Moreover, you cannot figure out how personal development, the exercise of your creativeness, can have anything to do with preventing nuclear war or reversing unemployment trends – except as an ineffectual reaction, an escape. In the middle of the night, you wake up wondering what is wrong with you.

That is what we are up against.

No consensus emerges in this section about the relation for feminists between political and creative processes: it would be odd if it did. Some writers (Joan Blaney, Gabriela Müller, Anna Wilson, Maud Sulter) are arguing that political struggle of different kinds is the source and basis of their creative work. Another woman (Ange Grunsell) describes her need for space within that struggle, for reflective time and emotional independence – a recent gain for some women and still beyond the reach of many. Catherine Itzin proposes a way of getting rid of internalised oppression (the source of destructive conflict) and for releasing one's creative and cooperative potential. Amrita Mohan finds her native culture informs and guides her creative output; this becomes contentious only because she lives and works in a society which discriminates against this culture. These models of creativity do not form a seamless fabric, they remain full of tensions in themselves and with each other.

But they start from the point that our individual lives and the way we live them cannot for a moment be divorced from the society in which they are lived; creativity may be mysterious but it is not mystical. Nor is it an abstraction to be endlessly defined and measured. Not one woman chose to spend time debating whether it really exists. This is not to say that 'creativity' shouldn't be problematised. One of the commonplaces about creativity is that it is somehow qualitatively different from 'work', both in the sense that it is to do with spontaneity and also that it is not functional but effete. Several essays tease out an understanding of how creativity coexists with a fully occupied, economically active life instead of the one being essentially inimical to the other. How creativity coexists with employment – or lack of it – is another matter; our degree of control over ends and means is the crucial element.

However, the comfortable assumptions at the back of 'we' and 'women' – assumptions that have grown out of a defensible wish to share and politicise personal experience and have become something of a convention in feminist writing – are exposed when a black woman speaks. Such generalising assumptions cannot help being racist; not so much by personal intention as by the passive perpetuation of those social codes and apparatus for whose eradication white women bear a responsibility. Joan Blaney's account shows her own radicalisation in the process of working for, and then leaving, a white-dominated community recreation and dance project. In comparing her account with Ruth Noble's who also works with movement, the difference in their premises and strategies for resistance is striking. Joan works in the West Midlands, Ruth in Devon, which is one factor. But the determining one, I think, is their different race: their different relationship to local and national power structures. The women Joan teaches derive great pleasure and meaning from the ethnic identity of the dance. But the need for her course was not evident until she offered it, and is still being disputed by officials in the local authority where she works, despite the observable success of the programme in providing a social and symbolic framework for some of Britain's least visible, least valued people – young black women. (Sport is a much less contentious activity.) This instantly problematises 'community art' – whose community? Who funds the activities? What are the objectives and who evaluates their success? Does 'community' cut across or restate the differences of race, class, gender, age, able-bodiedness? Who decides?

A Struggle for Recognition

Joan Blaney

For my husband Donald and my daughter Siobhan Marie,
in recognition of their love and support

'It's all-out confrontation now.'

I arrived in England from Port Antonio, Jamaica, at the age of nine.

At the end of my secondary school education I pursued a secretarial career for five years until I became dissatisfied with the mundane office routines and decided on a nursing career. I began and completed my training at the Queen Elizabeth Medical Centre in Birmingham.

I left nursing to start up a small business with my husband, planning to return at a later date for it was a most fulfilling and rewarding career.

After the birth of my daughter I began to contemplate my return to nursing but the appearance of public announcement on television, seeking volunteers to work with unemployed and disadvantaged people in a sports-orientated scheme, caught my attention. I was very much a sports enthusiast and so the idea of the scheme appealed to me. I answered the advertisement and was promptly put in touch with a local activity centre.

I worked in a voluntary capacity with the scheme for some months and came to the conclusion that, although my nursing career was one I thoroughly enjoyed, this was the field in which I wanted to remain and when a position for a part-time Instructor/Supervisor became vacant, my application for the post was successful. Nine months later, in March 1985, I took up a full-time post as a Community Sports Leader, employed by the Local Authority, and worked in one of the most deprived areas of Wolverhampton with a large black population.

The politics involved in providing sporting and recreational activities for the unemployed and disadvantaged people were apparent and in many instances the policies of the scheme were preoccupied with simply getting young predatory males off the streets and into 'drop-in' centres, with little regard for the plight of young women who do not usually constitute a visible 'problem'.

Provision for women was limited and there had been few attempts, if any, to involve young black women with little interest in conventional sport. It is acknowledged by workers in the field of sports and recreation that these young women are one of the hardest groups to motivate, but could this possibly justify the lack of will to provide for them?

My prime motive for setting up African dance sessions was not due to any conscious empathy with Rastafarian women or interest in the African Arts. For, in common with many West Indian-born blacks, I had no real concept of an African identity. In fact the first encounter between myself and Africa was during my second Christmas in England when I was asked to play a part in the nativity play. I first learnt of the character I was to play when a black class-mate of mine approached me in the playground and said,

'They want us to play Africans! the three African kings.' He was very distressed and on the verge of tears.

The next day I was approached by the 'third king' who said her mother was very upset by her role as an African and would be coming into the school for an explanation. I was unperturbed by the feelings of my 'royal colleagues' as the opportunity to make my stage debut was more important to me. I therefore kept the nature of the character I was playing from my mother in case this would jeopardise my chances to appear.

I still recall this story with some amusement but it does portray the sensitivities of some West Indians when there is the merest suggestion of a link with Africa.

Such sensitivities I felt would not be manifested by the Rastafarian women whose faith had already bestowed upon them their African identity.

It was my duty as a Community Sports Leader to publicise a whole range of activities and it was during such an exercise that I met a young Rastafarian girl and asked her about her sporting interest. Her response as I expected was negative until I mentioned the idea of African Dancing. She immediately expressed a strong interest and spoke of other young women who would also be keen to participate.

I contacted a local African Arts Co-operative who were willing to provide tuition and booked a room at a community centre to accommodate the activity. The prospects of having organised such a meaningful activity excited me and I was confident of its success. My optimism, however, was short lived as the first session drifted by without a single participant. I contained my disappointment and continued to promote the session but when the following two weeks brought the same lack of response the disillusionment was overwhelming.

I could hardly believe that the sessions had not gained the interest I expected and began to question my approach. Had I been too forceful and overbearing to those whose long isolation from the community had left them apathetic? And was I indeed asking and expecting too much?

Perplexed and a little disheartened I decided to meet with members of the African Arts Co-operative who continued to volunteer their services. They attempted to bolster my flagging enthusiasm for the scheme and invited me to attend a programme of dance in which they were taking part.

I attended the Sunday evening dance programme and was completely enthralled by the vivacity of the dancers and the magical and compelling rhythm of the African drums. A surge of unexpected determination suffused me and re-kindled my enthusiasm. I knew then that I had to sell this dynamic and beautiful art.

The following Monday with revitalised optimism I approached two young women outside a local school and spoke about the general activities we had to offer. I then mentioned, rather tentatively, the dance session. They responded with the fervency I had become used to and I gave them the time and venue of the next session, wishing that I had the power to impel their attendance.

The Friday afternoon of that same week, I was feeling a little indifferent when I arrived at the community centre and I was unable to decide whether or not it was going to be the last attempt to initiate the activity. The display of African dancing, the first I had seen, was to have a lasting effect on me and I felt a little sorry that the young women, whatever their reasons for not attending the sessions, were going to miss out on the enrichment and vitality of our common heritage.

Reservedly I made my way into the centre and was surprised and relieved to see that the two young women I had spoken to and four others with their children were awaiting my arrival. I was elated and triumphant.

The following weeks saw a dramatic growth in the number of participants and, from a total of 14 attending one session, seven young women came forward, committed and dedicated enough to form an African Dance Troupe. The troupe gave their first public appearance in August 1985 in front of a 300-strong crowd and their performance received rapturous applause.

Despite the success of the group I received no real support from fellow sports leaders and was met with hostile feelings and remarks whenever the dance session was mentioned. I was also reminded that there were other activities in progress – a fact I was very much aware of, because the dance session was only one of the successful activities I had been running at the time. The participants' dependence upon me as a leader was becoming more and more taxing and the lack of support and co-operation from my white counterparts made me ponder over my position within the scheme.

As the only black management member in a group of seven I began to wonder whether my presence was only required to perpetuate the façade of black involvement at such a level, in short nothing more than tokenism. The isolation I experienced was affecting me deeply and I felt unable to contribute effectively. I considered tendering my resignation but first had to analyse the true success of the dance troupe that could not be measured in numerical terms nor at the level of technical excellence achieved.

That success was the young women's newly found confidence and self-esteem. They had obtained a feeling of worth within a community which had long been denied them, and the spell of imprisonment within the walls of high-rise flats or some other modern slum had been broken. Even their children had been transformed from the quiet and withdrawn toddlers I had first met to lively and playful youngsters. I was the only witness to this true success and was alone in my joy and knowledge because the white workers within the scheme were unable to grasp the needs and the motives behind such an activity which was the fulfilment of cultural and spiritual aspirations that exist in the lives of many black people.

After anxious deliberation I decided to continue my efforts for the sake of the troupe and other participants who had placed so much faith in me.

A few weeks later a black colleague of mine was dismissed due to circumstances that had arisen out of lack of understanding and sympathy for his situation by my white counterparts. I resigned, for I could no longer reconcile my position within what was basically a racist system with that old and much abused argument of 'changing the system from within'.

I saw the haste with which my fellow sports leader began to plan cover for the sessions I had been running and concluded that my departure had been long awaited. I could well understand his need to maintain the sessions, for I had more than doubled participation levels in the area.

I was feeling very sad at the next African dance session and as I looked at the bright joyful faces of the dancers, there was a tired and empty feeling inside me. I had given all I could and in doing so had given so much of myself. There was still much to do and yet I was leaving. My throat felt heavy and I fought to regain my composure.

After the drummers had left and we sat down for our usual chat, I broke the news of my resignation. The silence that followed was profound.

'So that's it, then,' was one solemn remark.

'Hopefully someone will be able to continue the session,' I answered. That wasn't enough and I had to explain that I wasn't abandoning them but that my own principles were at stake which, if compromised, would make me unworthy of the respect they had shown me in the previous months. I so much wanted to stay but the price was too high.

'No one cared about us before and I can't see anyone else caring now,' was another comment and the most poignant one. There had to be another way.

I drove home that afternoon feeling numb and somewhat down-hearted, torn between my convictions and the knowledge that without understanding and sympathetic leadership the troupe would disband: although I knew that such leadership would not be forthcoming from my colleagues, I simply could not withdraw my resignation.

I began to recall the troupe's first public performance. It was a performance I wanted to relive again for its energy and splendour. The seven young women take the stage moving zealously and rhythmically in a beautiful array of bright and colourful costumes. They dance to the music of 'Kpanlogo', a popular West African dance. The series of pre-set movements are well timed and exuberant and as the language of the drums dictates the variation of movements the young women display elegance and virtuosity. The spirit of this high society ceremonial dance is entered into with pride and gracefulness.

Memories alone, however, would not bring me contentment when I still had a strong desire to remain with the troupe. It was then that I decided to continue my efforts in my own way and this was the beginning of 'Afeme'.

My keen interest in sports meant that I had very little time to contemplate the arts and I could never have guessed that my decision to stimulate a certain target group using aspects of their faith would have had such an immense effect on me for although I have always been conscious of myself as a black person the work I did with the dance troupe gave me a new insight and raised that level of consciousness.

Alienated by the racism prevalent within British society, large numbers of young black people have rejected not only the customs and values of their oppressors but also of their West Indian-born parents who often seem to parody the white middle class. To many in authority the rejection is very threatening, after all, black people were not given the 'benefit' of British colonialism in order for them to reject a whole value structure.

In Jamaica I was taught in standard textbook English, for the British culture had left its mark long after independence. Those born in Britain see the British people 'warts and all' from a very early age. There is no concept therefore of her being the benevolent 'Mother Country'. It is Africa that provides a sense of identity.

African Art is an important part of our heritage, a part which has been a target of oppression. For hundreds of years it has been a one-way traffic; blacks are expected to acknowledge the greatness of European culture, but, while ballet and opera are universally accepted as art, that acceptance is not forthcoming from Europeans for the dance and music of Africa. Could it be that to European eyes African dance is primitive and spontaneous? And is the lack of recognition of the existence of African history linked with Europe's reluctance to accept Africa's art-forms as more than the efforts of a subservient race? The truth is that there are dances performed in Africa which have been handed down over thousands of years, much longer than ballet in Europe, and they can be as technically demanding and complex as European dance.

'Afeme', from the Ewe language of Ghana, means 'home'. It is meant to offer the concept of belonging to those who are becoming increasingly alienated from society and to help encourage a more positive and constructive input into the community by the disadvantaged people of all races. Borne out of a struggle of black people to operate successfully within a white system, it is not racist in its motives but merely a reaction to the racism that black people face in their daily lives. It is seen as a threat because the white authority has imposed its own racist outlook and motives upon it. A group run by blacks without a white management team suddenly becomes radical. The 'colonial' and 'missionary' mentality of many in white authority finds it offensive when black people refuse to be patronised and declare that not only are we able but also equal.

The ideals of the scheme I had previously worked in were based on a principle of containment, the maintenance of the 'status quo'. In no way could its cosmetic approach alleviate the deep frustrations being endured by young black people who suffer a double disadvantage in a society that is full of inequalities and prejudices based upon class and colour. We are encouraged by the capitalist society in which we live to obtain a car, a house and other material goods for these are seen as achievements, an indication of our worth as a member of that society. Are black people so unworthy of such achievements that they can be pacified with fun and games without any progressive objectives?

'Afeme' differs from any other scheme the local authority can offer because it comes from within. For it is only those who have shared in the experiences of the disadvantaged people who can truly understand their needs. The oppressive system feeds on those who avert their eyes from the truth in case their material gains are threatened but in doing so serve only to perpetuate a system of manipulation and imprisonment. But my eyes are wide open and I take consolation from the riches offered by the art, dance and music of Africa. Riches which tangible wealth could not withhold.

If we are to accept people on equal terms then we have to look beyond a material plane because the world will never be equal on that level. Dance and rhythm are common to all people and all races and could broaden communication between black and white and help to enhance our multi-racial society.

If we, as black people, are to contribute effectively to the society in which we live we must be aware of our own arts, history and culture and must be allowed to express them without inhibitions.

Racism is based on fear and ignorance and if black art and culture was looked upon with the respect it deserves and brought to the attention of a wider audience then we would be on our way to eradicating such factors. Until such time, I will remain a proud black woman fighting for the recognition of my history and culture.

Postscript

Joan has had a prolonged altercation with the local authority, who disputed by every means available her allegations of racist and sexist practice within the leisure service provision. An all-party panel of the Wolverhampton council agreed to vindicate her report and to act on her recommendations; but withdrew this agreement at the last minute. The Guardian's *northern edition carried a report; the struggle has become bitter. There have been death threats to Joan. She remains committed – but now also 'cynical', in her words.*

The change from working within a statutory organisation to estab-
lishing an independent base has obviously to be distinguished from
falling in with government calls for more people to become self-
employed. Such a change is often sought because it involves working
collectively instead of hierarchically, in an enabling rather than a
competitive way which allows feelings and values as well as effort to
be part of the work environment.

Many women in this book work formally or informally in a co-
operative setting with other women and men; their work has a
dimension which engages directly with received social structures.
The principles on which sports leaders and other community work
organisers are encouraged to base their work – 'motivation',
'participation', 'target group' – are precisely those that Joan Blaney
discarded because of the racist assumptions behind them. Turning
people's needs into demands, turning round the formulations of the
world that are presented by those in power as the truth, is an
increasingly important way of taking the political initiative.

In the next article Ange Grunsell opens up the discourse of space:
the narrowing space left for thoughts and actions which challenge
dominant values. Her theme explores the consequent need to think
and act in the margins.

The Tory government has won the battle of opinion about the state
being on the side of the private individual against the 'mob', the
enemy of freedom. That now appears to be the major function of the
state, as its welfare role is squeezed. The emphasis in what is left of
public funding is on short-term contracts, on maximising profit and
on increasing the proportion of private contractors. By promoting
unproductive competitiveness, these strategies are hostile to real
freedom and growth. Finding ways of sharing and passing on
information (in its widest sense), of defending what has been gained,
is crucial in maintaining the possibility of progressive change in
individuals and in society.

For feminists, this means continuing to work under beleaguered
conditions, they can't 'just get on with the job'. Their work is always
put in some category or other which manages to downgrade it – and
here is the paradox of feminism, that in making the necessary
challenge to this relegation, this Otherness, a huge amount of
creative energy is tied up. Ange points to the reasons why 'creativity'
and 'art' are much less exclusive frames for women: they are
impelled to make connections between their creative experience and
its social context, their jobs, the shopping, the child-care. Much of

women's work, into which a great deal of creative energy is channelled, is immediately consumable – meals, household organisation – or privatised – crocheted antimacassars, patchworked quilts – or invisible – child-care and emotional sustenance. It is instantly marginalised or else translated in a depressed and discriminatory job market into sold labour which creates surplus value for somebody else. The process of politicising what has been constructed as 'natural', i.e. the type and location of women's work, both paid and unpaid, and thereby freeing creative energy, depends on insisting on these connections.

> *The most dramatic finding . . . was that all women with paid jobs, whether . . . part-time or full-time, have less free time than men . . . The concept of women's leisure as being, in effect, vicarious enjoyment of their family's leisure activity, legitimated by the service they provide, may go some way to explaining the differential leisure behaviours of men and women . . . The majority of women follow family leisure patterns, with only men and few, more privileged, women having the supportive networks and freedom to follow individuated leisure patterns.*
> *(Margaret Talbot,* Women and Leisure; *see Bibliography.)*

Not surprisingly, current government policy under Mrs Thatcher has deepened woman's economic oppression, as Elizabeth Wilson's evidence in an article in The Socialist Register 1987 *(see Bibliography) shows; not so much (she says) by deliberately relocating women in the home – Mrs Thatcher acknowledges the desirability for middle-class women at least, to 'develop our talents' outside the home – as by confining the majority to low paid part-time work in the service sector, by deregulating employer/employee relationships, by cutting public childcare provision, by diminishing health, housing and social services, at the same time as increasing relative and absolute poverty; all of which adversely affect more women than men.*

This is a class as well as a gender issue, as Ange Grunsell intimates – middle-class women haven't done as well under Thatcherism as their men, but they've done better than working-class women. The gap between middle-class and working-class women has widened. This has been disrupting for feminists in their relationships with each other: appeals to personal experience may be neccessary, but are not sufficient, in coming to a shrewd and solid understanding of the world.

Breaking Out, Breaking In

Ange Grunsell

For Val and Stephanie, my teachers

The Cage

There is a fenced square of tarmac outside our school. They call it 'The Cage'. It is the single most coveted piece of space in the school, which is open-plan indoors and has a field and large tarmacked areas outdoors – nowhere else is there a clearly defined and boundaried rectangle. There, every playtime, some of the third- and fourth-year boys play football. It is held by the biggest and strongest and any new boy wanting to prove himself must do it in that form in that arena. The girls who cluster round the walls of the building, as in most playgrounds, yearn for that space – and say so. Some strong fourth-year girls request they be formally given a share of it. They are given one day in the week. But once there they do not have a conspicuous and instantly unified use for it and many don't dare approach this powerful piece of territory – and those that do sometimes merely gate-keep and let in the boys of their choice (who then play football). Sometimes the arrangement lapses altogether and the girls give up. Perhaps the staff should be defending the space for the girls, 50 per cent of the time, by using their authority; even if only one girl chose to use it and she chose to sit motionless in the middle all playtime. But what a phenomenal personal endurance that would be! To occupy that stage – to redefine its nature and use – and take it for yourself! A friend, on becoming head of another such school, used a simple and effective tactic. She simply removed the football every time boys alone were playing – and the protagonists in the space quickly changed, though the game didn't; it was still football.

One day we did the exercise of planning and drawing the ideal school. The boys were full of ideas and skills to put them into practice: space, they felt, was clearly a dimension they could create and manipulate. Wondrous shaped ground plans mushroomed – each a mixed school with cricket pitches, computer rooms, projection rooms, break dance areas, even launch-pads for school journeys in outer space. The girls, with no exceptions, planned a single-sex, girls only, school. They knew they needed that – but what to put in it? They didn't, couldn't tell, apart from repeating familiar features from their own experience; and most found it hard to grapple with the skills demanded by the task.

Breaking Out – Breaking in

So the public space – the world – is owned and shaped by the boys, and, so far, the most successful of tacticians have only managed – sometimes – to get a few girls in on the same game. Men, whatever their class or culture, have a sense (which is sometimes more a pretence) of space and freedom both physical and psychic. It pushes you off the pavement, away from the bar; its voice edges you out of meetings, its outstretched legs kick you accidentally beneath your own table. That space may be little more than the pavement and the pub; if you're black, in Capetown and in Brixton, it is less still than that. But whatever men have, women always have less. Those with power define and restrict the space of others: Show your pass! Wear your veil! Give us a kiss darling!

We decorate spaces (with care and nice handwriting), clean them, squeeze ourselves into other people's – and can only win through to the smallest portions through intense inward and outward struggle. I sit in the dog-filled, train-filled, siren-filled Holloway night with my friend and she says, 'In Sudan or Saudi you'd be a prisoner in your house', and my children sleep upstairs and so do my neighbour's and her neighbour's and we all sit indoors alone (except she's come to see me because her daughter is away). She fears, as well she might, the night walk home along largely unlit streets (well, we called the council eight times in the last four weeks but nothing has come of it). We both fear for our daughters, fledglings of the tube and the bus stop, free only to exercise self-defence and walk along the centre of Dunford Road because the lights are still out.

It is intolerable, wholly inequable, to be thus caged; to face what world we pass on to our daughters, still unable to build a Lego house or change a bicycle wheel. We none of us need to look far to recognise *why* it is that in the classroom-improvised drama 'Breakfast Time', where girls and boys decide to form separate groups, these seven-year-old daughters endlessly enact a no-story-line of wiping and washing and setting the table, while the boys in their playlet are fighting an outbreak of fire within five minutes of getting up, or dispensing with breakfast altogether to leave the house and go motorcycle racing. It doesn't seem from the snapshots of our daily lives given to us by scenes like these that either sex is internalising any sort of whole or practical model of approaching life to build on. How can we ignore the urgency to do something about it?

Yes, I've been active with my sisters – I demonstrate and remonstrate about sexism and racism at work and on the street. I stick stickers on pornography and campaign about children's books. I give lectures to teachers and write articles. On the whole I've replaced being man-focused and dependent with the support and company of women. I know what the problem is out there, and the pernicious effects of a white middle-class male status quo. But I spin like a gyroscope balancing along a wire and cannot find a way to take my own space – a room of my own.

My only room is late night or early morning; is a shut door against the cries of 'unfair' without and of 'selfish' within. It is the space between me at work, me cooking the dinner, me listening to you and you and you – and me. The stolen hours for which I have only myself to blame, I sell myself so short. It is changing cafés near Oxford Street as soon as I get to be recognised by the regulars. It is the glorious singularity of moving in the gap between on my motorbike, my beautiful nifty one-seater which stands outside the house ready for me to take off and weave carefree among the clumsier traffic; and on which there is room only for me. These are the rare hours when I cheat myself and the rest and for once don't turn to the demands, the temptations, of the draining board, the washing machine and the knock at the front door.

'Oh ho,' says me to me. 'Spoilt bitch; so you crave space. You with the wealth of owning half a house; who have the luxuries of children, an interesting job, a motorbike even. You are white and educated and extravagantly fed and still you whine.' And what have I made of so much wealth? Like women everywhere I must still work to find a way to make and defend my own room, alone and with others. Making space for creativity, reflection, transformation. But many elsewhere do more. The women of a village in India threw sand into the new well, secretly, night after night. The well was planned and built by men in consultation with a white male 'development' worker – so thoughtfully, to 'improve the quality of everyones lives', to save them time. Time for what? For other tasks. For more hours doing agricultural work. The women's choice which their action achieved was to be able to walk, once again, twelve miles a day with their sisters to fetch water away from the village; to take their own time and space. This is organisation and action more radical than I have yet been capable of. Defining, reorganising and defending what constitutes real quality of life is a complicated and collective matter. Water is heavy to carry.

I check my digital watch, pay for my tea and scuttle home obediently to take food from the freezer. 'But why do you fabricate this trap?' the other me persists. 'Your partner shares child-care, housework and shopping too, and still you complain for lack of room.'

Finally I know it is myself I must struggle with. A thousand years of my mother's mother's obligation, dependence and bound feet hang heavy in my soul. The cornflake ads fill me with shame at breakfast time. My children have only me to defend them from E numbers and lung cancer (from all the cigarettes I smoke over their infant heads). With greed and in confusion, I want to raise my children well; to cook and to provide, to garden, too – at the same time as earning money and fighting for the girls, in the classroom and on the committee. I have helped to build my cage and reel drunkenly and erratically within it, promising more to everything than I can fulfil, weeping over the burnt cake, the unfinished article and my stuttering son. How can I write and dance and sing? To whom can I make love with this lot?

And reeds, I'll whisper to you . . . maybe, just maybe, I'm afraid of the chill wind of the plain, without and within, should I dare to choose – to take my own room (with or without £500 a year). Maybe I should be blown away. Better to snarl at my captors than walk 12 miles in the sun. And then, our children must be welcomed from school and the home fires lit. Who else will do it?

A Small Space

But suppose I do dare to choose to take some room for myself?

Suppose I stop moving for long enough to acknowledge all that I stay in touch with in my own life. The cost of being unable to go 'all out' for any of them brings important insights as well as confusions. It adds up to more than simply the variety of contradictory perspectives involved in cleaning the lavatory, teaching 25 inner-city children and chairing a committee. To be doing all these things and to be counting as work 'everything I do' is, in our time, a predominantly female condition. Most of us can only take on wider areas beyond those we conventionally construe as ours if we have the capacity to pile them on top of those we know we have to do to look after ourselves and those dependent on us. Not so for most men, who are commonly provided for throughout their lives in matters of toilet cleaning, food and the details of shelter – other than during interim conditions. For them, 'doing', 'working', is far more exclusive and specific, and the other areas of human experience are an unimportant backcloth which will somehow be woven by somebody else. I was unsurprised recently by the outcome of a 'futures' exercise with a mixed class of ten year olds; for the boys it was exclusively about jobs and possessions, for girls it was jobs *and* families *and* homes. When I asked the boys did they care very much about money and status, they replied, 'No miss, money isn't everything, you need a family to look after you.' But creating the 'looking after' was not their responsibility.

So locating the meaning of the diverse tasks in our lives and their relationship to each other becomes an issue important for personal orientation and survival, of peculiar necessity for women to do – for me to do. Women of my generation, raised with conflicting messages about how to realise ourselves as women, are constantly faced with the task of making that meaning and developing it – whatever choices we eventually make as to where our priorities lie. We find ourselves asserting, defending, having to take decisive action to protect our hard-won decisions. Moreover, we find that it is this relationship between tasks and priorities that occupies much of our conversation and with other women.

Out of all that talk a vocabulary of individual and collective understanding is slowly born. And if the me that wipes bottoms and cooks meals could be fully there in the me sitting at the department meeting, what might that mean, not just for women but for everyone? But I must make room to absorb that understanding and to articulate it into a deliberate effort to transform the way in which separate activities are pursued.

For there are many things I want to assert. But if our power, my power, lies in the knowledge of all the different things we/I do, then getting at that knowledge demands *not* doing some of the time. It means resisting any intrusion for long enough to recognise, first, that it is an intrusion and, second, the importance of resisting intrusion! We women who shape houses and lives yet have our designs negated must not continue to negate ourselves, our full selves. We must take and shape the space we inhabit and fashion it in a way that does not muzzle or deny whole areas of experience. But we can only do it if we hold on to the self that thrives in cubby holes and secret places, and struggles. We can only make a start if we ignore our guilt about not doing, harden ourselves for long enough to step out of the web and take time.

The well and the washing machine; even the motorbike – alas the motorbike – can undermine our own sense of value and competence as providers and convert us into servicers and inter-mediaries for which the requirement is constant motion, not owned strength.

From the vantage point of a piece of personal territory won and maintained, I could begin to explore the issues my experience forces me to contend with. I could look for ways to make visible the connections between roles, and the real costs of ignoring those connections. How can the interdependence of different tasks be properly acknowledged? What are the implications of valuing a wider range of human activity for the public as well as the private world? For in the securing of that precious space – which will always be too short, like a sunny day on the beach – lies the essence of recognition. The space between birth and death is short, limitations are constant, life itself is a precious gap.

I do not need (like D. H. Lawrence) to punch a hole in my umbrella to see the sky, I can see clearly from my kitchen window what Toryism is doing to Britain. But I can hardly bemoan the limitations of young girls' visions and present them with a model which confirms these. I must take my own time – first to prove that I can exist in my own space, then to find the words not of reaction but of initiation.

My starting-point has to be claiming as mine a piece of the house where I live. A place to do nothing in or to do a lot; a place to withdraw. Establishing this has to be a prerequisite for creating anything else. Virginia Woolf, how right you were about a room of one's own – even though that's something most of the world has never known and a whole room just for me is not possible for me either.

I wanted to set about making some small piece of the house mine. Not the kitchen, which is the engine room and the heart of providing in the household. Not the bedroom, which I share with my partner daily and in its very smell sums up the part of me that is us. I can't take the living room, where all the members of the family and household come to relax in various sociable and noisy ways. But, I discover, I can take part of the living room. A curtain to divide the space; a table and chair by the window; some shelves; plants and pictures that are mine. I've made it. The space is also used for music-making (the piano, my piano, is here) by other members of the family – but that's negotiated now on my terms. No one else uses the table to write at or sits in the chair.

How long it took me. I sit here and look at my encouraging Alice Walker poster, her smiling gesture at the list of titles which are her witness, and realise it's taken me months of small steps, painting the walls, putting up the curtain, the shelves, the pictures. Many declarations of intent foreran these difficult acts – and how much effort it took to remove myself from the heart of activity on to the fringe. Much easier to watch television, find reasons for staying in and around the kitchen, to phone other people and invade their spaces. How many false starts before I could write this piece; how difficult to abandon rhetoric and to think. The pleasure of discovery that I still do exist when I withdraw is a heady one. Into this small space crowd so many questions, so much pain and doubt, yet so many ideas. They have been beating at the margins of this piece. I have made my room and now I must furnish it without abandoning those commitments which made me seek it. I'll have to take that risk. The excitement is all my own.

'This place would be here, whether we came or not,' she says. 'No,' says Helen. 'I don't think it would altogether. I mean of course it would exist, but only as the other side of somewhere else.'

Frankie Finn, *Out On The Plain*

Catherine Itzin's essay continues the meticulous reformulation of what is 'out there' and what is 'in here' – of how creativity might be made to relate to politics. The importance of a personal environment we have helped to create, in its emotional as well as material sense, is that it can reflect us back to ourselves instead of swallowing or stifling us; it can give us confidence and help us to stop sabotaging our own work. The idea of a residual true self which underlies the accretions of conditioning and which can be construed as a birth-right to be reclaimed has had a powerful appeal for women as they try to discover and then express what they deeply want and need; but it can be contrasted with another important principle, that of demythologising bourgeois notions of self as unified, constant, bounded and reliable.

This is perhaps one form of the necessary discussion of the relationship between spontaneity and control. The emphasis which the contributors give to either of these polar aspects of creativity is no doubt partly a question of temperament, of how each woman perceives herself and her history. Additionally, though, there are philosophical and political positions at stake. 'Every human being is an artist' is one (Joseph Beuys). 'Artists are the antennae of the race' (quoted by Ezra Pound) is another. '. . . art is always a social servant and historically utilitarian' (Leon Trotsky); 'In art, as in love, instinct is enough' (Anatole France) – what people choose as the defining characteristics of creativity is a sure give-away of what their political programme is, or would be.

Head, Hand, Heart –
and the Writing of Wrongs

Catherine Itzin

Her heart had always been in the right place.

By very early childhood, she had acquired a sixth-sense set of antennae tuned into the plight of people who were mistreated in any way.

To children who were bullied or ridiculed. Negro slaves in the South. The poor. People starving in India and Africa. Jews exterminated in the concentration camps. Jesus Christ on the cross. All victims of violence and injustice.

Holocaust, Hiroshima. Each new and horrific discovery of 'man's' inhumanity to 'man' sent a shock through her system. Terror.

She felt pain as if it were her own. She knew it mattered, even though the lives of adults went on as if such things hadn't happened, weren't happening. She knew that the possibility of personal happiness in a world that could tolerate such suffering, and the causes of it – the inequality – were minimal. She also knew deep down that none of it was necessary and that something could be done about it.

She was ten then.

Eventually she found that the injustice was closer to home, in her own life, in the present, not just past history in faraway places in the lives of other ('different') people. She became increasingly aware of the 'position of women'. The real hardship of being born female and raised feminine. The limitations imposed on her, her sister, her mother, her grandmother by the oppression of women. Subtle, seductive, but nevertheless systematic invalidation, humiliation, brutalisation.

She came to connect the poverty in her parents' early lives (and its emotional legacy in hers) with capitalism. She came to realise that her family were working class (as well as raised poor) and regarded as inferior, looked down upon by people higher up the class hierarchy. Coming from the farms of the midwest USA, she endured a form of 'regional class oppression' that characterised her and her beloved family as stupid and unsophisticated and insignificant by comparison with East and West Coast USers – and Europeans.

'It's not fair,' was her childhood refrain.

The ultimate insult to her intelligence was the conviction of the Catholic church that her failings (or feelings of failure) were her fault, that the state of the world was predetermined by a vicious and unbreakable cycle of 'original sin', in some way a loving God's perverse will.

She was sixteen then. She started to smoke. It made her feel better, more superior, sophisticated and significant. Cigarettes stopped her feeling the pain. A welcome fog, numbness: keeping the fear at bay.

She knew she was not prepared to wait for a better life in the next world – despite the fact that smoking, and the later periods of alcohol abuse that acted as an additional anaesthetic, hastened her in its direction. Her heart alternatively ached and raged and, in spite of the burden of internalised worthlessness, hopelessness and powerlessness (commonly known as guilt), she always nurtured in her heart a passionate belief that the wrongs of the world could be righted.

She maintained a burning sense of indignation in the face of overwhelming individual and institutional indifference. Her intuition told her that speaking out, truth-telling, revealing the obscured facts about reality and providing information about the nature of oppression was a key to changing the world: that writing – from the heart – could right the wrongs.

She'd known all this almost as if before she was born. But she could never, until a few years short of her fortieth birthday, find the words, or the form of words, to express her feelings and communicate what she knew. Any attempt at writing was a terrible struggle. All she could do was hold her breath (smoking helped) and hope for the best. Her head (her thinking) and her hand (her writing) were somehow not connected with her heart (her feelings).

She is me.

I run now in the mornings around my local park. As I run, I breathe regularly, I feel my heart beat, and I begin to think. Thoughts come into my head, words, phrases, sentences, paragraphs. Running is my own private space – time and place where my attention is only on myself. When I set (get) my pace, my running rhythms right, body in tune with brain, my thoughts flow. I am wholly with, in, of and for myself. When I can no longer contain my thoughts, I go home, sit down and start writing. I have discovered that my thinking is my writing. It is no longer a struggle. It is a pleasure.

This profound change is the result of five years of using a process that has enabled me systematically to reclaim myself and my creativity. A process that has enabled me to begin to collect my thoughts and reliably connect them with my hand.

For nearly ten years before this change, I wrote and published for a 'living' (i.e. low and unpredictable income – the pattern of women's work). But my writing, although very readable was not my thinking then. Not in the sense I see it now. It was the thinking of others.

I was a theatre critic for a national weekly for those ten years. I wrote regularly, even elegantly, often persuasively: but always about other people's thinking. I edited a much-esteemed international theatre magazine. This involved selecting and editing other people's thinking for publication. I even 'wrote' a couple of books – based on interviews with people about their lives and work. I chose other people's experiences and ideas to write about because in a very real sense I had no thinking of my own – or rather I did not have access to my own thinking.

Over the past five years – during three of which I did no writing at all – I have discovered why this was (and would have been) the case, and I have been able to begin to do something about it.

Mind you, I don't denigrate the 'writing' I did before. I'm proud of it. It has been much appreciated by other people (critics and readers alike), it is 'required reading' in many academic institutions, and I *do* value it. If that was the only way I could communicate my 'lost' thinking then – second-hand through reviews of other writers' writing and through interviews with other people's thinking – then I think I was mighty clever to have figured out a way to get on and do it.

It amuses me to recall how some reviewers of my book *Stages in the Revolution* would, in the course of their almost unanimous enthusiasm, comment on how difficult it was to pin down *my* point of view – as if this had been some deliberate, particularly clever and praiseworthy aspect of the book. The reality is that I didn't have one that I could put into my own words! Of course, I always chose to review plays that 'reflected' my thinking, or allowed me to 'reflect' my thinking and to interview people whose experience and thinking were close to my own. In any case, I was not consciously aware of what was going on.

The first stage in my 'awareness' was an overwhelming need to say 'no' – to stop editing, reviewing and interviewing. I remember saying to a fellow critic (they were and still are mostly male) that I was planning to 'retire' from my theatre writing. Surprised, he asked why. When I said it was because I felt that I'd never written a thought of my own in my life, he laughed. I had a reputation for being quite a radical and forceful thinker. Certainly a lot of my readers could have told me what they thought I thought.

Having said 'no' and stopped trying to 'think through others', I found myself alternately in despair and panic. I sank into a deep depression – what the mental-health system labels 'breaking down'. Without the prop of other people's thinking, I became acutely aware of the absence of my own. This confrontation with my empty head was terrifying and I found myself constantly shaking. I cried often and uncontrollably – from the grief of the loss of my thoughts. I lost my sense of time and space and place, would awaken in the early hours, body tense, 'mind' racing (the nearest I could come to thinking).

I had such strong feelings. And I knew I had thoughts, but they were always scattered. As if my brain had been smashed, my thoughts in fragments – like a comic-strip character, knocked senseless, reeling, seeing stars. I didn't then know what had hit me. With these symptoms of 'clinical depression' I felt that I was 'losing my mind'. Now I know that I was just beginning to find it for the first time in my life – and that the crying and the shaking were an essential part of that process.

It was during this period that something called Re-evaluation Counselling was introduced to me by a friend – as a 'tool to assist people to think more clearly and to function better'. I was understandably intrigued by what sounded like a solution to my troubles, and decided not to allow myself to be put off by a terminology that was occasionally reminiscent of US encounter groups and sixties counter-culture. I also resisted my usual aversion to anything remotely resembling 'therapy' (acquired in previous brief, relatively mild, but extremely distasteful encounters with the mental health system). I was assured that, any superficial appearances to the contrary, this particular theory and practice might be therapeutic, but definitely wasn't therapy. Putting aside my scepticism proved to be a wise decision for it has been the use of Re-evaluation Counselling that has freed me to begin to become the thinker and writer I always knew I was, and know every woman to be.

The major contribution of Re-evaluation Counselling to the liberation of me and my creativity has been its understanding of oppression and the connections it makes between oppression and internalised oppression:

– how individuals are, from the beginning of their lives, systematically mistreated initially as young people and then as members of sex, class, race or religious groups or as people with physical and mental disabilities;

– how this mistreatment is institutionalised and reinforced by structures of society which determine that members of some groups have access to economic and decision-making power denied to members of other groups;

– how the institutionalised oppression is internalised by individuals.

And most important of all:

– how the internalised oppression can be eliminated through a natural (albeit often inhibited) process of emotional release or emotional 'discharge' – specifically and quite simply: crying, laughing, shaking or trembling, sweating, and even yawning. (See the Endnote for a fuller explanation of Re-evaluation Counselling and how it works.)

The process of my 'creative' transformation over the past five years has come about through a regular use of Re-evaluation Counselling and a continual process of this emotional 'discharge' and spontaneous revaluation. It has been a period of new discoveries, new information, new points of view, new decisions, new directions.

An early stage was to make a decision to 'trust my own thinking' – always and in every circumstance, however confused or 'blank' I might feel. This felt at first to be a near nonsense. I had no sense of having any thinking of my own to trust – and the notion of trusting myself seemed almost absurd. As a mother, I trusted Dr Spock. As a patient, I trusted the doctors and nurses. As a student, I trusted my teachers. As a citizen, I trusted politicians (well, some, sometimes). As a child, I'd trusted my parents. I've learnt now how my trust and confidence in myself and my own thinking and writing had been systematically undermined – by sexism and classism, and through the educational system.

An early long-forgotten memory that came to mind in my first counselling session was a 'little' incident when my first-grade teacher had humiliated me in front of the class for shaping some of the letters of the alphabet incorrectly. A couple of years of regular counselling, on and around this apparently trivial incident in my life, uncovered many previously obscured memories of how this woman had intimidated me and humiliated me and subjected me to mental and physical violence. A part of this was her telling me always that there was something wrong with how and what I wrote.

She was so dismissive of my first poem as 'not being a poem at all' that I never dreamt or attempted to write another poem again until, in counselling groups on writing, I took the direction to trust not only my thinking but my 'first thoughts'. By this time I'd acquired an insight into the reality that my 'thinking' included my 'intuition' as well as my 'intellect'. Trusting my thinking meant 'trusting my first thoughts' as being the natural combination of both my 'intuitive' and my 'intellectual' knowledge. I discovered that my first thoughts in this case came out in the form of a poem – this poem:

Women's Intuition

I know:
Women are mothers.
I am a mother.
I must be a woman.

I think:
Women are beautiful.
I am a woman.
I must be beautiful.

I think:
Women are powerful.

I am a woman.
I must be powerful.

And so
I must conclude:
How I feel
(Inadequate, unattractive,
unloveable, self-critical,
helpless, powerless and
hopeless, for example)
Doesn't make sense.

It's simple really,
Logic.
When you trust your intuition.

(1983)

I could see unequivocally in this situation that my thinking was my writing, that in this case my thinking was a poem and therefore that I was 'a poet' (and now indeed with two poems published) in spite of what that wretched woman had done to me when I was six years old.

Gradually I have 'discharged' the *internalised oppression* – the damage of these truly annihilating early 'hurts' (they never are just 'little' incidents) – enough to see how they had made me internalise some very false notions about myself and my ability to think and write. Freeing myself of this *internalised oppression* through the 'discharge process' has enabled me to see the *oppression*. In the educational system for example. It has enabled me to write my thinking about it. No surprise that my latest book is about young people's experience of the educational system and what parents can do to improve it!

I have also used counselling to 'discharge' the enormous extent to which I've internalised and lived my life on the basis of the invalidation and misinformation of sexism. How, for example, it falsely teaches us that men can be writers (or certain kinds of writers) and women can't. How it invalidates the writing women have done most easily within our oppression – diaries, letters, journals. And, of course, how the oppression also excludes women from the opportunity to write at all by filling our lives with other work.

More recently, as a result of discharging the hurts I experienced in an 'upwardly mobile' working-class family, I have come to see more clearly the classism which creates and maintains the pretence that writing is something that has to be done in a certain style, using certain kinds of words in a certain kind of way and usually done by certain kinds of people: middle class and often academic. This is all a lie. Because writing has been appropriated by the middle classes, there is a tendency to think that writing itself is middle class, therefore to avoid it or even dismiss it if you're working class. This is a mistake. As our writing is our thinking, it is a powerful tool in our own and everyone's liberation.

For myself I've stopped trying to write in any particular way, and act on the direction to write what I think in whatever way, wherever and to whomever I wish to share my thinking. In the process, I've reclaimed my potential to write as a working-class woman – personally, directly, without the 'artful' or 'clever' trappings and turns of phrase that I learned in order to compete and succeed in the literary and academic worlds. It's a relief. And my writing has improved enormously in my view.

A parallel part of my 'creative' transformation has been on a seemingly less political, more personal level – the piecing together of my fragmented thinking process. Fairly early in my counselling experience I uncovered an obscured incident in the very earliest months of my life, when my life was seriously threatened and I nearly died. It was, I am sure, the incident that 'smashed my brain and scattered my thoughts' – the terror that paralysed my thinking process. As I began systematically to discharge the fear (and other distress) connected with that life-threatening event, I began to breathe again. Taking the direction 'to breathe and think', slowly and in that order, my thoughts have gradually come more and more together. (You'd be surprised how many people stop breathing – hold their breath – when they're struggling to think and write). It's been a long and developing process. The 're-writing' of my 'schools' book' involved so many stages of re-ordering paragraphs and pages that the scissors and pasting created a final manuscript of the normal 70,000-word book length – but nearly three feet thick! And I was counselling up to four or five times a week on occasions as I wrote it, rather than the usual – and more typical – once or twice a week. It was a triumph, of 'discharge' over the 'structural dyslexia' (the right thoughts but in the wrong order) that I believe resulted from the terror of that very early (pre-birth) life-threatening experience.

Learning to breathe and think has, incidentally, benefited not just writing, but my very well-being. For in the process I have eliminated the 20-year smoking addiction I now see as being attached to the 'terror' of that early hurt, and subsequently reinforced by the constant invalidation and intimidation of oppression. It's no accident that the heaviest smokers are women and working class!

You can't breathe and smoke at the same time. Smoking stops your breath. It fills you with numbness (the chemical anaesthetic) that stops you feeling the terror – whatever *your* terror may be. If you breathe – take in and let out air continually – you literally *can't* smoke. You feel the terror and you 'discharge' it: laugh, cry, shake. Finally it's gone – and so is the 'need' to smoke. It *is* simple, but it requires that initial decision to breathe. And a particular quality of attention (available from other counsellors) that assists emotional discharge is an important, helpful part of the process. But the process is possible – and it's accessible to everyone, anyone.

Needless to say I used to 'have' to smoke to write at all.

Now, looking back, I see some more 'method' in my choice (albeit limited) to write about the theatre. For I have always regarded myself as a playwright: that is my identity and my aspiration.

I have done a 'bit' of playwrighting – and had those plays produced. But this is just the tip of an iceberg. My filing cabinet is full of 'promising' (even award-winning) but unfinished dramatic business. I get just so far – but never quite finished. A recent insight: for a play to be a play at all (never mind 'good' or 'bad'), it has to have a certain structure: order of events, thoughts. It may just be that I haven't been able to finish my plays because of my inability to order my thoughts. If so, it is now at least possible, increasingly certain, and possibly even probable that I may – using the process of 'discharge and re-evaluation' – collect and order my thoughts into the form of my plays. Then I think the characters that continue to live and speak in my head year after year will connect with my hand and come out on paper.

The next stage in the process? The final transformation? I'm learning not to set limits. I assume there is as much I don't know now as I didn't know then. Creating myself is a continuing process of discharge and re-evaluation.

Internalised sexism and classism (and racism too, of course) define the limits of success and install a fear of stepping out of line. In addition, very early life-threatening attacks can install a terror of the public visibility that is a consequence of success and leadership. These barriers can also be dismantled and the isolation made to disappear.

I know I'm not on my own any more.

I meet regularly with other writers in two support groups that I have organised for myself. Some of them are counsellors and we specifically use the discharge process when we meet. Others are contributors to this book. We are in our late thirties, early forties, all of us successful, and fairly well-known writers of one kind (children's plays, literary criticism, poetry, non-fiction), wanting to become writers of different kinds. We all are – and also call ourselves – The Mothers.

I also have a sense of being in the company of all women. Every woman has experienced her life uniquely: the wrongs of oppression as well as the benign reality of being human in a world that could be the way we know it should be. Every woman is a thinker and every woman is a writer waiting for the opportunity to reclaim the connections between her heart, her head and her hand – and to write our wrongs.

A Note on Re-evaluation Counselling

This is a process that offers the opportunity for personal and social change. It consists of a basic theory and a simple, but reliable, practice.

The theory is based on an understanding of human beings as essentially intelligent, loveable and loving, eager to learn and co-operate, able to function well. It assumes that everyone, however, has been impaired – emotionally and intellectually – by the distress acquired in the process of growing up in a society structured on inequality and injustice. Everyone also has the ability to recover from these hurts. This occurs automatically when the process of emotional release – or discharge – is allowed to happen, and results in the elimination of internalised oppressions and in the ability to think and act more effectively.

A major part of the theory and practice is based on a detailed understanding of oppression and internalised oppression.

The process of recovery can be learnt, usually in groups, in most parts of London, in many parts of the UK and in over 40 other countries. The skills acquired can then be used on a regular structured basis. Contact Catherine Itzin, Dept. of Sociology, University of Essex, Wivenhoe Park, Colchester CO4 3SQ, for more information.

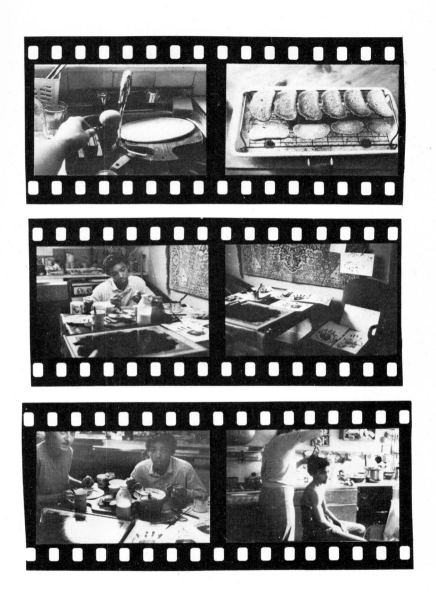

The Everyday Creative Process (my son Samouri and myself
photographed by automatic release). Gabriela Müller

Power and Powerlessness. Gabriela Müller

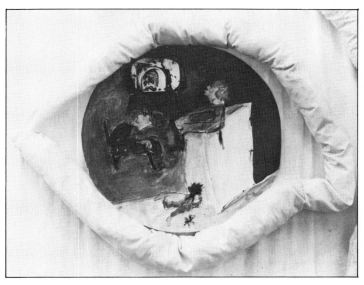

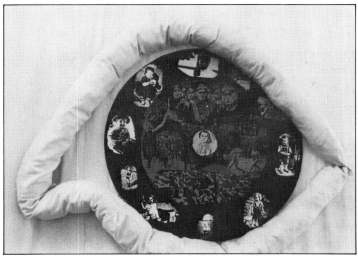

Power and Powerlessness (details)

Receive the Sacred Body of Christ to eat

The One God

and His precious Blood to drink

The One Male God

pray to Him, love Him, endure His punishment

The One White Male God

Blessed are the Poor for theirs is the Kingdom of Heaven

Go and feed the hungry
Go and clothe the naked

Go with the Holy Book and take their Land . .

Gabriela Müller
The Catholic way to White Heaven: photographic images created
in a phototherapy session with Rosy Martin

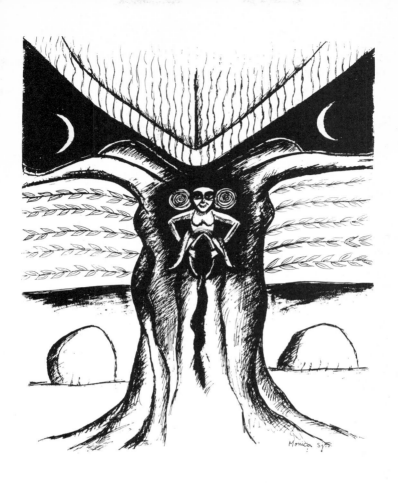

The bleeding yew Mother Tree on Nevern graveyard,
Pembrokeshire, S. Wales. Monica Sjöö, 1983

THE FACE OF "WYRD" (THE UNKNOWABLE
ONE ~ THE DARK MOTHER) AS SEEN IN
CERRIG CENNEN CASTLE CAVE & WELL AT
IMBOLC 1985   Monica Sjöö

The face of 'Wyrd'. Monica Sjöö, 1985

and there lay my son, never to open his
eyes again on this Earth plane – all my prayers, love
& hope crushed. We put flowers in his place & on his
blind eye, a leaf on his chest – & he went soaring
on great white wings into the great light beyond.

Monica Sjöö 1986

NERTHUS & FREYIA

Monica Sjöö 1983

How class divides women is painful. Many of us are wounded by the conflict. Working class women still need to assert themselves and their experiences against the complacency they meet in middle class women. Many groups are working to free themselves from the internalised oppression Cathy vividly describes, creating new forms of expression in the process, as working class women's writing and exhibitions show.

There is another dimension to Cathy's discussion. The validation of rationality and the exercise of intellect – around which, from a combination of historical and ideological factors, has grown a palpable distrust – are desirable counterbalances to an emphasis on women's capacity for feeling. In recognising some kind of tension between our thoughts and feelings we are not bound to define this as a symptom of mutual incompatibility, which after all is another dualistic convention. Indeed there are reactionary consequences from doing so. The aggressive anti-intellectualism of Thatcherism – its denigration of philosophical inquiry – is ill-disguised by the pretensions of the so-called New Right thinkers and is a trend against which we have seriously to defend feminist ideas.

Education is a realm where a simplistic opposition of feeling ('ideologically untainted') to intellect ('oppressive', 'imperialistic') has far-reaching and unwanted consequences. To insist on rejecting the need for institutionalised education is in effect to persist in supporting prevailing power structures. It is a mark of privilege not oppression to be able to refuse, at least in theory, the small but significant advantages gained by 'equality of opportunity'. The fear of acquiring knowledge and expertise which, as Catherine's article showed, is a sign of damage early done, is sometimes held on to as if it were a mark of political sinlessness. What is entirely necessary is to change the ends to which people put their expertise and the structures within which they operate; hardly an original thought, but worth restating.

How this is done depends on how well the validity of others' experiences can be tolerated. Catherine's understanding of internalised oppression – how we learn to oppress ourselves – is also an understanding of the mechanisms by which we oppress others. Catherine uses the term 'intuition' to distinguish certain perceptions she regards as reliable from those which she realises result from pain or some other distortion. How we decide which perceptions are reliable (and what we call them), and how we evaluate the fact that ideologies may stimulate as well as repress creativity, are questions that need to accompany an exploration of political difference between women. Insights that are crucial for one group of women at one moment are unlikely to be the salient ones at another moment or for another group of women; this truism is sometimes buried under an overwhelming need for the expediency of 'sister-hood'.

Amrita Mohan does not class herself as a feminist; her allegiances are framed by culture and family. Her work with young children embodies a commitment to honour those allegiances; to counteract in the classroom those forms of oppression that silence, label and betray young people of colour. Behind and through this daily interpretation of a job, she cherishes a vision of an enriched social equality; but she has few illusions about the existing barriers of apathy. Amrita Mohan and I taught at the same school for two years; it is also the school which our four children attended as infants.

Away from Home

Amrita Mohan

(An interview)

L.S. Why did you decide to come to England?

A.M. I was a student of English literature and really loved it; I wanted to study a bit more. The other reason was that my husband, Surinder, wanted to do some further study in engineering. We were too young, too inexperienced – we didn't know what it was like, going to another country. We thought we'd study for two or three years and come back. Once we were here, we realised it was going to be hard. Because we were not indigenous students, we would have had to pay the full tuition fees – which we couldn't afford. We got whatever jobs were going; this meant working in factories at first. Then I got a job in the Post Office for a while. By then we had the children and it seemed that we were stuck. I didn't do anything about my education . . . Before I came here, I was a lecturer in English in a degree college. The difference between that life and my life here was tremendous – shocking. Eventually I took it on as a challenge; I decided that as I am a teacher, I could learn to teach young children too. I stuck at it; I worked very hard. I did a diploma in teaching English as a foreign language. And at the same time I was teaching Indian children in a language centre. That kept me going, I felt I was doing a worthwhile job. Those children needed somebody they could identify with. They needed to feel that they belonged somewhere, that whatever they had got to offer was valued. If you do not value them, you develop a negative attitude in the children – they withdraw, cannot do their best. Their language, their culture, needed recognition and since I belonged to the same culture I tried to involve them by using our common background – songs, stories, plays, cookery . . . Some parents valued this and even participated in the lessons, but others felt I was wasting time – the sooner their children learned English, the sooner they could move into the main school . . .

L.S. How had racist attitudes affected you personally?

A.M. Before I started teaching I'd come across lots of unpleasant experiences personally. I was aware of discrimination: in the language centre I felt that the majority opinion was that the children should abide by the rules of the prevalent culture, that they should conform now they were in England and forget what they were, where they had come from. We had Greek and Portuguese as well as Indian and Pakistani children. I resented this, I must say. I tried in my own way to help the children maintain their identity – because I felt what they were going through . . . Just before I left the Post Office to go into this job, the assistant post master called me into his office. 'Oh, Mrs Mohan,' he said 'I didn't know you were a teacher, I didn't realise you were so well qualified!' I'd been there for nearly two years and he hadn't wanted to know anything about me. After that, he became very friendly! We – the Asian community – come across that the whole time, these preconceptions . . .

L.S. Now you are working as a class teacher in the main school, with white children as well. You are still committed to teaching Asian culture. What responses do you get to that?

A.M. Yes, I am committed – for two reasons. First, there will always be some Asian children in the class: at no time is there an all-white class. Even if there are only two or three of them, they will celebrate their Diwali or their Eid – it is important to talk about those festivals as well as Christmas and Easter. Though they are a minority, their need is just as great and that need should be met. They are individuals, not statistics – as we recognise already in terms of children's academic needs. Cultural needs should be met, too. The other reason is that the countries of Asia – and India in particular – have a lot to offer to the world. They are not recognised for that because they are economically not as strong as Japan, for example. Because India is a poor country, people in the West think it has nothing to offer. In my very small way, I hope I can bring that to the notice of little children. When they grow up, perhaps they will look upon people coming from India or Pakistan – or any other country – as people equal to them, who have something to offer. So there is no harm in exposing English children to our culture as well – it can only broaden their horizons . . . When I came to the main school, the Head was sympathetic to my ideas; she always appreciated the stories or music or plays that I performed with my class. I don't think I came across any opposition from the other teachers; once or twice some (white) parents objected. The teachers could have done more, perhaps – it was much more pleasant when the whole school was involved, like when we had our Asian Days.

L.S. What struck me about those occasions was the need to go beyond that; we ought to be integrating what we did rather than leaving it all for one day of the year. It was noticeable how the Asian parents – particularly the mothers – felt involved and welcomed in a way that is not customary the rest of the school year. Perhaps we need an explicit policy that we would all be committed to?

A.M. Yes, I feel there should be – in all schools. It's time that the indigenous community, indigenous teachers, started taking notice of our culture. You've got to make the children feel proud of themselves. One example is my own son Viki. We have a Punjabi dance called a *bhangra* – it's a very lively dance and whenever we have parties, we get together and we dance. He used to join in, but not very enthusiastically – he'd say, 'Oh, I can't.' He's usually very proud of his cultural inheritance; and he's good at all the western dances! The students had a function in their school, a revue to raise money for the school fund. Some Indian girls and boys got together and said, 'Come on, let's do a *bhangra* dance.' It had never been done in that school before! It was beautiful, absolutely lovely; and since that day, Viki has wanted to learn *bhangra*. Why? Because it was accepted, acknowledged and valued in his school. You can explain; but explaining's not enough. The children must feel it. There's so much lying dormant among these young Asian boys and girls. It could be tapped, through the right channels . . . I used to be a student of the Indian dance called *kathak,* so when I can I use the dance movements with the little ones, to illustrate a story. Children always respond to it – it's so expressive.

L.S. There's nothing quite like it in the rest of the infant curriculum; there's self-expression through movement, which tends to be rather rudimentary, or there's P.E., which is skilful but not very expressive. But this seems to offer a structure and a meaning, as well as pleasure.

A.M. Yes; I can remember an assembly I did about the festival of Diwali. One white boy was so taken by the story of Ram and

Lakshman that he would keep asking to hear it; he was so taken by the character of Ram that he wanted to act the part. When he grows up, he won't find those stories alien; maybe he'll want to explore them further. That's what my job's about. When we did the story of the Taj Mahal, the children were so engrossed I don't think they were aware of their parents sitting and watching them. They said, 'Mrs Mohan, when we grow up, we want to go and see the Taj Mahal for ourselves.' . . . When we took water as a topic, I played *jaltarang* for them – bowls of water which you beat with little metal sticks – so that that should be part of their learning about the topic.

L.S. Let's now turn to the question of women . . .

A.M. Going back thousands of years, the status of women in India was very high. Their position changed when India was attacked by Muslim invaders who looted cities and dishonoured the Indian women. They would do, any outside invaders do that – throughout history, women have been the easy targets all the time, haven't they? Indian society was shocked and took the solution of withdrawing women from society altogether; that's when the veil was introduced. Women lived inside the house. Some good things happened too from that invasion – a beautiful culture sprang up from the combination of Muslim and Hindu ways; and we often managed a mutual understanding. But woman has never resumed her original place! Indian women are powerful in the family, they have strong family support. Their position is not feeble. Their needs are different from western women's. The first need is for contraception. But western feminism is catching on.

L.S. What effect has emigration had on that family bonding and protection?

A.M. Young couples do not know what it is like when they first come over and live in a different society. I felt it more than Surinder – the sort of support you get in India when you have children is just not possible here. For forty days you're not allowed to do anything when you have a baby! But when I came home from hospital and gave Viki his first bath, I was shaking like a leaf. Surinder was very supportive, so I have been lucky that way. Not all Indian men are like that . . . My brother wrote a poem about our mother – 'mother' is an extremely respected figure in Indian society. The kind of sacrifices a mother makes for her children would be unheard of in the West – say she hasn't got enough money and she wants her children to be educated, she would do anything possible; sell her gold, work at menial jobs in her spare time to earn a bit more money. And not only the financial things, but the quality of emotional and practical support is something I haven't come across here. Because the Indian mother goes to all lengths for children, she is held in deep reverence. You can find that in many poems and stories. My brother's poem starts with how good his own mother was to him, then he goes to the universal, as it were. He says whatever I am it's all because of you. You have given me the ability to express myself; there's nothing of me in this poem, it's all yours and I'm giving it back to you. Every mother is an artist – in the form of a child, a mother writes a poem, sings a song. Day by day she refines her creation.

L.S. That's a beautiful idea . . . but it causes me some difficulty. You have written poetry yourself – is there a conflict, do you think, between being a creator in the sense of being a mother and being a creator, being a poet yourself?

A.M. Not a conflict as such, but being a mother and having to give so much to your children because you want to, you feel drained or that you've lost something. The children need the best from you if they are to grow up into good human beings; it takes up a lot of time and energy to cultivate those values – it won't wait. And by the time the children have grown up you might feel it's too late for you. But perhaps if there was really something in you, you might be able to call it back. I don't know. I would like to, I don't know whether I will or not! . . . Music, drama, literature have been my love from the start. I used to train the college students for the annual young people's arts festival. I used to contribute essays to journals and I had a contract with All India Radio Jalandhar for the equivalent of *Woman's Hour;* I would be asked to discuss cultural topics, such as comparing Punjabi women writers with English ones. It was very exciting – then I left it all behind! . . . Now I belong to a writers' group, The Progressive Writers' Group, which is a national organisation with local branches. Surinder and I both belong. We write poetry or essays to be read and discussed at functions. The majority of the members are communists, so we celebrate May Day and I wrote something for that. Then once we had a famous Punjabi woman poet coming, Amrita Pritam, whom I was asked to introduce . . . We have unfortunately just two other women in the group, out of about 18 members. The men are asked to bring their wives along, but they give the excuse, 'Oh, she doesn't understand much about poetry, she doesn't want to know about poetry.' I say, 'How do you know, till you bring them?' That is my one argument with them.

L.S. What makes *you* feel valued, gives you a sense of pride and worth? You try to give that to other people – what nourishes you?

A.M. When I have involved my children in something and they enjoy it, my first reward comes from that. Then if my colleagues enjoy it, that's good too – we all thrive on a bit of praise! I remember once the Head said, 'You know, children, you are very lucky to have Mrs Mohan as your teacher because she doesn't only do the things that everybody else does, she always does something different, something extra.' That was very nice. Apart from that, it's my home. We are all so committed to this, the support I get from home keeps me going. I feed myself on Indian music and Indian dance – I've got some lovely dances on tape.

L.S. Is there just one out of all the traditional tales that you would like to pass on, one that the children love particularly?

A.M. Well, they like the one you acted with them – you know there is a summer festival in India when sisters tie a ribbon round their brother's wrists and pray for their good fortune and long life; and in return the brothers promise to look after them and grant their wishes. It originated many centuries ago. This tale is set in the time of King Porus, a brave and just king of India. The warrior Alexander was gathering his armies to attack India – it was his dream to conquer the world. While he was planning the attack, his girlfriend Rukhsana started to think that if King Porus was all she had heard him to be, Alexander might well be killed instead of conquering. She had to act quickly. Somehow she smuggled herself into India in disguise. She came amongst the crowd celebrating a festival, there was merry-making and street-people selling *rakhis,* the ribbons that sisters tie on their brother's wrists. She asked what was happening, and someone explained the custom to her. So Rukhsana formed the idea to appeal to King Porus in just that way. She brought a *rakhi* and went straight to the palace. She walked through the halls until she came to the king's chamber. People made way for this unknown woman because her demeanour was so determined, yet calm. She came to him and asked him to hold out his right arm. She tied the ribbon round his wrist and said, 'You are now my brother. I need your help.' King Porus replied that he would honour her request because it was the tradition. 'What do you need, my sister?' he asked. Rukhsana revealed who she was and told him of her fears for Alexander's life. She begged that if he died in battle, he would not die by Porus' hand. He gave his word. When the battle was fought – it was a fierce one – Porus and Alexander eventually came face to face; though Porus had the advantage, he remembered his promise. He let his sword fall. He himself was taken a prisoner. Alexander asked him how he should treat him in captivity and Porus is alleged to have replied, 'As one king should treat another.' Alexander was pleased with this answer, and set him free, saying, 'I would rather have you as my friend than my subject. India shall go free as well.' And Rukhsana had brought this about . . .

L.S. When you take up writing again, what would you like to do?

A.M. When I go back to writing, I will write in both languages, Punjabi and English. I want to write about my experiences in England – the good and the bad experiences. I want to write for ordinary women; and I have been thinking I would call it *Away from Home* . . .

Joan Blaney, Amrita Mohan, Gabriela Müller and Maud Sulter engage with the deep-seated racism in our society in very different ways.

Gabriela as a white woman closely related to black individuals pulls apart her own whiteness and surely offers white women one way of being actively anti-racist. At the same time she relives, through memories of her childhood, the aftermath of Nazism in Europe – a legacy many of us feel we do not yet know how to turn to some comprehensible good. She does not attempt to be dispassionate; caught up in history not of her making, she nonetheless assumes a responsibility to change, in however small a way, how the present and future may be lived and understood.

In her art therapy work she believes in making extremes (of feeling, image or value) approach one another, as part of a personal and cultural healing process. The concept which underlies this is again that of responsibility – for the life of society as well as for oneself – to which several other articles also appeal. It relies for its emotional force on two assumptions: one, that symbolic power is equivalent in effect to actual power; two, that both society and the world can be thought of as if they were alive, organic. It would be shrewd to debate the arguments in support of these important assumptions, if only because such assumptions can be, have been, used by apostles of fascism to license their brand of social organisation.

By portraying violence and brutality, Gabriela takes the psychic risk of embracing it; she says, in effect, that people are susceptible to becoming brutalised, inhuman, not through original sin nor by mysterious external forces, but because we allow ourselves to be divided from each other. She proposes that we do not need 'easy consciences' – the liberal compulsion to be Mr Clean – in order to survive intact; but nor must we collapse under a masochistic sense of guilt.

Gabriela writes about preparing for two exhibitions – Love, Sex and Romance *and* Realising Power *– both held at Brixton Art Gallery (now threatened with closure) in the autumn of 1985 and 1986 respectively. The form she has chosen springs out of her conviction that*

> *It is necessary to remain open to pre-verbal impulses and fantasies and therefore extremely emotionally exposed . . . When we are open, confrontative and honest about ourselves, we are not just*

united in our anger but ultimately in our struggle against that which is meant to divide us. (In Women's Work; *see Bibliography.)*

When horror becomes unimaginable, it wins its final victory, because when the imagination is overwhelmed we begin to give up, to shrug our shoulders, to accept the omnipotence of evil . . . In this century it has often seemed that subjects too colossally vile to be grasped, things beyond words, have come into the world, like forerunners of the apocalypse. (Salman Rushdie, Guardian, *7th November 1986.)*

Washing the Linen

Gabriela Müller

1.

I am five and a half years old. I feel mischievous. Grandmother and Auntie are watching TV while babysitting me. They haven't noticed I am watching too from behind the door.

I am terrified. What are these images about? What is 'German', 'Nation', 'the World', 'POWER'?

Why are so many people dead, killed?

I am frightened . . . I scream . . . I am found out . . .

Grandma and Auntie look shocked. Tell me off, then try to pacify me.

Grandma tells me a story which begins: 'I once had two close friends . . . They were Jewish girls . . .' She has tears in her eyes and her voice trembles.

I imagine masses of people looking, seeing, stirring – passively, powerless. Seeing, watching. How can their betrayal ever be forgiven?

When I grow up, I will transform the world.

2.

Seven a.m. Saturday morning. I woke up early today because I want to be creative. Hmm. My first cup . . . I am fighting the urge to get the hoover out and tidy the living room before I 'make myself big'. (And then the kitchen and then . . .) I have been shifting the furniture around, finding new corners to look from, different ways of seeing my space (yeah, and cleaning those corners).

Time is running on while I wake and dream. At least and at last I've awoken to a few words which don't feel like enemies. It is nearly eight a.m. and I still don't know what to do.

Sunday. I am working for a collective exhibition. The theme is Love, Sex and Romance. Today is the day all my creative work is supposed to be finished. Ha ha ha ha. I've done the sleeve of the catalogue. I can do it because it's not 'my' work. I am angry with myself – undisciplined, lazy, escapist, my internal Father says. What the hell is going on?

Why don't I get up and work on this wall, the one I cleared for this purpose? Three weeks ago I chased everyone out of this room . . . Is this the old fear of seeing myself out there, big, and I'm really so small? Exposed to myself and the world?

I'm filled with ideas now. It's noon. Sue will be coming soon, there'll be no time. My son demands a haircut.

Those three white spaces are silences staring at me. I don't like the way I've filled them. Art therapy has taught me something very important. I have learned how to continue, not to stop in despair. As therapist I ask myself, what is this despair about? Keep on asking. Keep on, keep on . . .

I don't feel much yet. I feel outside it. The only association I have is the blue – a baby-boy suit! Do I have to produce a baby boy to take on the world for me – to express my dreams? I am escaping into colour separating. I can take a colour apart and merge it into any possible shade. Pushing this green into turquoise and then into a deepnight blue. Defence or virtue, or both? I'm lost again.

I see an industrial landscape, my home town, behind the baby-boy suit. I am wandering off to the town I came from, near Patric Henry Village in West Germany. Born into the *Wiederaufbau* – the Rebuilding – after total destruction. A couple of big bad boys had broken everything, I'd been told. The Americans are still there.

This piece of writing is nothing special. My creative process at its most ordinary. Let me celebrate the ordinary. The ordinary is never the norm or the normal. It is the simple stuff in life that is so difficult to understand and in this lies its magic. How to put that across?

I have an image. Two women riding a tiger, one with a snake and the other with a bird.

Monday morning. Of course I'm not finished and ready. Far from it. I spend all morning painting. I'm exhausted, empty.

The mail came. A letter from West Africa. I felt heavy. I sensed it. Ya Fatu Khan has died. Could I send the last photographs I had taken? A piece of my life has gone. I'm shocked. She was one of the liveliest women in the neighbourhood. Every time we meet we tell jokes, gossip, tease, sometimes dance, argue, hug and kiss. 'You moved to Uncle Job's house,' she said the first time we met. 'You live here. You are one of us now.' She looked serious. 'You will learn how to cook, to wash, to pound the rice and couscous in this pot.'

I didn't know what to say, did she really mean this? I hadn't come to Africa to be a housewife! As if hearing my thoughts, Ya Fatu released a thundering laugh – 'Hahahahaha . . . Why did you come here?'

The last time we went back to Serekunda I learned she'd had a stroke and was paralysed. I was used to see her storming out of one of the rooms with a flying buba, her wide African dress, and a headtie like a huge swinging sculpture, leaving a scented trail behind her. Mesmerised, I would fall into Ya Fatu's arms. 'Ya Fatu ...' 'My picken, my child. Is peace with you? How is my husband [meaning my baby son]? How is your husband, how is Ya Awa, how is . . ?'

Ya Fatu had two girls close in age who were always sticking up for each other. Together they did most of the household chores and as teenagers they were always giggling. 'Kikeriki, kikeriki,' Ya Fatu called them jokingly. I waited for a long time for Ya Fatu to be rolled out of her bedroom by the two daughters. They must have taken all this time to dress their mother, put powder, make-up, perfume on. Ya Fatu looked immaculate. 'You are the prettiest in town!' I greeted her, something I always said when we met. 'And the best perfume.' 'My picken, come, come,' she whispered, tears in her eyes. 'I thank God to make me see you before I die.'

3.

> I've been growing up
> in second floors
> of apartment blocks
> cop car sirens
> as my night music

the shambles of the second world war
were my playground down the road
ruins
in my memory of growth

The river bank
with trees surrounding
my lived fantasies
soft little body and soul
combined
with fears of dirty men
snakes and rats
were my reality
and tears
my happy childhood loneliness

That is how my poem called 'Africa' begins. It is a long poem: here are some extracts from it.

I gave my love a name
I called it Africa
tam, ta, ta, tam

I carry your child in my belly
I brought it for you
to be delivered
take it from me
it's yours
tam ta, tam tam
I am here, I am here
I am here...

the drum beats
talks to me
takes me
to a land of spirits
who greet me
'yam man ngam
njam ma rek'
are you friendly?
is peace within you?

or did you come to steal
to plunder?
is peace within you?

sleep, sleep, sleep
an old woman
opens her arms
'come my picken
you my picken now'
the spirits drift
away . . . dancing . . .
I am here I am home.

4.

Thursday afternoon. I've been printing and typing for the exhibition. My own piece is all in my head – a bed. The myth of privacy, the bedroom, not a safe place for peace, pleasure and love but where ideology is perpetuated and challenged. I feel tense. Maybe I am excited, yes, I am excited. My mother is coming tomorrow.

Friday. My mother arrives from Germany. We are glad to see each other. Later we have our first row. I told her I haven't much time yet. I'm nervous about the exhibition. It doesn't look right yet.

A friend said I could borrow his cot. I want a bed. I don't want to give birth to a baby, I am making art for once. I need a bed. I am angry.

I'm hurt. My son always has to reject me when his gran arrives. I am going to escape. Find some solitude in Brixton.

The underground is filled with policemen. Brixton is burning. The air smells of fire. Not sex, love and romance but killing, rape and hatred. Police had entered Cherry Groce's home early in the morning. She and her three small children had woken up to the forced entry of these armed men. She was shot in front of her children. Another racist 'accident'. The riot flares.

I feel upset. I think of the phrase 'art cannot change the world, it merely states what is'. 'What is' must be very different in different places. No one riots in Cork Street. The police don't shoot an innocent black woman there. Art there is apart from reality. I can't bear to collude, by my silence, in the injustice, the humiliation and oppression that affects us. As a white woman I am safer if I keep my mouth shut. I simply have to refrain from speech, save the taxpayers' money and be a quiet cog in the machinery. Make art – Art – which is pleasing, don't ask myself too many questions. I'm hurting all over. I go to the gallery and put a newspaper on the bed. The page shows five young black women being dragged and beaten by police. I know this will not heal any wounds. It just acknowledges the pain and condemns the violence.

I am furious. I leave the gallery and walk through the streets. I'm aware of my whiteness. I'm aware that my mother wasn't shot in the back. I'm aware that my black son is more vulnerable to racist attacks than I am.

The newspapers are playing on the rape of a white girl, an MP's daughter. I know all this psychological warfare stuff and yet I feel scared. I could be the target of some angry black youth. How easy it is to fall into the trap of racist stereotyping. My own son is part of this 'black youth'. 'I am not the colour of my skin!' I want to scream. Race doesn't make for racism.

But how do I explain my privileged position? I can't, I don't want to. I want to destroy this destructive world I can't escape from. Transformation seems far away. Art seems meaningless. My bed will not silence the daily racist and sexist oppression. My bed is not a sanctuary where Beauty is an escape from reality.

5. Towards an Anti-racist Way of Realising Power

I am a white racist woman. As a little girl I am taught to be racist. Rebelling, I am often defeated.

I am white and therefore have the luxury to see myself as an individual. I forget that I am white and part of a white culture in power.

I choose to focus on my oppression as a woman. Not on how I am oppressing others or misuse my power.

I hold on to my guilt. Guilty and stuck, I don't act.

I don't like to identify as white. I deny my whiteness by talking about the many times I was not seen, heard; I was abused, hated.

'White is ugly' – guilty about the privileges I have got, I feel sorry for myself for being white and part of a racist group in power.

6.

A week before the opening of *Realising Power*. I am a ball of tight
knotted confusion. Don't know where to begin. I'm still stuck in
the publicity work for the group and won't miss an opportunity to
have yet more work dumped on me. It seems hard labour to get my
piece on white racism out in the open after such long silencing.
Somehow my workshop 'White women – white racism' gets left
out of the printed programme. Accidentally. I am told that I can
always print an extra leaflet announcing the workshop. Yes, extra,
apart from the other art, the other women, the other white women.
I feel excluded. Is it me or is it the discomfort 'white racism'
causes?

'Everyone is overworked – we've had lots of accidents.' I don't
believe in accidents. I phone one of the white women I trust most
to understand my pain and anger. She confirms my feelings. I'm
not crazy after all. Then she adds, 'I don't trust any white woman.'
'What about me?' I ask with difficulty. She changes the subject.

This is the true state of affairs. We white folks, including women,
don't trust each other. We've projected our hostility on to the
whole world. In removing the hatred from those we've projected it
on to, we are left with the hatred we inflict on ourselves. The
mistrust is so deep. This is how it feels. I can't change alone. I feel
abandoned, devastated.

The exhibition opens. I've worked to the very last minute.
Friends, colleagues arrive. I don't know who to talk to first. Linda
Malone and a friend play conga. Another woman sings, some
dance. I run around serving wine, keep everyone happy. My son
sits down with a long face, says he is bored, wants to go home and
watch TV. Three women from the collective come over to say how
much they like my work. Others sip wine and ignore the work.
Linda has to go to another gig. The music stops and suddenly
people say goodbye. Within ten minutes, it seems, everyone has
disappeared. We pick up the empty glasses.

7.

Another lousy day. Rejection from the Riverside's 'open exhibition'. What do I expect? Can't I do something about the great
mother goddess, something positive or pleasing, something we

could stand back from and enjoy? Or something framed by a Lacanian discourse rapped-up in art-iculated language, where feelings are anal-ysed into constipated rigidity?

I'm furious. What *did* you expect? You made a shit and didn't wrap it up! The big bad world isn't a nice mummy or daddy excitedly yelling, 'Look what our darling's done!' No. They say, 'Oh this stuff about white racism, we aren't in South Africa here, we've got our anti-racist policy. We take a more positive view, we don't go on about white folks' racism. We promote Black Art. We promote colour reversal. Black had to be white before, now white has to be black, sorry, multi-cultural. Dressed in "ethnic" clothes, dancing to "ethnic" songs. We eat oranges from Brazil, not South Africa. Let's have more art entertainment. Where's the black goddess? Worship her, don't bore us with white racism!'

The art of being an artist, if you weren't born in the right place, is to be able to live through rejections. A lot of them. To be able to speak when silenced. To be able to hear when not being heard. To be able to see and make seen when no one looks.

8.

Sunday 12 October. Two days after the opening. Like clouds after a storm my thoughts are flying past . . . here and there . . . I was trying to change the cross. Always behind time. I didn't like the way it looked and the text was missing which is an important part of the piece. There I was sitting on the bench trying to find bits of the appropriate text. Tiptoeing on the edge of propaganda. I don't want the audience to agree with me. I want good attention. I want us to speak of the silences, the things which keep us apart.

As I sit in my creative mess, Lesley arrives. We talk about the exhibition, the collective, this book. Somehow it feels now, now I can write. The process is not at an end but a circle has been completed. I make plans for the future and sit back and say, so far . . . this is it.

How wonderful of Lorna to come and sew the lip of the face on as it was hanging down with the weight of paper. The moment we sat inside the bed-sheets sewing and chatting felt like the little girls that had been there before. We didn't argue but talked about the politics of everyday relating, our favourite valley of exploration, our favourite adventure playground. I asked Lesley to take some photos.

A week later. I'm trying to get some feedback from my work. I get lots of non-committal responses which feel like insults: 'Oh, okay,' or 'Yeah, good . . . nice.' Well done. Pat, pat. Some white men hissing, 'Stupid rubbish,' when they look at the 'White male god culture' piece. It's almost a relief to hear this. It's honest. A priest comes in and has a long look at the cross. Some women come and tell me they are Catholics too. I'm aware that I've committed a cardinal sin. I ask if they are practising Catholics. To my amazement some of them say they are. I can feel the guilt in my stomach. 'Don't you feel offended by this?' I ask. 'No, no – I can really identify with it.' Support where I least expected it!

9.   'Imagina'

discovering
the warmth and darkness
underneath
a big castania tree

I am filled with silence

the deep dark sound
you taught me
the one
which
enters as air

into my mouth
breathfully
fills my body
passes through
my vagina
out

transforming
my world
your world...

wet paint touches
my skin
as I push
the brush gently
across the paper
the red flushes into
the blue wet shape

suddenly
there it is
emerged
birthed
images
surfacing
coming out
opening
like flowers
in the beautiful
dark night . . .

Many women in this book reiterate a sense of being silenced; of having to make the space and find the words to speak some truth which is unacceptable – whether about class, or race or sexuality. Anna Wilson works simultaneously inside and outside the tradition of the novel, writing novels partly in order to break the silence which that tradition has imposed on lesbian experience and values.

On Being a Lesbian Writer: Writing Your Way Out of the Paper Bag

Anna Wilson

Let me add up the silences, the denials.

I have just been travelling, a white tourist forced to inhabit the official culture of foreign places, having no access to life beneath the surface. In China, there are no lesbians. Women hold hands in the streets, there are no lesbians. In the disco boys dance with boys, girls with girls – it's more decent that way, of course. During the slow numbers the girls hold one another close: I am the only one staring. No one sees what I see: it does not exist.*

In the Philippines there are lesbians – well, no, there are no lesbians, there are 'tomboys'. Tomboys are women who dress like men, look like men, act like men. Often they have been brought up as boys – that is where their identity lies. In the Philippines I too am a tomboy: you can tell by my short hair, by the fact that my clothes do not emphasise my waist, by the bra I do not wear. The remainder of my identity as a lesbian does not exist here, I am simply a woman who wants to be a man.

Travelling downriver, an alien landscape passing on either side of us, I have a conversation with another British woman. She challenges me to itemise my oppression as a lesbian – she cannot see it. At random, I mention the problems of employment. 'Couldn't you just not tell them?' she asks.

Silence begins at home. My mother keeps her copy of my first novel in a brown paper bag at the back of her bureau. This is because it is a novel about lesbians. I have not told her of the things

---

*In case there is any ambiguity here, I should say that of course, I know there are lesbians in China. But as a white tourist I could not meet them or even know who they were.

I've written since; nobody wants a bureau littered with brown paper bags.

In common with other oppressed groups, lesbians have always suffered from the hostile and damaging definitions of mainstream culture. In addition, because we are not born into our own culture, we suffer the absence of a self-definition. As a young woman, inching reluctantly toward acknowledging myself a lesbian, it was all I could do to refuse to go and see *The Killing of Sister George**; refusing others' negative definitions was the height of my self-preservation. We had no positive images of our own, it being a question only of how deviance from the norm was to be explained.

With the women's movement came a sudden rush of a particular kind of fiction by lesbian writers. The authors all seemed at the time to be 25 years old and their novels all autobiographical. The first, overpowering necessity then was simply to say what we had not been allowed to say for ourselves, to describe the undescribed, to render normal the abnormal. We felt the need to explain ourselves to each other, as well as to the rest of the world. Read now, the text of those novels is, 'Look, we're here, we really exist!' Beneath the surface there lies a subtext that asks anxiously for a place in the world: 'See how easy it is for almost any girl-child to turn into a lesbian. There's really nothing odd about it. We're quite normal really. Charming even, harmless, loveable.'

All this begs the question of whether one ought after all to be so concerned to be explicit about one's identity. The expectation persists – is continually reinforced – that as a writer one should be addressing oneself to the universal audience. In reality what is being challenged here is one's capacity to write for the white male establishment; the question only arises if an author is black, homosexual or female, working class, or any combination of these things. The pre-supposition is that any non-white, non-male, non-heterosexual writer will produce material of at best reduced relevance to the real world simply because she is not of, and does not represent, it. Obviously the intended target, audience or subject for what we write will vary; the point is that there is an automatic assumption that what we write is not central. The universe turns out to be those in power; clearly, if indeed I did set out to address

*A film which accurately reflected and reinforced the stereotypes of the sixties concerning drunken tweedy butches, fems whose emotional development was arrested in childhood, and the general misery, jealousy and indignity.

this audience it would be, once more, in their terms; a return to self-denial. I have sat at a feminist writers' conference and heard women talk about how important it is to write about men: by doing so, and only by doing so, they felt, would they achieve breadth or truth. A man may write about a silkworm and be profound. To even approach his significance, I must write about him.

It is necessary, also, to fight off the assumption that as a writer one should rise above the particular in search of 'the wider vision'. My vision is no wider or narrower than anyone else's, but because it is a lesbian vision it is perceived as more limited than a heterosexual one. Language reflects the process whereby the lesbian is marginalised, whereby marginalisation is institutionalised: it seems absurd to qualify 'vision' with 'heterosexual' – a heterosexual person's vision is simply that, a vision. It stands on its own.

Perhaps I should define myself as a human being, first? After all, in essence . . . There is a school of thought that believes that this would be a rare leap of faith: no one else may think that lesbians are human beings, but we at least ought to set the rest of the world a good example. Unfortunately, this seems to me another doomed survival strategy, very similar in effect to hiding in closets in the hope that one will pass for something else, for the term is currently meaningless, in that it does not describe the realities of power, the realities of how anyone is actually seen. It may theoretically be useful as a way of distinguishing people from animals, but in practice we are differentiated from animals as either men or women from the day we are born – and are seen as more or less distinct from them, depending on into which category we fall.

Perhaps then, I should try to see the world from a woman's point of view. After all it has long been the concern of lesbian feminists to reclaim female territory as our own; we call ourselves woman-identified, some of us claim a greater depth of understanding of what a woman can be than our heterosexual sisters. And on the other hand we get exploited, threatened and raped as women, as well as as lesbians. Certainly I do not wish to claim membership of Radclyffe Hall's 'third sex', having special knowledge of the interior lives of both men and women by virtue of inhabiting a shadowy region in between. And yet, I remain other than Woman; there remains a distinction between what the world expects of a woman's view – and what I see. Merely in having chosen, been cornered, forced, obliged, been sufficiently contrary (all of these) to define myself as a lesbian, I have made a particular protest against women's role in this culture, against the restrictions of femininity, against expectations – I have refused to live as a woman.* This puts me somewhere else than squarely in the centre of even feminist culture. I am not going to pretend to be a woman because, again, that comforting label lies about my experience.

If it seems important to retain my sense of difference, to guard the oblique angle from which I see the world, what does it mean that I write as a lesbian?

We were once accustomed to thinking of writing as the tool of politics: there was a time when the women's movement discovered its anger through poems; when a line could jolt the reader into sudden awareness. We snarled our rage and hymned uncovered strength; words were immediate, personal, awakening. There was a time, too, when lesbianism was a life-choice waved tantalisingly under the noses of heterosexual women: open the box and a new world of intensity and passion, gentleness and completeness can be yours. 'Every woman can', and should, and secretly wanted to – heterosexuality could be shucked off like an old itchy skin and women face the world in new bright flashing colours. The hint of danger was part of the lure.

That time of exploration is over. Who in this climate chooses to be a lesbian, chooses to put herself out in the cold? It isn't safe or fun out here anymore (we have given up the insane optimism that pretended otherwise), and I cannot expect many to want to join me.

Since the need to say we exist, or the expectation either of being able to create the revolution or to bring heterosexual women into the fold, seems at the moment less immediate, perhaps there is no longer a clear imperative text for lesbian writers. In the long run it does not seem desirable that we should all be writing of the same things, or in the same way. If as lesbians we share a common oppression, that bond does not necessarily of itself create a common heritage. How do we find or recognise, then, some particular lesbian vision, that clarity of view that comes from a position beyond the pale.

*There are a number of quintessentially female experiences – as our culture defines them – that require, if not an actual heterosexual relationship, a heterosexual attitude to men, which I have not had nor wanted to have. I live in a heterosexual culture and am all too familiar with it, but there are acts of submission – ritual and real – that I have never had personally to make. No doubt there are, too, positive experiences that I have missed.

It is a reductive move, I think, to equate this possibility with the expectation that I will write about the only area in which lesbian experience is commonly perceived as being different from anyone else's, i.e. sex. I appreciate that there are some valid reasons for this: the subject still has rarity value, after so long a period when lesbians could not write explicitly as lesbians at all, and least of all about that. But, while descriptions of sex may be superficially radical, delivering the shock of the familiar to lesbians, the shock of the alien to the rest, it is another matter to believe that the topic has transcendental power. Lyrical, evocative, violent or whatever, such descriptions remain locked into the deadening cycle of lesbians writing, doing and being what is expected of them.

Clearly, the possibilities for lesbian writing are as yet far from realised. One should not be surprised that attempts by lesbians to construct the future in fiction remain so resolutely earth-bound, that fantasy struggles weakly into half-life littered with visions of women in infinitely extended long-term relationships. The existence of a deliberate, self-conscious lesbian literature is painfully precarious: a decade or so is not much of a base from which to leap into the unknown, not much of a past. We stand behind the flimsy dam of the last ten years of consciousness, watching the waters of centuries of hatred, sickness, denial building above us: is there time, is there time to think before the wave breaks over our heads? We have hardly begun to consider our possibilities. Who can imagine, their mind half closed down, what a lesbian might be like in a non-hostile environment – we know as little about it as we know of the effect on plants of the absence of gravity.

We are all in retreat, trying to merge with the wallpaper, get jobs, say nothing. Danger distracts one from abstract thought. I have to keep thinking. Dare I write another lesbian novel? What shall I live on if I do? This narrows my choice of subjects, whether I decide to take the risk or not. For all that, it seems the more necessary to go on, not to fall silent, to lay claim to the right to have something worthwhile to say about everything. Even if increasingly I have the sense of being in hibernation, of sending out arctic bulletins.

It is to radical lesbian theory that feminism owes some of its most incisive insights – about the construction of sexual identity, about the economic relations of marriage and motherhood, about the norms and practices of reproduction, about the forms and incidence of male violence towards women – which has the rider that for white heterosexual feminists there is always a danger of allowing, coercing women with deeper oppressions or who have made more dangerous choices to be their consciences: to do their work for them without acknowledging that their peace of mind exists indirectly but precisely at the expense of those others'. Or else lesbianism is denoted as a matter of sexual preference, something which can be ignored once mentioned. This lets heterosexuality off the hook as another kind of sexual preference, 'just a question of choice'.

What lesbian sensibility permits – as well as having opened the way for the practice of 'woman-centredness' – is a point from which to see how women, in and through their sexual and economic relations with men, have been continually constructed as alien and other. Moreover, it shows how women's own creative energy has not been available to them, but has been taken up in the maintenance of this alienation. This surely means that women are inescapably polarised, passively or actively, to the culture which has formed them. They have a dis-identity. At its baldest, the choice seems to be between existential inauthenticity and continuous, total opposition. So there can be no simple 'going with the flow', creatively speaking: sexuality – and the expression of body through art – is the prime site of politics.

A question then, for any feminist, is to work out how not to get stuck in reactive strategies; how to escape the undertow in her work of hatred and fear; how not to have pain at the centre of her being. Or, to put it another way, how not to fall into the temptation of rendering the account of women's lives as a prolonged romantic agony, ahistorical, unbreachable. It would be hard to ignore the challenge of making art which emerges from a fully realised analysis of women's changing heterogeneous history, an art which embraces one's own sorrows or happiness but is not identical with them.

To develop a proportionate sense of one's own and others' oppressions has been an integral part of feminist intention not always matched in practice. Black women have long been demanding and creating space for their work but white feminists have too often withheld a welcoming response. The background to the next article includes the prosaic fact that the proportion both of black

*people in the labour market and of racist employers has remained
unchanged since the legislation intended to counter racial discrimination was passed in 1968. Recent unemployment figures show
that Afro-Caribbean people are twice as likely to be unemployed as
whites; and Afro-Caribbean women one-and-a-half times as likely to*
be unemployed as white women (from Black and White Britain,
published by the Policy Studies Institute; see Bibliography).

*Maud Sulter proclaims creativity in its widest and most basic sense
– surviving; refusing the identity which will keep you quieted, invisible; sticking your neck out, saying with persistence, even when it
seems fruitless or fatal, that your perceptions and demands are valid.
Her rhetoric is that of liberation, not merely equal rights.*

A Portrait of the Artist as Poor, Black and a Woman

A Creative Challenge to Myriad Contradictions

Maud Sulter

As women we must be true to ourselves. Love ourself before others, acknowledge our worth, and place our experience centre-stage. Throughout the journey of this life we experience a constant transformation. Nothing can halt it yet we so often try. From the woman who was our mother sprung the foetus from the womb the child the girl the woman. For our creativity to shimmer golden through the white fog of mediocrity we first have to recognise that for many of us our life will be a constant battle. Inside we feel the need to fight and for a time, and possibly for ever, it is possible to be frozen by fear without recognising why we are afraid or what it is we must fight. Not facing up to the continuing contradictions which face women living globally in the late 1980s and beyond will not make them go away. Strength can be gained by facing up to those factors which conspire to contain us. Racism, class privilege and sexism are just three of the forces which conspire to keep us in our place. Therefore the only way forward is to forge our own place. Our centre. The need to be centred should not be under-estimated. That is our spiritual home within this body and the spring from which our creativity flows. Lose touch with your centre and you lose touch with yourself. A very dangerous situation for a woman to find herself in. Think back. What damage have you done to yourself or others when you have felt out of touch, out of control? It is never too late to take an active role in your own transformation.

Recognise that your every action, process, practice, decision, experience, is filtered through that white fog with which society tries to stifle us. The duality of confusion and guilt should not surprise us. Challenge it with simple common sense, i.e. how you feel at your centre about the situation and, after an initial fightback, which as you have been warned about therefore can prepare physically and mentally for it, both confusion and guilt will back off as neither can survive a challenge that springs from your centre.

As a blackwoman actively engaged in cultural production, writing, performing, skill-sharing, making pictures, my work has to be placed within the context of my environment. That environment is European, within the Western perspective, urban and moving steadily towards the Right. I am not safe on the streets. I am not safe in the home. I do not have free speech. I do not have freedom of choice. Those democratic rights are a fallacy. Yet I struggle to make my thoughts heard. Fighting isolation is not easy. Do not let anyone tell you that it is. However once you find your voice you know that you can never be passively silent again. Your spur to creation is the desire to communicate. To have a meaningful exchange with other people in order to develop yourself and therefore your work even further. So much to do yet so little time? The only answer is DO IT NOW.

Our priority must be to give ourselves the space to create. Physical and Psychic space to work within. No one else, unless you believe in fairy-tales where a damsel may come to sacrifice herself for the sake of your art – and believe me she'll discover womanism and tell you to piss off and quite right too! can. So if the laundry needs to go to the launderette, or all you and your two kids have to eat for tea is a tin of beans and some stale bread, make a conscious decision. Either you go to the launderette or supermarket or you don't. If so, DO IT NOW: if not, stop dithering and get back to work.

THIS IS A PUBLIC HEALTH WARNING. CREATIVITY IS DANGEROUS. Being visible when you have found your voice in whatever metier can be frightening. Let others help you. I have voices I call on when I am troubled. In this instance Audre Lorde's 'Litany for Survival' from *The Black Unicorn* reminds me that:

> when we are alone we are afraid.
> love will never return
> and when we speak we are afraid
> our words will not be heard
> nor welcomed
> but when we are silent
> we are still afraid

So it is better to speak
remembering
we were never meant to survive.

Other words speak to me as clearly. Over the past few years Blackamerican writers, female and male, have made a significant niche in my psyche and influenced my life's direction. That too was painful at times. Recognising that to survive both Richard Wright and James Baldwin suffered rejection from factions and communities which should have recognised their wisdom and worth. Exile from the land of their diasporan birth offered survival. Would this fate befall me? How could I tell without making those first few steps towards creating words on a page, a song on the lips, an image in mixed media?

As a blackwoman I can make connections with the whole world. All creations, civilisations which pre-date history, people everywhere. All has sprung from the blackwoman's womb. And yet at the moment we do not have our sorrows to seek. In April 1984 I reviewed Pat Parker's collection of poems *Movement in Black* for *Spare Rib*. In that review I said that I too hoped for the day we could leave the house and not leave some facets of our personality by the faucet. Am I any more honest with myself than I was then? If not, why not? Yes, being visible can be dangerous. But being invisible eats away at your soul. Night and day. Obviously we have things to lose; lesbian mothers their children, people we believed to be friends who will not accept our true selves and many other horrors beside. Yet given the boundless gains to be made can we afford to remain silent any longer?

Women's Liberation is worthless if it does not allow women the space to develop their potential. There is no one politically right-on way of being unless we want an army of clones. From experience I suggest that they would be a 'colourless', privileged, reactionary set. As violently against blackwomen's creation for liberation as the present status quo. We would find no voice within their ranks.

My writing takes several forms. Poetry, prose, fiction, journalism. I hope to expand even further into writing for the stage and television. Mass audiences appeal. Reading my work in public, facilitating writing workshops, talking with friends, all provide stimulus for yet more work. Never let yourself be compartmentalised. In the West they love to label you. Then the state believes it can deal with you. Step out of line, out of category, and they do not know how to handle you. Be careful. This can lead to diagnosis within the myriad categories of madness. I have been mad at several points in my life. Madness can be productive. However, being poor, black and a woman, often the only treatment offered has been drugs. Now an interesting contradiction exists around drugs. If it is on the street it is illegal. If it is prescribed to sedate the populace, especially women, drug abuse is legal. If you refuse drugs they often refuse treatment. Believe me, being drugged out of your mind seldom helped anyone. Refuse to be controlled. If the pressure has got you hooked on drugs, alcohol or individuals, seek help from self-help groups. Kick the habit and you kick back. Madness is a normal reaction to the times we have to survive in.

In fact you would have to be mad not to go mad occasionally. Believe me, I have been there. Women and madness. Take Virginia Woolf for instance. Now her madness was condoned because she was white, middle class, and an artist. It was no less painful for her. But she had net after net of security around her. And as for her suicide? Was it madness or was it free choice? Who can say? No one. We shall never know. I however will allow the two options to stand equally in my mind. Give women the right to choose. Are we brave enough to choose to take control of our own life? How much support do you offer others?

My work must stand alone in the world. I cannot be there to explain every syllable. As in any journey of exploration sometimes I cannot see the wood for the trees. Sometimes the cathartic reaction of working with groups of writers takes weeks to recover from. Abreaction, the free expression and release of previously repressed emotion, is all very well but if the energy simply flies out into space rather than being channelled on to page, canvas or suchlike the price can be too high to pay. Therefore collective work and skill-sharing has to be balanced by time on one's own to keep in touch with that centre we recognised in the beginning and actually get down to some serious work. Because, believe it or not, it will not write, paint, draw itself.

So we have found our centre. Reclaimed the power to name our self. Taken the space to create.

Decide on the initial form you want to direct your creativity towards. Organise space. The kitchen table perhaps. Time between the hours of midnight and two, six a.m., four o'clock in the afternoon. Even if it is only half an hour make a deal with yourself that come that time nothing will distract you from your goal. A short poem, a line-drawing, an outline for a story, anything. If after several attempts you still do not make the space for yourself have a serious talk with yourself. Get in tune with your centre. You obviously do not want to venture into uncharted waters enough. Why? Only you can answer that. If you still do not get your shit together, forget it.

The practical organisation has been done. Now comes the question of sacrifice. Writing is cheap. A pencil and some paper does for starters. Maybe later you would want to get a typewriter. If money is tight choices have to be made. You still have that power. Poverty is relative. The cost of living is high. I would suggest creative liberation but getting caught is always a threat and the only legitimate targets are situations where loss is written off against tax. If you have ever had your home broken into you will know the utter sense of violation. Too often these days the poor steal from the poor. And remember wealth is also relative.

So having found your voice what do you want to say? At the time of writing I am working around issues of sexuality and desire, fighting pornography, sexual abuse especially from a perspective of child/racial dynamics. Dealing with anger. Like in *The Color Purple* by Alice Walker. When Celie makes a stand against Mr –, he laughs and asks her who she thinks she is. He accuses her of being poor, black, ugly and a woman: nothing at all.

Too often in everyday existence we are confronted by that attitude. It comes from men black and white. It comes from white women and ironically and sadly from blackwomen too as a by-product of that internalised self-hatred that sometimes means we most effectively attack each other. Doing the master's work for him.

Celie however found her voice.

She acknowledges the truth of what Mr – says. She knows what she is, that she is poor, black and ugly, and that she can't cook, but she also knows she exists and survives.

Alice Walker, her writings, her life, is yet another weapon we have in our fight for self-recognition.

Unfortunately at the time of writing I can offer few blackwomen writers working in Britain as examples. Buchi Emecheta, Barbara Burford are two strong writers of fiction, poetry and plays. There is a very important void of younger writers born and brought up in Britain. Perhaps because we have grown up amongst them and know even better their ways we are being silenced and will continue to be silenced as ours is the voice with the most incisive truth. Britain fights hard not to recognise us. Always imposing categories of 'otherness'. Repatriation still threatens our security. Institutionalised racism goes unchecked. And the growing threat/ actions of racist attack and discrimination looms ahead. Creativity can help us all recognise common experiences and offer some means of communication for change and liberation.

Living with contradictions is not easy. But it is too easy to fall into the trap of self-censorship. Money, education and desire all bring their share of pressures. Every woman needs money to live. If you have ever gone without the memory haunts you throughout your lifetime. When the cupboard is full you worry. When the cupboard is bare you worry. When it is half empty you worry most. Caught in a dilemma of apparently irrational fear.

Education can free your mind yet distance you from your family and friends. Working-class guilt is such that to achieve can make you feel as bad as any academic or material loss. And there are always those who will try to buy you off into the middle classes. Remember class is a state of action.

Desire. You are a blackperson and you can sing and dance. Now you know that the myth of the 'singing/dancing darkie' is just that. A myth. Created by white people to categorise and control. You want to be an actor. Contradiction. You are a blackperson and you are good at academic subjects. You want to be a lawyer. Now you know that the myth of the 'Uncle Tom' is just that. A myth. Created, in this case by Harriet Beecher Stowe, a white American woman, to categorise and control. How do you fulfil your desires amid this minefield of contradictions?

I have no easy answer. Personal integrity has to be your key. And recognising where your talents lie will give you greatest satisfaction. If you are struggling to make this world a better place the path should become clearer as you go towards your goal. Have aims and objectives but never be afraid of adapting them along the way.

Travel is important to me. It helps me put my experience into a global perspective. As a teenager I wanted to visit Russia. I was in love with the Tsars, although a committed socialist at the time. Of course that in itself was a contradiction but I sailed on. Scotland is a cold country by repute. I was born and brought up there. Having lived in London for several years I can take solace in the fact that it doesn't rain as much up north as down here. Anyway to fulfil that desire it had to be snowing. What is a trip to Russia without snow? So I arrive in Moscow. It is −20°. I enjoy every moment of it. My ever-active mind consumes opera, ballet, art, architecture, politics, food, different ways of being. Preconceptions are challenged from many perspectives. Back to Britain. Now I can use that information and inspiration to work towards constructive change. 'Okay Maud,' says I. The USSR, as I now know to call it, is white. It is time to go to Cuba. Time passes. My flat is burgled by heroin addicts, black male white female, all I have is destroyed. Luckily I am insured for some of it. Not the emotional devastation, or the irreplaceable losses. The money I decide will not be spent replacing the steam-iron so I go on a women's study-tour to Cuba. Cuba is wonderful. The Cubans are wonderful. The tour a disaster. Racism, prejudice, heterosexism, it is all there included in the price. Fourteen white feminists and me.

That trip over the USA awaits. So I go to visit my blackamerican lover and friends in New York. Is New York America? Anyway again I had to challenge preconceived ideas and prejudices. All is not bad in America. Just as all is not good in the USSR. The potential for global change is always with us. We have the power to work together towards a brighter future. Not tomorrow but starting today.

So now Africa awaits. The Continent of my father. Although I have been to the north that is not enough. Someday I shall go to the newly freed Azania. That time will not be long but the road will be bloody. In the meantime I must return to see the line of my grandmother's brow, the skill of my father helping the sick heal themselves. Remembering of course that he may never be able to heal the wounds he inflicted on others. No, my return to Africa is not simply biological. It is cultural, spiritual, intensely personal. Remembering always that

> As a blackwoman
> every act is a personal act
> every act is a political act
>
> As a blackwoman
> the personal is political
> holds no empty rhetoric.

Whatever the reappraisals feminists have had to make as a result of challenges from inside the movement (to white middle-class assumptions, for example) as well as from outside (from a hostile domestic government), feminism is still about agitating for changes, envisaging resistances, cherishing and modifying ideals; about seeking liberation as well as working for equal rights. These activities by definition can only realistically be undertaken collectively. The fact that there are many and fragmented beliefs and tactics, and that accountability is difficult in theory and practice (an obvious example of the latter being the cessation of WLM national conferences), is no indictment of feminism's failure but an indication of the immensity of any such undertaking in the eighties. There must be elements of idealism in any agenda: we are experimenting with what it is still possible to imagine as well as to do.

At the same time, we are obliged to take on the implications – for ourselves and our work – of the current acute fragmenting of feminist and socialist opposition.

In replying to a questionnaire I circulated, many of the contributors expressed feelings of isolation. One woman said, 'In some way I feel I personify isolation.' The women who do not share these feelings are either performers or identify closely with a definable group. Clearly the question of audience is crucial to women's perception of what they're doing – audience in the sense both of 'constituency' and literally of other people being present: 'My Muse really is my audience at any given time. They and the music are my inspiration.' None of the contributors seemed to be interested in entertaining narrow definitions of the word – they ranged from 'women everywhere' to 'anybody' and, 'Oh, everybody. I wish I were free of a need to conquer the establishment but I'm not, though I know they'll never listen,' to 'All those people who ever yearned, and failed, and tried again . . . life after life'; however much they simultaneously acknowledged the likelihood that in practice and for the moment it meant 'people like me' or even people who are 'out there, picking my writing apart . . . on political grounds, as they have the right to do'. It seems there is no pre-existing arrangement of readers or viewers that can provide a sufficiently homogeneous or sympathetic gallery. Which presumably means that audiences have still to be created, not found.

HOLLERING FOR THE EARTH: FORM

Diaries, journals, autobiography are devices for breaking barriers of isolation; at a minimum they reflect the writer back to herself – 'I write for myself,' said two women whose work is in fact well-known and loved – and in a developed form these devices have become part of the structure of feminism through their substantial contribution to the theory and practice of consciousness-raising, without which feminism could have been a restricted ideology, a top-heavy edifice.

If for a moment you consider the articles themselves as artefacts you can see that many of them are in that 'confessional' form. Some of them are even written in the present tense, in the current of the river, not from its bank. This phenomenon is not fully explained by saying that that's what I asked for, since one of the few things I specified was that the contributions could be in any form the writers chose. Feminist writers and their audience alike have recognised the transformative power of 'truth-telling' – telling it like it is – and they have been reluctant to disappear behind defensive façades or to dissemble themselves with the scarf and robes, the sonnets and realpolitik *of the oppressor. And they have developed the allied knowledge that by thus exposing the contradictions in her own life a woman can contribute to a collective understanding of how political structures work, which understanding in turn illumines and challenges her experience – 'the personal is the political'. Moreover, some of the terror of writing, to which several contributors attested over the blank and strenuous months of composing their articles, comes in part, I think, from an impression instilled in women of always being the Other, of not having a fully realised subjectivity to project. Writing themselves on to the page is a rehabilitation, painful in process but exhilarating in achievement.*

This 'truth-telling' persona can temporarily ignore the fact that autobiography is a discourse as much as any other form of writing; it is characterised by a certain stylistic innocence (there are exceptions) and freighted with urgency, freshness, intensity, a passion for getting it right; it exacts a reciprocal response from the reader. It has given women a way into literature, made practitioners out of readers. These seem to me to be positive, not pejorative, attributions.

But of course – as the astonishing amount and range of their fiction and poetry published in the last decade and a half shows – feminists must also be highly conscious of the need to question and subvert just such forms of expression; the border between them and the stereotyping agenda of female writing as spontaneity-plus-candour is easily crossed. Fiction and poetry are the obvious locations for playing with identities; for asking, 'Who is this I? What can it not think or say or imagine? How many times can it multiply, fragment or reflect itself? How far can the references between the personal I and the poetic I be dissolved?' Such experimentation demands but also expands confidence, opens up distances, explores space. Girls at school, as Ange Grunsell has pointed out, often have difficulty making up stories, making things happen.

But fiction and poetry are the nearest means at hand for people who are materially dispossessed; you need only a pen and a piece of paper: the back of an envelope in a tight moment or a prison-cell wall in extremis, as Irina Ratushinskaya demonstrated. The means of production and distribution are arguably the least esoteric: access to a photocopier – even a word processor – is a possibility for a growing number of people and the publisher, if you can get one, will bear the cost of large-scale production – unlike, say, being a painter or sculptor where the considerable expenses are all your own.

In shifting the centre of interest away from the author's own consciousness, narrative fiction has as one of its concerns the public display and evaluation of shared experiences: it tries to assemble a new consensus of reality. This is a political act of self-determination; the impact of The Color Purple *was to 'change lives', not because women put down the book and took up revolution as if it was a manifesto, but because such novels generate meanings with and for their readers. First, in the very act of breaking longstanding silences and, second, in annotating the many kinds of violence. Decolonising the present, re-peopling the past.*

The Swamp

Nadine Otway

'When a slave died my grandfather didn't replace him, so the work-force dwindled, and when they were set free, he only needed 25 men to run the three plantations, so he told the rest of them they could clear off the land. The Queen in England had set them all free, so they could damned well learn to fend for themselves.'

Great-aunt Martha would pause, then with venomous satisfaction she would continue: 'Within a week they were back, begging Grandpapa to take them back. They'd had enough of their wonderful freedom. Yes, sir! They were starving, because they'd never had to do a thing for themselves. They were worse than children. But of course Grandpapa didn't want them. "You free now," he told them. "According to the English Government you were all desperately unhappy and ill-treated when you were slaves, so if you have any complaints take them to the Governor in Kingston, make him look after you. Now, get yourselves off me land before I set the dogs on you."

'Some didn't want to go and Grandpapa set the dogs on them. And some were even stupid enough to try to walk to Kingston. Imagine! Over those mountains! Of course most of them turned back, or died, but they were free, nuh, so they must have been quite happy.'

Aunt Martha's chuckle always caused the grown-ups in my family to exchange amused looks. They all admired her gutsy frankness, while pretending to be horrified at her open hatred of her grandfather's slaves, who had had the temerity to crave their freedom.

One hundred years after the slaves were freed, the ghost of slavery still lingered broodingly over the plantation. There were reminders of the violence and cruelty of that time everywhere. The grove of tall *lignum vitae* trees beside the Great House where slaves were hanged, whipped or branded, within sight of the house so that the master and his family could witness for themselves justice being done; the cold, damp cellar beneath the house which still had chains bolted into the wall; the whips and old muskets which Aunt Martha had unearthed and arranged in a glass case in the drawing room.

'In those days,' she would say, pointing at the case with her thick walking-stick, 'in those days Jamaica was a disciplined place. None of this thieving you see now went on then ... They wouldn't dare steal even a mango off a tree, they'd have had their hand cut off. And a good whipping into the bargain. Mind you, I've taken my whip to a few of them in my time, I can tell you. Once I caught a fellow beating my horse and I took my riding crop to him, and rode him down with the very same horse he'd been mistreating. Laid him up for months, – I don't think he ever walked without a limp after that. And do you know, his wife, well, she called herself his wife, but you can't take that too seriously, she had the nerve to walk up here and complain to my father. Well, he wasn't a man to tolerate that sort of impertinence. "Take any grievance you have to the Constable," he told her, "and on your way you can take your husband with you. I don't want either of you on my land."

'Of course she didn't complain to anyone; even if she had, she wouldn't have got very far, the Constable played cards with Papa every Friday night. But what I'm saying is that we need a lot more discipline in this society nowadays. Bring back whipping. That sort always improves with a good hiding now and then. And that includes you, young lady.'

Aunt Martha was not a great believer in tact. Some years ago my father had run away with the postmaster's daughter, a brown-skinned woman with no redeeming family connections, and no wealth at all. They fled to Cuba where I was born and where they both subsequently died. My grandfather brought me back to live with him and his spinster sister, Martha, who never let me forget that in her opinion I was not as good as my cousins. She referred to me only as 'that one', or 'the child', and could hardly bring herself to speak to me directly.

Her open hatred secured for me the sympathy of most of the workers on the estate. From Maude the cook and Fox her husband who was also my grandfather's foreman, down to Claudie, the man who was in charge of opening and closing the gates, who also fed and trained the dogs and slaughtered the pigs and chickens.

Claudie taught me how to climb trees, kill chickens quickly and handle the dogs, so that when my cousins came to visit from their neighbouring estate and began their favourite game of teasing me and laughing at my lowly relatives in the village, I was able to set the dogs on them and watch with great satisfaction as Brutus, the most savage of the pack, took a chunk out of Tony's leg and sent the others screaming in terror back to the house.

Fox, the foreman, was my greatest friend and ally. He taught me to ride a horse, and to play chords on his home-made guitar. He took me with him as he went over my grandfather's estate, telling me about the crops and the soil, and the fertilizer best suited to each one. 'You listen to what I telling you, because one day all this going belong to you, and you must learn so nobody could take advantage of you.'

'I don't want it. As soon as I'm old enough I'm going to leave here. And I'm never coming back.'

'So where you going?'

'Don't know. Maybe New York, or London,' I speculated.

'Mustn't do that,' Fox cautioned. 'Can't be really happy in somebody else's country, you know. Stay where you born and grow – where everybody know you. Besides, them country them too cold and the people not nice. All them want to do is make money and fight war and all them things. No man, you much better off here.'

Fox told me stories of Br'er Anancy, and African folk tales handed down to him by his slave ancestors. Once I asked him as he sat sharpening his machete: 'Did they really hang slaves from those *lignum vitae* trees over there? Hang them till they were dead?'

'So they say. I don't know,' he replied, reluctantly.

'And you know that big gash in our dining-room table, is it true that it's the mark of a machete, where the slaves cut off the overseer's head when they had a rebellion?'

'Who telling you all these stories?'

'Tony. And he said that after soldiers put down the revolt they tore the slaves' tongues out and fed them to the dogs for their supper, and that's why dogs always attack black people – because they want to eat their tongues again.'

'Lord God! That Tony, him is a worthless little brute. Him only trying to frighten you, you know. Remember the day you set

Brutus on him? See here, they was bawling with laughter down in the village when me tell them.'

'Tony says they never found the overseer's head but people see it if they're going to die or have very bad things happen to them.'

'That's all rubbish,' Maude called from the kitchen, 'people love to tell stories like that to children and frighten them, but nothing like that is true. Now come inside and have your bath.'

'No, I hate baths.'

'Go on,' Fox nodded to me, 'be a good girl and tomorrow me take you down to the sea.'

The sea was about a mile away by a path which led from behind the house through the groves of lime trees and past the well which no one used since a woman had thrown her new-born baby down it. The path followed a stream which became a river in the rainy season, a tributary of the large River Cobre which had provided water for the plantations for centuries, and then ended in a mangrove swamp.

The swamp was a brooding, silent place where twisted trees clawed at the dark green stagnant water which made sinister, sucking noises as it heaved its yellow slime against the shore. It was in this primeval place that runaway slaves lost all hope of freedom, as they splashed desperately through the swamp, dogs baying hungrily behind them. They must have looked with longing to the sea in the distance, less than an hour's walk, but generations away. The white foam hissing on the shore had rolled uninterruptedly from Africa, and the strong breeze which deformed the sea grape trees on the shore had blown the slave ships with their tormented, dying and diseased cargoes to this fantasy island. The hunted slave would have one last, desperate look at the sea before he either drowned in the swamp's slime, or was cornered and savaged by the estate dogs, or, worst of all, recaptured and brought back to the estate for mutilation, torture and death. An example had always to be made of runaway slaves.

Occasionally, after a long drought, the swamp would give up a few bones or a skull, and the workers on the estate who hated the swamp anyway would not leave the estate after dark until Fox had buried the bones, and Henry, the obeah man, had poured Katanga Waters on the surrounding area.

When independence became a real possibility my family laid elaborate plans for hiding in the mangrove swamp, should the workers go berserk and attempt to slaughter us all in our beds.

There were bitter denunciations of the British Government who were 'selling us out', and scornful laughter at the very idea of a Jamaican National Anthem or flag.

'As long as I'm alive the only flag I'll every salute is the Union Jack, and the only Anthem I ever standing up for is "God Save the Queen". That's what I fought in the last war to keep, and no jumped-up politician is going to tell me any different.' My Uncle Richard had been in the Coast Guard Reserves during the war, and had, in his own eyes at least, seen 'active service'. He regarded England as 'Home', though he had never set foot there, and personally identified with the Monarchy.

'You think the Queen going to be happy to come and stay at Kings House with a black Governor General? You mad? She's too much of a lady to openly object, but she going tell them exactly how she feel in a subtle kind of way. And you mark my words, not one member of the Royal family going be here for the Independence farce.'

'Only because they don't want to witness the blood bath we going have here once the Hampshires march out. Who going keep the peace then? The West India Regiment?'

In the event, Independence did not bring the hordes of cutlass-wielding peasants baying for blood which my uncles had confidently predicted. Nevertheless, 'Black Power' scrawled on walls in Kingston, and the occasional shouts of 'Black man time now!' were enough to convince my family that it was time to sell up the estates and leave Jamaica. The land was sold during the short boom that immediately followed Independence and before currency restrictions were imposed, and the entire family decamped for Canada.

It was ten years before I returned. The village seemed very much smaller than I remembered it, but otherwise it remained untouched by the huge change which had taken place in Jamaica, and despite the immense leisure complex which a multinational company had built on the estates we had owned.

I enquired at Wong's rum shop for Maude and Fox.

'Dem gone long time now. Have one little plot land up in hills. Never see dem long time now. You go to hotel, Miss, see how everything change up. All better now. Pull down old house, make all new hotel, have everything. Plenty peoples come all time stay by hotel. All over world they coming from.'

Mr Wong's English had changed as little as he had over the

years. He revealed the secret of his perpetual youth. 'Take new wife soon as old one get too old. All time have new, young wife. Send old one up to hotel, she get job.'

'Do they employ many people from the village up at the house, then?'

'Only womans, make bed, sweep floor. Hotel don't take mans, so all day they sit outside play domino, take rum. And never pay bill. Good thing mans from hotel come down here some nights play Peok a Pow, drink little rum.'

'Welcome to the Overseer's Head', the sign blazed above the huge white iron gates, and lower, only slightly less garish, 'The Most Haunted Hotel in Jamaica'.

The uniformed security guards at the gate hesitated before lifting the barrier and allowing me to drive in.

'What happen, Miss? You was lost, you take the wrong road?'

'That's the rough road you come on, you must have missed the turn-off from the airport.'

'No, I didn't miss the road,' I replied. 'I was visiting some friends in the village.'

The men exchanged knowing glances. 'You don't have to go into that village for anything, you know,' one man volunteered. 'You can get everything you want right here. Anything at all,' he stressed in a meaningful way.

The Reservations Manager was an urbane Jamaican, who spoke with an occasional American accent. 'Hope you'll enjoy your stay with us at the Overseer's Head. I don't know if you know anything about the place, but I can just fill you in quickly on the background, and there's plenty of brochures and things if you want to do an in-depth kind of study. It used to be an old slave plantation, you know. Where this hotel stands was once the great house, where the master and his family lived. If you look in the Freedom Lounge you'll see the whips and chains they used in those days. Have a rum punch on the house and you could sign up at the same time for a guided tour of the cellars, where most of the ghosts seem to do their haunting. Ha Ha!'

'Why is it called the Overseer's Head?'

'Well, you see, long ago the slaves had a rebellion, and they cut off the head of the brutal overseer, and a local folk legend has it that it's bad luck if the head appears to anyone. All along people had been really scared of, you know, ever coming across this thing, because it would bring bad luck. Well, when they were building a

golf course and filling the mangrove swamp they found a skull, and
everyone said it was the overseer's head. The chap who owns this
place was there at the time, and he said: "Bad luck? We'll just see
if superstition could beat good old hard work and the free
enterprise system." So he urged the contractors and builders to
work twice as hard and finish the hotel before sched. And they did!
As a joke he said that the poor old overseer had done him a favour,
and he'd return it by naming the hotel the Overseer's Head.'

The Freedom Lounge held all of Aunt Martha's macabre
collection as well as other 'souvenirs of slavery' which the management rightly assumed would appeal to the guests. Slim-hipped
waiters in clinging white trousers paraded through the Lounge
bearing cooling and intoxicating drinks for the guests, while full-
bosomed waitresses bent over the guests on the terrace by the
Olympic-size pool flashing white smiles at the tourists who,
aggressively aware of their own power, demanded drinks, sand-
wiches, salads and fruit.

The groves of citrus trees were all gone. Instead of the musky
smell of nutmeg, the pungent odour of chlorine hung over the
rolling lawns. Even the mangrove swamp was gone, filled in to
provide an eighteen-hole golf course. Only the *lignum vitae* trees
remained.

I asked Mr McDonald, the affable Reservations Manager, why
of everything on the old estate, they alone remained unchanged.

'Couldn't get those damn trees down at all,' he explained.
'They'd nearly finished building the hotel before they decided they
didn't want them there at all. They interfere with the view of the
sea, you know, and while the guests prefer to bathe in a swimming
pool, they still like to look at the sea. But they were afraid to use
dynamite in case it damaged the building, and they didn't want to
botch the job and leave some ugly stumps, so they just had to
forget about the trees and leave them right there. Now they say the
roots might damage the foundation of the hotel. With all this new
technology you'd think they could do something about a few old
trees. If they can put a man in space a few *lignum vitae* trees
shouldn't give them any trouble.'

'I suppose it's a blessing for the village that your hotel is here,' I
ventured.

'I don't think it makes any difference to them one way or
another,' he shrugged.

'Well, you provide employment and I expect you must buy a lot of vegetables from them, and the fishermen have a market for what they catch. That sort of thing is what I had in mind.'

'No, no,' he laughed. 'We're quite self-contained here. We don't have a thing to do with the village. We get all our meat, fish, vegetables, even most of our fruit, flown in from Miami in freezer containers. As for employing the locals, well, even though I'm a Jamaican myself, some of my countrymen, to be honest, they just downright lazy. They don't want to work. Any day you drive down there you see them outside the rum shop playing dominoes. The middle of the day, grown men siddown playing games. I ask you!' His American accent disappeared in disgust.

'Why don't you employ them here, that would give them something to do?'

'What? Here? At the hotel? You mad? That lawn-cutting machine you see there, for example, is a complicated piece of machinery. Lloyd, the fellow who runs it, knows what he's doing. We sent him on a course to Miami to learn everything about it. Everybody working at this hotel is a highly trained, skilled person, all have training of one sort or another, except Pepe who cleans the pool, and his uncle is a local Union man.

'We don't need to employ any benighted people just because they're locals. We get all our staff from the Hotel Training School in Kingston, people who know what they doing and how much the tourist means to this island. Suppose we pick up some man from the village and he stupid enough to upset a tourist. The tourist go home and tell the newspapers, and next thing you know, everything crash.

'All of us, the entire island, depend on Tourism. It's the dollars that tourists bring in that buy the food, build the schools, fix the roads. If Tourism fail, and that could easily happen through bad publicity, then they could put out all the lights in Jamaica.

'This is a hard business, and sometimes it just seem as if everything is against us. Take for example the golf course. Dollars the owners poured into making a beautiful eighteen-hole course. It was one of the best in the world, a miracle of modern engineering, because they filled in a massive swamp to get it the right size. And you know what happened the last rainy season? The land started sinking. The swamp taking over the golf course again, and I don't believe there's a thing we can do about it.'

I met Fox and Maude in the village a few days before I left Jamaica for the last time. In ten years Maude had become a wizened old woman, and Fox had become a gaunt old man.

'Is now times hard for true,' Fox told me as we sat in Mr Wong's shop drinking Red Stripes while Maude self-consciously sipped at a 'Nu-Grape'. 'All the progress they talking about don't mean a thing to people like us. And every second word you hear nowadays is "Power this" and "Power that". "Black Power", "People Power", Tide have "washing power", Mackeson give "Man power". All kind of power about, except living power. Because we only surviving from day to day. We not living any kind of life here at all.

'Hear me now. If I could sell me crops to the hotels I maybe would have some money to buy fertilizer to grow more crops. But the hotels import everything, and even if I did sell them anything, I can't buy fertilizer because the Government say it can't afford to import fertilizer. Jamaica supposed to feed herself, but everything you see in the shops they buy from abroad.'

'Has nothing at all changed since Independence?' I asked.

'Independence! We change one set of masters for a different, hungrier bunch, that's all. And this lot of them smarter. Any which way the wind blow, they going with it. Make I tell you. The first election, one fellow came up here telling us to vote for him, how he going bring schools and business into the area, fix up the roads. He was even going to bring hospitals and dentists, and put up health clinics all 'bout. So we walk 13 miles on voting day to put we "X" beside he name, and you think we ever see him after he win? Him turn big-time Minister, but he never do one single thing for us. Not one! The next election another rascal from a different party get in and the same thing all over again. Plenty promises before, quick get-away after. I tell Maude after the first rogue that I would never pick up myself and vote for anyone again. I must walk all them miles so those lying fellows can go live high life in Kingston and fly up and down in aeroplane? Not me!

'But you see, what happen is, these politician fellows they quick to spot any advantage. Now everything is reggae and Rasta, every politician want to say how he more "roots" than the next one. But ask them how to plant a yam, or when to sow a seed in the ground, and they don't know. And don't care, neither. If something not happening in town, to them is not happening at all.'

'And they well wicked in town,' Maude interrupted. 'All town people do is walk 'round, thief and smoke weed.'

'Hush you mouth, woman. How many times you go to town in

your life? You don't know what you talking about,' Fox silenced her. 'So what going happen to us now, tell me that,' he continued. 'Donkeys' years now we been on the land. First as slaves, growing cane for the white man; then as labourers on the boss man's estates. You think anything change since then? Not one God thing! Look at us, free to starve on a plot of land that with a little fertilizer could feed most of the people you see in here.

'They say everybody have a say in Government now. But who speak for us? Who is there to talk up for us? Where is our voice?'

Maude paid for the round of drinks Fox insisted was theirs and mounted the bus after him, a small indomitable figure.

For people for whom the significance of their culture has been bent to the white person's, the finding of a personal voice and the reclaiming of historical facts are interdependent. Reclamation is both painful and joyful; what is reclaimed, complex and ambivalent. The major project is to bring the invisible ones into focus but from an unsentimental angle; not idealising their oppression, for being oppressed impairs people. (What purpose, otherwise, in becoming emancipated?) There has to be critique as well as love, distance as well as identification. It is through style and stance that these nuances are communicated.

The form of expression that is simultaneously a suppressed tradition, a record of history and a survival strategy, stirs its listeners to love and anger; carries its practitioners to realms of self-transcendence and also depersonalisation. Women blues singers have been performers of startling talent, but they also were promoted as emotive symbols of a certain kind of suffering femininity or of a sexuality alien but attractive to white folk. Deciding to participate actively in this tradition means finding personal ways of sorting the shit from the stardust, and both from something more real.

Sandi Russell amalgamates tradition and personal expression for her audience in clubs and halls; her article achieves the same synthesis for us listening, as it were, at a distance.

Minor Chords – Major Changes

Sandi Russell

'That can't be right; what are you doing?' Mrs Prenshaw ran to the piano and checked the music. 'Fauré would never *write music that way. Why are you singing like this?'*

It seemed to pour out of me. I had no intention of singing the song differently, but somewhere within was a need for me to express, embellish, create. Without the merest hint of embarrassment, I said, 'I think Fauré would have liked the new changes!'

Pamela played the piano in strict, box-like time. 'Now, try it again Sandi; sing the song like it was written.' Taking a deep breath, I readied myself, my body rigid to aid in the 'straight' rendition. Half-way through the song, Pamela lunged forward on the piano keys. 'God help you, you're a jazz singer.'

I don't know when it started, or how. Mom says I started singing before I started talking. A slight exaggeration, I'm sure – but close. I was a delight to have around; little talented Sandi Russell. 'Sing for them Sandi; dance for them Sandi. Isn't she wonderful?'

On occasion, Dad would take me with him to the nearest bar and hoist my four-year-old body up on the long, smooth, wooden surface. Glasses were moved aside, I was given centre stage and told to sing. All would applaud and exclaim. Dad beamed.

But later schizophrenia set in. As I grew to love my talents, I also grew to hate them. As my teachers singled me out as a prize pupil, my friends sat back and glowered. I loved singing, but not at the expense of losing my friends: I stopped tap class, ballet and singing lessons.

Growing up in Harlem, one could not escape the sounds of jazz:

through windows it textured conversation; 'How you doin' girl?' It was four-three-seven today, warming cold, large clubs filled with last night's whiskey and smoke – it caught you, grabbed you up, made your pulse beat faster, and floated away the ugly constraints of poverty and the fact that drugs were taking over the neighborhood.

I heard it before I knew what I was hearing. It was just there – everywhere, and it seemed as if it was a necessary fabric of life. Everybody I knew listened to it; talked about it. It was *our* music, not *theirs*.

Singing in the church choir was moving, exhilarating, beautiful. The spirituals lifted me, brought a lineage of proud and creative people to my present life. But you still had to follow the score in this enlightened, progressive Young People's Baptist Choir. Now the Gospel Chorus, *that* was the choir that sang from the knowledge, the life of the soul. These older women with the sure-footed step and uplifted shoulders carried us through the history and out of the pain to that far-flung freedom so impossible to attain in the streets of the everyday. With shouting and humming, swaying to a music beyond the hearing, they improvised a life of before and a life to attain. This free music was the one to stir me, to stay.

The Savoy Ballroom in Harlem was swingin' that night. A handsome, light-skinned twenty-seven year old was showing his girlfriend the new dance steps. The Chick Webb Orchestra played and Ella Fitzgerald was eagerly awaited. Henry was excited as he whirled Edna around the floor. 'I can't wait to see her. She must be beautiful, with a voice like that. Her tones are so pure and clear.' Ella was announced and a squat, short-haired, dark-skinned woman appeared on the stage. My father pulled his arms from around my mother's waist. Shoulders slumped, he headed for the bar.

I watched Sarah Vaughan singing on television. I couldn't get close enough, hear enough, feel enough. Dad walked in and said, 'Turn that thing off. She's nothin' but a whore. Black women in show business ain't nothin' but dogs. We know how they got there.' I stared at my father, my tongue dry and my throat clotted with pain. 'But she has a great voice Dad; listen.' 'I don't care what she has, she's no damn good. Turn that crap off.' He walked out of the room, and I spun back to the TV screen. Sarah was gone.

I don't think it was defiance, this need to sing jazz. It just seemed to have so much going for it. You were free to invent, create, on the spot. The music *sounded* like my people's voices, the way they spoke to one another; that rhythm, that cadence.

Slowly, though, I was moving away from the familiar sounds that affirmed my existence. I was learning that 'my world' was not enough to grant me the better life my parents had envisioned for me. Classical music took precedence. I listened to it, sang it, and made myself *love* it. I was deeply moved by much classical music, yet I was forcing myself to believe that this was the only music; the one to be taken seriously, the one that endured.

The cutting-off point came when I was accepted to a highly acclaimed, specialised school, New York's High School of Music and Art. There amongst many whites and few blacks I learned music theory, how to *hear* Palestrina and Poulenc, but most of all, the proper way to sing. This was the beginning of bridled creativity. It was carried through during University, where I studied liberal arts and trained intensively as a classical singer. The clear, smooth, soaring tones became more bell-like and compelling with each year; but the heart of my music was harnessed and choked.

My mother was a domestic worker, and one of the people she worked for was Bernard Greenhouse, the cellist of the renowned Beaux Arts Trio. My mother listened and learned, brought back all the information she thought 'necessary' for her daughter, to help her get out of Harlem and Blackness. She listened to classical music with an avidness I had never seen in her with any other kind of music. Her hard work and acute ear enabled her to recognise a Mozart sonata long before I could. My mother was speaking to me through a music that came from neither of our lives.

Ingrid Bergman made her way into our home, gesturing and breathing through the 24-inch screen. 'Look at her, isn't she beautiful? She doesn't even wear make-up!' Dad leaned forward, looking as if he wished he could fade out of our lives and into the arms of 'white purity'. 'Listen Edna, you know that these black women are no good. Look at them on the streets; drinking, talking loud, on Welfare, having babies left and right. They're just pigs, dammit.' My mother got up from the couch and quietly touched my father's arm. Her very white hand belied her Native American heritage. 'Henry, how can you say that? Your daughter is sitting right here!' 'Oh Sandi, she's different.'

In many ways, for my generation of black women, I did prove different. Because of my looks (I have been mistaken for every type of olive-skinned person imaginable), doors opened more easily for me than for my darker sisters. I dated white men and no one on the streets noticed or cared. I dated black men and all eyes turned. I didn't marry; I had a relationship with a woman. And I continued to love jazz.

Many black women I knew in show business had long lost interest in this freedom of expression and pursued the 'fast fat green-back'. Rock had taken over the world, and there was big money to be made. Little did they realise that there would have been no rock music if there hadn't been the blues and jazz. I wanted to sing from the source: only this medium gave me the right to express who I was, in my own way. In the mid-seventies the jazz clubs were closing, but the inward and outward pressures were on me to sing.

I argued with my friends and myself about the newest musical rage: disco. But for a few exceptions, this music was monotonous. It challenged no one; just bludgeoned you with a loud and insistent beat. It was a surface, slick dance music, giving no room for artistic expression. There was nowhere to go and nothing to say except, 'Do it to me,' *ad infinitum.* Even under an alias, with the prospect of good money, I side-stepped the offers.

With many club doors closed, I went on tour as a lead singer with a pop group. Dressed in a crimson hot-pants jump suit and black boots, I sang the songs of Stevie Wonder and Roberta Flack, among others. Feeling lost and alienated as I travelled from one indistinct American town to another, I learned what the American populace wanted; or what the promoters thought they wanted: tits, not talent.

During this time, I hurled myself on stage, screaming through the music that I was Sandi Russell. Listen, my voice begged, listen to *me.* I can sing, I can give my own life-interpretation to this music; I am a musician, an artist. Notes falling on dull eyes and deaf souls, I continued, weary and wanting.

During a stint in New Jersey, I was trying to give new life to dead material. A representative from the largest theatrical agency in the world came up to me and introduced himself. He said I had a fabulous future ahead, but that I needed a gimmick. 'No one wants to just listen to a voice.' I asked what he had in mind. 'Listen, honey, I've got the answer. You should call yourself "The Harlem

Hillbilly" – I'm tellin' you, it will go over real big.' I got up from
my seat, fluffed up the Afro that I had worked so hard to achieve,
and told him I was Sandi Russell, and that was all I intended to be.
Somehow, I couldn't quite see myself in a low-cut frilly blouse,
mini-skirt and holsters.

The road was eating me up, using me. I had learned the ropes of
stage presence, but my musicality was stifled. I was bored,
uninterested and empty. Churning out the same songs in the same
way rendered me numb.

Back in Manhattan, I settled down to jazz singing and poverty. I
found fairly quickly that those men who could 'aid in your career'
needed to know much more about you than your singing talents.
'Show me your legs,' was a remark I still heard on a return trip to
New York in the summer of 1985.

My world was beginning to spin. Circling round and round, there
seemed nowhere to grasp hold. Slipping in and out of slime seemed
to be the only reality. Slime in the form of agents, managers,
'holders of the dream'. My body spoke to them, even though words
came from my mouth and song from my soul. It was my anatomy
that held the all-important key to recognition and stardom.

Once, engaged in conversation with a well-known agent thirty-
three stories above the ground, he made an unexpected move and
my eyes snapped at the penis that was prodding its way into my
pupils. Startled and sickened, I got up, told him a few choice
words, and left. He screamed at me as I walked that never-ending
corridor towards the elevator: 'You're nobody, and you'll always
be nobody.'

I kept on singing, with my pants on. People listened, people
cared. My name was in lights on marquees of well-known New
York clubs. I was getting famous and staying poor: 'You're new. I
can't pay you what I'd pay Dizzy. Don't worry – in a few years
you'll be making great dough.'

There are very few women singing jazz today, and even fewer
black women singing it. I know of only two other black women my
age singing in Manhattan. I spent most of my working time with
male musicians. With them I learned, they learned, and we all
respected one another and gave each other space. *No* musician
tried to hand me a line about etchings or trap sets. They respected
my musicality – me. Making music with men was the only time I
experienced equality in an otherwise racist and sexist environment.

The billboard read 'JOHNNY HARTMAN and SANDI RUSSELL – next week – OSCAR PETERSON'. That was enough to make me want to run and hide. How was I going to hold my own with the great jazz singer Johnny Hartman? But I stayed, and got to know one of the kindest, most caring individuals in the business. Johnny's manner was soft and gentle, as was his singing. He took me under his wing that first night. He always had time to talk, to listen, to help in any way that he could. I could never just go to a club and listen to his brilliant renderings; he always asked me to sing. He gave faith when there was little hope.

I continued to see my name in and around town. People wrote little columns about me and, on occasion, furnished pictures. They said I was great. Did I have a record? No. So I tried.

As far as the recording industry was concerned, *nobody* wanted me to sing jazz. They wanted disco, fusion, soul, soul/pop, easy listening, country and western, *anything* but jazz: 'Can't sell it, nobody listening.' I said, 'How can they listen, there's only one jazz station playing it, and only for a few hours, at that.'

It had never entered my mind before, but politics and the white establishment played a huge role in determining what people looked at and listened to in America.

So, when the ONLY jazz station in New York City went off the air at 12 noon (no previous announcement), and country and western music came on at 12:01, I knew my career and the music I loved was in jeopardy.

Jazz is an Afro-American art form. It is not just entertainment. This art form has affected virtually all the popular forms of music to emerge from the United States. It seems that it is all right to have Grace Jones sing 'Pull Up To The Bumper, Baby' five times a day on the radio, but to have Abbey Lincoln sing 'Freedom Suite' is not what the American people want. Who are the American people anyway, and what do the they *really* want? Nobody bothers to ask. The disc jockeys, record producers, company managers, decide who gets recorded and who gets aired and who makes the money. You hear the same uneventful five chords contained in 20 records all day and all night for months. The decision-making is *not* done by the people.

Jazz is about freedom: freedom of musical thought, rhythmic inventiveness, varying moods and participation with others. The concept of freedom seems to be diminishing in the United States and, as I sense and see, in Britain as well. It is much easier to structure people's thoughts, drone out their desires, blast away their political actions with constant thump and clash.

An English friend of mine, visiting the United States, urged me to try a new landscape, a quieter setting: 'Leave New York.' It was apparent that my nerves were tattered, racism was making me bitter and that I needed to get away.

I came to Northern England to write, live a quiet life and try to obliterate all the past injustices and painful experiences I had known. No longer seeking a singing career, I went to hear a local jazz band. I found, on arrival, that my story was already known: I was 'the jazz singer from New York City'. Urged to sit in with the group, I eased into song once again. This time though, it was solely for the sheer joy of singing. Money, although important, was no longer paramount and status held no sway.

The response from the listeners surprised me. They really wanted to hear jazz. There was a genuine interest; a real desire present. But I was soon to find that there was one outstanding problem: there were hardly any venues for the music.

Agents in the North have bubbled over with enthusiasm, yet say there is nowhere to book me. 'The people don't want to hear jazz.' Obviously, we do not know the same people. All those I've encountered are saddened by the paucity of places to hear it. There is a huge and vital interest here, which no one is really addressing. The few places available to jazz artists have been severely damaged by the cuts in Arts Council funding. Consequently, they play the game safely, only hiring 'names'. This attitude exists not only in Britain but in the United States as well, and makes the continuance of this important art form more and more difficult. Carmen McRae once said to me, 'Who's going to carry on the tradition?' I and many others desperately want to; it is essential that we try, for jazz is an honest music, a felt music, a song of the spirit. It can be clapped to, tapped to, danced to, but above all, there is something to listen to: an ever-changing exultation of life.

When I first started singing jazz, I didn't know how long it would really take to call myself a 'jazz singer'. It wasn't just the songs I sang – it was *how* I sang them. Sarah Vaughan had sung them, Billie Holiday, Ella Fitzgerald, Carmen McRae, to name just a few. The challenge was how to make them mine.

At first, I took very few liberties, changing only a few notes here and there (very often the wrong ones). I found myself listening to saxophonists more than to singers. I realised I wanted to recreate their sound. Embarking on this new musical discovery, I jumped in and tried to take those musical flights, swirling as only a good jazz saxophonist can. All too often I gave emphasis to the words that carried no weight, and great importance to those that were just connectors. It made musical sense – but not fully. I hadn't yet learned to wed the words with the melody.

The technique got better, and I was nearer to home, yet it was a hollow attempt somehow. I realised that even though the *notes* were free, I wasn't. I was still bound and shackled by guilt. I didn't believe in myself. Did the audiences see me as my father saw all black women performers? It was this blurred vision that sent me careening into years of self-destruction. Unable to shake off the images set forth by my father, I chose to live with men who abused me. The 'business' aided in my self-deprecation, and when I fought it, it slammed its doors in my face. I stopped singing.

The voice fell silent as I clung to the guise of respectability and a 'straight' job. But the music never left me. It tugged, it cajoled, it screamed. I started to write. I wrote voraciously: poems, poems, poems. Tryin' to get the music out. Setting the writing aside, I read. Books written by black women were appearing everywhere: I devoured them. Their words sang to me, released me, allowed me to breathe.

These women told the stories of self-doubt, of self-hatred, of overcoming all the obstacles and emerging whole. I was hearing myself, and I was all right. They wrote as I had tried to sing; carried on the cultural traditions of black music through their words: Toni Morrison giving space to let the reader come in and participate; Toni Cade Bambara riffing with language as John Coltrane did on his best solos; and Ntozake Shange giving back the rhythms of my everyday speech and making song. Because of these black women writers, I knew I could sing again and, this time, sing with the whole of myself. What I had to relearn was how to be free. Free inside, unashamed. It was *all right* to be Sandi Russell.

The 'business' is behind me now. In New York, it seemed as if a cloud clung to me: I had to 'make it'. The 'making it' far outweighed what I really had to give and how I presented it. It wasn't about the music, it was about the 'personality', the name in lights. It cluttered my mind and strained the sources of any creative energies. I had to be a 'name', not a singer of jazz. The effects of this tore at my insides and wasted my time. I didn't want a gimmick, a costume, a heading. I just wanted to be myself and sing the music that I loved. So I left the bright lights filtered by coke-chasers and image-makers. I said, 'To hell with it, I'll be myself, and give my music to the ears and hearts that want to hear it.'

There is one reason, above all, why I sing jazz. It demands that I confront the *all* of me; the deep, internal, *fearful* side, as well as the exultant exterior. Audre Lorde would call this deep-delving the *erotic:* 'The erotic is a resource within each of us that lies in a deeply female and spiritual plane, firmly rooted in the powers of our unexpressed or unrecognised feeling.' Although her essay 'Uses of the Erotic, the Erotic as Power' is somewhat polemical, she examines white patriarchal suppression of this power in women (I argue, in some men as well) and sees in it a means of oppression and powerlessness; a distancing from one's full self.

When a male Afro-American jazz musician in the early twentieth century picked up his horn and played, his intent was to imitate the sounds of black women singers. The sounds brought forth by these voices used not only notes, but a rendering of that 'unexplored' place in all of us; where the screams are, the howls, the inexplicable. This linkage with the 'erotic' was a continuation of a world and culture lived in Africa. During the 1920s Harlem Renaissance, when whites came in droves to Harlem to hear this 'jazz music', they related to it as men do now when they confuse the erotic with the pornographic. They listened with half of themselves, enjoyed the veneer and claimed their superiority by calling it 'jungle music' played and sung by 'primitives'. This distancing from all that the art form embodied negated enriching engagement and relegated this powerful music to an inferior status.

This continues today, as bits and pieces of the 'sound' are used for commercially viable recordings, recordings that adhere to a plasticised, inhibiting musical structure. The *erotic* is twisted into mere sexiness. Gone is the real surge of feeling that can startle and alert. It is understandable that a society that wants to keep a people oppressed should thwart such emotive power.

When I sang popular music, it was not only the confining structure of the songs that plagued me, but the unrelenting knowledge that I was going further and further away from myself. I knew that in order to 'live', I had to have this 'going-in-ness'. The only means available to me to express this fully was jazz. No other musical form allowed this kind of energy to be expressed. Without it, there is an all-pervasive greyness: the sharpness and the vibrancy of life dissolve.

The sounds still come from the well-trained voice, but the heart and head have changed. Dipping deep into my soul, I now let it all come forth. It isn't as dangerous as I had imagined. Sometimes the sound is light and frothy, and at other times it screeches, assails, cries out. I let the blue-greens wash over me, let the blood-reds fire me up and give me new strength. I let these feelings go out, hoping that those who listen will release their own well-watched feelings and join in with me. I don't do this music just for me. It isn't to hear my own voice that I sing; it is to see others' eyes light up with recognition and a shared oneness. To give and to have it given back.

A woman artist I know came to hear me sing. I had seen her most recent exhibition, and it was filled with vivid colour. After my performance, she came towards me, eyes sharpened with discovery: 'Your music, your singing has helped me to see colour in a new way.' She was excited, full. She rushed away brimming with musical ideas with which to fill her canvas. I had done my job.

'I Got The Music In Me' was the title of an American popular song during the 1970s. It aptly sums up the way I feel. I have it and I consider myself blessed for being given it. I'm not going to muzzle it, mangle it, misrepresent it or manufacture it. I'm going to let the cries and the fears, the pain, the years of struggle and searching come, as they must.

I now let the music take me where it may. I soar, as the mood and the melody carry me to new and unexplored places. I become the saxophone, the trumpet, the bass, the blues singer, the church shouter, the woman of sorrow and joy. I speak to the people that want to hear what is inside us all, and if I get there, they speak back.

Sister Brown jumped up from her seat. Reverend Thompson was sweating: 'I've been through the muck and mire. Jesus took my hand, oh yes He did. Praise God, hallelujah. He talked to me, raised me up, cleansed my soul. Took the burdens of the world away. Praise His name, children. Shout glory, hallelujah.'

Reverend Thompson's voice no longer was his own; a fire was in his throat. Sister Brown sprang from the pew and raced back and forth in the aisles. 'Oh yes Lord; praise His name, praise Him. Sweet, sweet, Jesus.' She jumped, her body flinging itself as if there was a raging wind blowing her about. The congregation hummed, punctuated with resounding 'Yes Lords'. I clung to my mother's sleeve with tears in my eyes. 'Mommy, please take me home, I'm scared.' 'Hush now, it will be all right soon. Sister Brown is just gettin' happy.'

It took years before I could watch the 'Sister Browns' without fear. Fear that I, too, might lose myself to that wind, that force. It never happened in church, but I've gotten 'happy'. It happens when I give praise to the music that sets me free: then I am no longer just me – I am travelling to another sphere, another land; taking with me all the 'Sister Browns' of this world, living and gone. I celebrate all of us: Bessie, Ma Rainey, Maya, Aretha, Billie, Betty Carter. All of these women jump up from the pews and join me – come into me. I sing for the named and the Unnamed. I give praise and glory. I carry on our freedom.

Finding one's own, one's unmistakable freedom – how often is this echoed throughout this book ...

But engaging directly – not only with tradition but with audience, too – sketches boundaries; a scrupulosity about voicing the half-tones of every thought and feeling is perhaps something of a luxury, best reserved for intimate audiences or readers who can turn the page when bored. It might also be said that an obsession with the riches of the inner life requires not a private income – women rarely enjoy that – but an economic marginalisation, the epitome of which is to be occupied solely as a housewife/mother. Earning your money through your pen or your voice enforces some kind of accounta-bility, though at first it may only be of the market-place.

Viv Quillin makes her living as a cartoonist; her work, because she earns an income from it, confronts the economics of creativity – which turns out to be another of those silences that need breaking. The commodification of art, in such a way that paintings become investments and the revolution of yesterday is today's harmless and unalarming chic, has been avoided by women artists to the extent that they are marginalised. Examining the tactics and ethics of earning money by one's brush, the 'wheeling and dealing', may sound like a luxurious consideration – I should be so lucky! – but is entailed by taking seriously Anna Wilson's observation, 'I am silenced by the necessity to make a living, which I cannot do by writing.'

Much has been made of the humour gap, feminists' supposed lack of wit. As Viv herself says, 'My income is living refutation of that idea!' While not wasting space countering the silliness of the dour feminist stereotype, we can note that for each of us there may be silences of tone as much as of subject – things that we each feel should never be made fun of or only in a particular way. Viv relishes illustrating topics such as premenstrual tension with funny pictures.

She reveals the underside of women's circumstances, the things that continue to give rise to feminist demands for liberation; she also pokes fun at the solemn or pretentious or downright batty bits of the feminist creed. She is also working within the almost completely male tradition of political cartoonists. She works to change the way women – and men – are depicted in cartoons, on birthday cards and in people's minds, but she also wants to give her readers 'a bedtime laugh after a day's hard slog'. As you might expect, she didn't find her own sense of humour under a cabbage leaf . . .

Being A Cartoonist Sort of Person

Viv Quillin

I'm a cartoonist. I've drawn cartoons since I was a little girl and I'm sure it is not coincidental that cartooning is the only talent I remember my remote and disapproving father admiring in me. From an early age I felt I was approved of when I was being funny and I think this has been important in me developing my talent for humour.

I copied him in drawing caricatures, not necessarily kind ones, of family and friends. At school I remember feeling popular and rather special when I drew cartoons. As this experience was repeated as often as possible, not surprisingly my work improved rapidly.

In junior school my male teacher reprimanded me for drawing bosoms on my women. I was very angry at this denial of reality but felt quite unable to say so. Perhaps he was denying girls' ability to have something he couldn't have!

Having planned a career as a fashion designer, I left school abruptly at sixteen to marry and have a baby hundreds of miles from everything familiar to me. The cartoons changed radically; ceasing to be rather pointless caricatures, they were a life-line, the expression of intense feelings. The marriage was not a happy one. Pent-up anger and bewilderment were released in drawings of women feeding armies of babies, placating demanding husbands, washing conveyor-belt floors.

My own blackening humour was shared and fed by neighbouring housewives. We made the most dreadful statements in bad-taste jokes that we could never have said straight. Laughing about my anger and hopelessness helped to reduce my fear and keep some perspective in my life.

After the marriage broke up I went to art college and was the only student on the course with children, a daughter of 11 and two sons aged nine and six. It was a difficult time, trying to be Wunder Mother to assuage the guilt of being at college; trying to be Wunder Student because I was the oldest one on the course and I felt I should automatically know how to do things better than the others.

I now had an audience of tutors and students to share my humour with. It seemed acceptable to express my plight through cartoons – nobody likes a moaner, everybody enjoys a laugh. It was easy to show people my cartoon sketch books although I couldn't share the serious painting and writing that occasionally burst out. It was a good way to wrap up a bitter pill in sugar.

For every serious project we were set I had a sheaf of cartoons around the subject despite the desperate lack of time at my disposal. I would literally have to empty my head of cartoons on to paper before I could get on with the 'serious project'. Looking back, I think I was probably very afraid of competing as a straight art student and was escaping like mad into my cartoons, the one area where I saw myself as good.

After completing the college course I dutifully toured the studios with my portfolio of designs – and a carrier bag of dog-eared cartoon books. To my amazement I began to earn a tenuous living as a cartoonist. At this point I followed an undercurrent in the bottom of my mind – that I was just keeping the kids and myself going until . . . someone came along to rescue me. It was really quite embarrassing, having become a staunch feminist, to realise that here I was waiting for a knight in armour to save me and earn my living for me. I'd been brought up to get a man, not a job. It was both exhilarating and terrifying to realise I could decide to support myself. If I wanted a holiday or a car I didn't need to hope somebody else would give it to me – I'd damn well get it for myself.

Without realising, I'd regarded the cartoons which paid bills as a kind of self-indulgence, a hobby I enjoyed, grateful to be published let alone paid adequately. I'd trivialised my work, yet I knew quite clearly that the drawings were one of the most important things in my life. From that time on I became much more professional in my outlook, insisted that my kids gave me the space and co-operation I needed to earn our living. And charged sensible amounts for work instead of deciding on a fee and then asking half of it.

This was particularly difficult as my own lack of self-esteem made me feel nothing I'd drawn could be of much value, as I wasn't myself of value. Also, women aren't taught to see the worth of their work in monetary terms as we are trained from very small to work 'for love' and not to expect any reward except gratitude. How many middle-aged secretaries boast that they run an office single-handed, protect an inefficient boss, haven't had a wage rise in years – and expect to have their loyalty admired?

Discussing how work is valued in the economic world would take a whole book. It is enough right now to know I was afraid to say, 'I want a lot of money for this cartoon because it took a lot of feeling and experience and skill to make and it's a good one.' What arrogance, how unfeminine; nice women wait to be asked. Much safer to say it was only a scribble on a piece of paper and let someone else decide what it's worth.

A fairly typical job can run like this: a magazine rings me and asks for a cartoon to illustrate an article on the problems of women who care for elderly or disabled relatives. We negotiate a fee and deadline and they send me the copy to read. The difficulty in this particular job lies in wanting to show the unacceptable conditions put on to carers, whilst not wanting to portray elderly or handicapped people as problems in themselves.

I put my wellies and mac on and go for a walk. This is a very effective way of thinking – while my body moves along, my mind grinds into action too. Each piece of work is like an act of faith in myself, trusting that if I let my mind open and relax, the creative solution will gradually come. I need something succinct and funny, not a literal illustration of the situation. Into my mind swim images of cantankerous bed-ridden old men – funny, but not what I want. The essence of the job is the difficult situation of the carers; I don't want to suggest that the cared-for should behave better to solve the problem. How can I separate the two? I'm stuck.

Thoughts slide vaguely to a cartoon workshop I'm going to run for girls in a local comprehensive school. I think angrily about the pressures put on girls in their career choices. I've been reading up on conditioning in education to prepare for the workshop . . . more musing, thoughts rejected, then suddenly – 'Care of the elderly and disabled as a career for girls.' This way I can describe all the drawbacks of unpaid work, no pension, etc., without denigrating the relative who needs and is entitled to decent care and attention.

After hot-wellying it home, I use another couple of hours

designing the drawing to fit the page, getting the schoolgirl's and career officer's expressions right. This involves some pantomime in front of my mirror while I act out the career officer, noting the stance, expression and accent required for the part. The work is finally packed up, invoiced and taken to the post. This time I haven't got to get any reference pictures and there were no interruptions to my train of thought. In one cartoon I've drawn on experience in motherhood, working with handicapped people, my children's education and the hard thought out feminist beliefs.

I've led a number of cartoon workshops now and hope it is as enriching for the participants as it is for me. Lots of women are inhibited about doing cartoons as they feel their drawing ability isn't 'good enough'. With cartoons, the priority is the idea and the drawing can often be more meaningful when proportions and perspective are 'wrong'. (Think of how expressive a child's painting is.) One very good way of getting humorous ideas going and by-passing the drawing 'block' is what I call 'Wantonly Defacing Advertisements'. The materials are women's magazines (the more sexist the better), scissors, felt tips, glue and speech bubbles. Teenage girls whose consciousness hasn't risen above their stilettos and ankle bracelets will come up with some side-splitting captions for pictures. This leads very easily into supplying their own drawings of whatever is needed to add to the picture and sparks off other cartoons which are, by now, unselfconsciously sketched out. I like to think the media will never again have quite the same influence after one of my workshops!

It's difficult portraying women because of the stereotypes, i.e. blonde means stupid, glasses mean swot, big breasts mean sexy. I try and draw all shapes and sizes and convey the kind of person I want by the way they hold their body and their expression. Facial expression is crucial and I may reject several before getting the one that feels right. I'm told that I wear whatever expression I'm drawing which must be entertaining for passers by my studio window.

The work is very much a reflection of my whole self. Everything that I experience and learn goes in, like a compost heap that gets a lot of rubbish dumped on it, which in time filters through and recycles as something enriching. Very often when I get bogged down about what I'm trying to say in a cartoon it's because I've touched an area in myself which is in confusion. I've recently written and illustrated a year in the marriage of Heather Aspic –

unpaid mother of two, wife of Richard. Heather is very much a description of myself as a young wife and mother with no knowledge of feminism. In the cartoon I'm working on, Richard has taken her to the Royal Corgi for a drink with his chum Basher. In the men's conversation Richard isn't being intentionally unkind, nor is Basher. I'm making them seem brutal when that isn't what I feel about them.

Back to the towpath for a walk in me wellies; what is it I'm trying to say through Heather? She isn't angry at that moment so what is the essence under the words and scene? I go back to myself as a young woman in the men's place, the pub. It's coming back to me, the kindly patronising of those in charge, who run the world, to me, the sweet funny little wife who has to be looked after – the powerless one. Heather doesn't understand her feelings of discomfort yet – as I didn't – she only knows Richard and Basher are being 'nice', but somehow it's not okay. I want my reader to identify with this and now I know exactly what I'm putting over, Heather's face is doubtful, puzzled and slightly put down. She is the outsider. Richard and Basher, stand together, confident: they know who they are. It's hard bringing out subtleties under what appears to be an innocuous situation. Through working my cartoon, I have understood a little more about my own conflicting responses when I get that double-edged offering of kindness and superiority: I'll be better equipped to deal with it. Sometimes I feel quite embarrassed at seeing my hang-ups coming out in my work. On a good day the humour allows me to love and accept myself as an ordinary fallible mortal!

Recently I began to find the language of cartoons very restrictive. This was terribly frightening. Not only have I invested a lot of time and effort establishing myself professionally but being a cartoonist is a big part of who I am. I gradually felt more and more pressured by the need to be funny. It was also becoming very laborious having to translate everything I wanted to say into cartoon language – pictures and minimal words. I considered the possibility of giving up cartoons and moving into other areas without the need for humour. It was only then that I realised my clown's outfit was both my armour and my security blanket. I protect myself and other people from what I see as my unacceptable serious side, nobody will find me interesting or lovable if I'm not funny: the little girl acknowledged only for her entertainment value. I can excuse the seriousness of my comments by trivialising them – 'It's only a joke.' I hadn't dared admit to taking myself seriously or expecting anyone else to. This looks very simple and obvious written down but it took months of patient thinking – and not drawing cartoons – to work out. I am beginning to accept that I am valued in many ways; I'm not dependent on humour to be loved and acknowledged as worthwhile. It is no longer a cage in which I've locked myself up but a valuable tool I can pick up if I choose to.

Current projects are a book on women's sexuality, getting into animation, and understanding more about envy. I see myself stumbling from puddle to puddle in my trusty wellies with occasional bursts of sunlight . . . I may do a few cartoons about it.

To change the way women are depicted is a long struggle not certain success. After all, you want people to look, or listen. Part of the creative struggle lies in marrying politics with aesthetics – propaganda versus entertainment is a dilemma (often a false one) that never seems to go away. You must get used to people accusing you of preaching or selling out, or both.

But even when you're satisfied that you've got the characters convincing, the plot crisp, the dialogue alert, the issues clear – it's just the beginning. You are dealing, from the list of characters on the title page to the final curtain on the last performance, with the politics of representation. Will people like it? Which people? What does it mean if they don't? How far are you prepared to go to give them what they want? Shirley Barrie is an experienced wrestler with these conundrums as a writer, director and stage manager for the theatre. In contrast with Ruth Noble, who starts with and from her body as dramatic resource, Shirley works with characters, situations and locations in the world – and then attempts to subvert the stereotypes they contain.

In this article, Shirley puts the writing of plays in its economic as well as artistic context.

Small Triumphs

Shirley Barrie

I always wanted to be a writer, but it took me a long time to find the form my creative compulsion should take. When I was about 11 I began several adventure novels. L. M. Montgomery's more obscure novels were my models: the *Emily* series and *The Blue Castle*. I never finished any of my stories. As a teenager I wrote morbid poems about death and how misunderstood I was. As an adult I turned to short stories. They were hampered by a stiff and verbose style and rejected by everyone. I tried again. For about two years I wrestled with an inchoate mass of material which was supposed to be a novel. Somehow I couldn't give it any shape.

Now for much of this time I was *fascinated* by theatre. Not that there was much of it in Southern Ontario in the fifties. However, every year in high school there was a school trip in the Stratford Shakespearian Festival. While a lot of the other kids shot spitballs at the actors, I was transported. I loved the sense of each performance being a unique occasion, the performance magic, the ability of a stage to contain *anything* if you found the right metaphor, the right style, the right characters. But it never occurred to me to be a playwright. At university I adapted Aristophanes' *The Poet and the Women* because it needed to be done and I was there, but I never saw it as a stepping-stone to anything.

I had been the co-founder of a theatre company and its co-director for two years before I seriously thought that maybe, instead of servicing other people's plays, I should start writing in the art form I was obsessed by.

I think part of the reason for this 'slowness' on my part was that there weren't any role models at the right time. There were lots of women novelists, and growing up in Canada in the fifties and sixties you couldn't avoid the fact that women were very good poets, but where were the playwrights? With the growing international reputations now of people like Caryl Churchill this is slowly changing, but *very* slowly.

The fact is that women, as writers, have taken much longer to break into theatre than into novels or poetry. This is partly due to the ways in which writing plays is different from other forms of creative expression.

A playwright is not entirely self-motivated not entirely her own-time keeper. Although she may sit in her room and write, what she writes is not a play in the full sense of the word until it is performed on the stage, and in order for that to happen a series of important collaborations on the work have to be made. It has to be accepted by a management who might suggest or require changes; it has to find a director who might have a different interpretation of the play; it is worked on further by a designer and lighting designer who visualise what the script suggests to them; and it has to be rehearsed and then performed by actors – sometimes of your choice, sometimes whoever is available and willing: sometimes they bring amazing depth and magic to what you have written, sometimes that special quality eludes them and you cut and shape and rewrite in order to find some connection between your intentions and their talents. All along the line there are a series of adjustments and compromises and in the best circumstances this results in a better play than the original concept.

Women are mistresses of compromise, you might think, and should thrive in these circumstances, but theatre is often very confrontational. Compromises can be hammered out in emotional scenes made more tense by chronic shortness of time and the playwright does not normally take the role of conciliator – she has a vision to protect. She may have to defend her play to everyone involved. 'Why can't this speech be cut,' says one. 'Why is this image so important?' 'I can't do this.' 'We can't afford that effect.' And most devastating of all, 'This just isn't working!'

Having a play produced is hard work. It is time consuming. There comes a time when you can't fit in what is required of you and your maternal responsibilities. Post-rehearsal conferences are crucial, overnight rewrites essential, complicated dress rehearsals are no respecter of children's needs. It is a stressful process in which you can get mauled and mangled. If you can't fight hard enough (and sometimes even if you can), your intentions can get misrepresented. It's also tremendously exciting and creative.

Theatre is also different from novels and poetry and art because it is an active medium. It is not most successful when it is reflective or introspective. Intentions have to be conveyed through action and words, not thought and words. Now women are very good at thinking and feeling since what we can develop inside us cannot be so easily circumscribed. But we have a long history of being prevented from acting and we don't do it easily. Theatre is about action. Playwrights have to express their ideas and intentions through action, and they must do this for both their male and female characters. There are still many plays, some of them written by women, in which the men act and the women sit by and watch. Bryony Lavery wrote in *Women and Theatre: Calling the Shots* (see Bibliography) about how long it took her to realise that women could be the main characters in her plays.

So a playwright who is a woman has to grapple with an active form and an active process and at the end of the day sits through the first public performance with an active audience who are experiencing and responding to the play *immediately*. 'They didn't laugh at that. Why not? I was sure it was funny.' Or, 'Listen to the silence. They're totally involved. It's working!' An opening night is one of the most exhilarating and frightening experiences I can imagine.

It's a lot to take on board. There are, however, increasing numbers of women eager to embrace the territory, but they are still having great difficulties in getting a script into performance. To achieve that, you have to persuade somebody with the *necessary resources* to put them into your play, and women are still losing out heavily in this area.

In 1983 the Conference of Women Directors and Administrators conducted a survey of plays produced in regional theatres and at the RSC and the National Theatre the previous year. All of the conclusions were startling, if not exactly news to any woman working in the theatre.

Out of the 620 plays produced in the Reps, 42 were written by females. Out of these 22 were written by Agatha Christie. 14 of the 42 were produced in Studios. None by Agatha Christie. Therefore 6 plays written by females other than Agatha Christie were produced on main stages. ('The Status of Women in the British Theatre 1982-1983', p.6)

Why is this? Well – in the vast majority of cases the people with resources to commit to new plays are men.

The survey demonstrates clearly that the more money and prestige a theatre has, the less women will be employed as directors and administrators; the less likelihood that a play written by a woman will be commissioned or produced, excepting Agatha Christie; and the less women there will be on the Board.

(Introduction, ibid.)

And since women, as they come to terms with the medium, are tending to write in different ways and from a different perspective than men, this can cause increased difficulties. The climate is not right for even well-meaning men, who have boards of directors screaming down their necks and funding bodies threatening to take away their grants, to 'take a chance' on a play they can't respond to totally. They're not able and/or willing to overcome their male bias.

In 1984 the National Theatre proudly announced its expanded line-up of directors. There were 9 beaming male faces selecting what the public saw at Britain's National Theatre. Now the National Theatre's past record on working with women was abysmal. The National produced 24 plays in three auditoriums during the year of the survey previously quoted. *One* of these was by a woman. (This made it a good year for women at the NT.) Out of 18 Associate Directors, one was a woman, and she was a casting director: she did not direct plays. There was no indication in this new announcement that things were going to be any better. The Women Directors and Administrators and the Theatre Writers Union demanded – and after several months got – meetings with the directors over this issue. I was a member of the delegation from the Union who attended. In the course of the meeting we naïvely suggested that the NT Directors should perhaps admit their male middle-class bias and do something about it. You could feel the hackles rise on the other side of the table as they collectively drew themselves up and pompously rejected totally the very idea of any bias at all. 'Come on,' I persisted, 'I'm biased. I admit it. On the whole I respond more readily to plays by women than plays by men. But when I'm in a position of choosing a programme for a theatre (which I was with the Tricycle Theatre for several years) that is not exclusively a theatre for women I have to deal with my biases in relation to the job I'm doing and the audience the theatre is trying to reach.' 'No, no!' expostulated the NT mandarins. 'We're not biased. We do the best that is available. That is our mandate.' The implication, of course, is that women do not produce the best and until some women get into a position to make some of the decisions this state of belief is unlikely to change. But how likely is this? Sir Peter Hall was 'keeping his eye on' about a dozen women directors, the women directors and administrators were told, but none of them met his criteria for the best yet.

Some might argue that it is pointless to storm such bastions anyway. But the National Theatre and the Royal Shakespeare Company etc., have access to resources and in theatre resources are relative to what you create. As an artist you can buy a piece of canvas and paint whatever you want on it: a single flower still life or a teeming cityscape. You can people your novel with countless characters in as many situations as you like. Your publisher may restrict you to 200 pages but within those pages you can make your scope as wide, as narrow, as public, as private as you need. This isn't the case with theatre. Plays require spaces and sets and most expensively of all – actors.

This is a limitation on all theatre writers, not just women. A few years ago there was a notice up at the Soho Poly Theatre: 'Wanted: One-Act Plays. Maximum 2 characters'. Women have done very well at writing intimate, small-cast plays for feminist companies, for small scale touring companies, for children's companies and occasionally for repertory studios. But what happens when you want to write a big public play that requires more than five actors and a skeleton set? You need a company with resources; and most of these – in fact, if not in intention – are closed to women. Catch-22 of course is that you hear it argued, by men, that women can't write 'big' plays. Is Louise Page's recent successful *Golden Girls* at the RSC going to prove them wrong or does the fact that the play is about women in sport make it, by definition, *not* a big play?

This limitation in scope can be very frustrating for a playwright. It means our wings are clipped before we get the opportunity to try them out fully. I have been working, for example, for four years in spare and stolen moments on a public play of 'female' epic proportions. I say this because I have been told that it doesn't follow the pattern of epic plays such as Brecht's; that there are scenes in it that men would never write. I find this exciting, but it might take me years to discover if I have, in fact, succeeded. The play makes (in today's terms) large demands, and most of the people who are excited by the subject matter don't have sufficient funds to take on anything so large. Well-funded theatres, so far, find it 'interesting' but not 'interesting' enough.

Infrequently a playwright may be asked to write a large-cast play for a youth or community (i.e. amateur) theatre. This does give you the opportunity of working with more actors, but it has its own limitations. It necessitates writing balanced roles and characters and situations that it is possible for inexperienced and untrained actors to manage. It is also often a part of the brief that the play should in some measure be collectively created. This can be extremely challenging and rewarding in its own way, but it does not always give the writer full scope for her own discoveries. It can also be very difficult to get funding bodies to help pay writers in these circumstances because the actors involved are not 'professionals'. So if we are determind to be 'professionals' we go back to writing small-cast plays for the few companies (usually impoverished) who appreciate our talents. Again from the survey:

> The greatest concentration of women occurs in the Alternative and Community categories of theatre. These are the least subsidised and least well equipped, and offer the smallest stages, the smallest audiences, the least predictable and controllable venues, the smallest budgets, the least likelihood of classical work; in other words, the most difficult circumstances in which to produce art.

Okay. It's difficult for women to produce theatre. But when they do, how do they write? When Lesley first asked me whether I would be interested in contributing to a book about women and creativity – about how we wrote as women – my first reaction was panic. It seemed to me that I had never analysed the how's and why's. I just did it. How could I possibly write about it? A good friend of mine who was visiting me at the time said that she thought this was the major difference between us. We had both begun writing for the theatre at approximately the same time. She, obsessed by why and how she as a woman could and should create, has produced very few plays. I have apparently ignored many of these issues and produced a lot more. I think, in fact, that it is a lot more complicated than that. Personal circumstances have a large part to play. She is a single non-parent, making her living (when not writing or acting) by teaching for the most part. That is, she has a mind attuned to analysis and the time to pursue it. I am married, a mother of two children and, until a year and a half ago, the associate director of a theatre company. I was, and am, also a playwright. I never had the *time* to think about the why's and how's. This was compounded by the fact that in alternative and children's theatre, writers often work on commission. You are asked to write a play on a theme which you agree with the company, by a set date – usually the day after tomorrow, or that's the way it often seems. I was often writing to a tight deadline a play that had been pre-sold, and often cast before anything more than a bare outline was down on paper. If I didn't come up with the goods, I was letting down an awful lot of people. All of these things together had the effect of concentrating the mind on what I was writing. The how's and why's did come into it but I tried to deal with them in a practical rather than a theoretical way. I have worked fairly consistently in children's theatre and it does seem to be an area of theatre that is more open to women than most. This is probably because, in England, theatre for children is given no status and very little money. I recently wrote a play for Unicorn Theatre, one of the biggest children's theatres in the country, and had the cast of the show cut from 5 to 4 halfway through the process in the theatre's frantic and continual efforts to make ends meet.

I have done a lot of work in this area of theatre and have sometimes not been taken seriously as a writer as a consequence; and, more often than not, have earned peanuts for the amount of work I've put in. However, I think it's a very important area of theatre to be involved in, because a children's writer has the opportunity to help shape the views of the next generation.

It means that there's even more to take on board. I believe that theatre must firstly be entertaining and it takes an enormous amount of deliberation, analysis and creativity to be entertainingly non-sexist when the patterns and stereotypes and short-cuts are so rigidly so. And here we get into the area of what we write as opposed to how we get the chance to do it at all.

Because theatre is about action – and theatre for children is definitely so – plays for children are often built around polarities of good and evil and I've been involved in many arguments about the virtues and vices of female and/or black 'villains'. I've written plays with both – because more often than not the villains have the most showy parts and women and blacks deserve them. Villains are fun to play; they have a great amount of contact with the audience. When I wrote *Riders of the Sea* for Theatre of Thelema the director refused to assign parts for the first week of rehearsals. *Everybody* wanted to play the villain, and I was really pleased when the part was given to a woman. But it's not easy to write an acceptable (to me) female villain. Again stereotypes betray us. In fairy-tales, evil women are step-mothers whose motives are position in the family or a perverse beauty contest. I sometimes think that the one positive thing Maggie Thatcher has done is to create a world-wide image of a female villain in a public not a domestic sphere. If women can be powerful, then they can also use that power for good or evil and it is important for children to understand this.

But it is not just the bad women who are creative problems; it's female adults as a whole. Playwrights are developing a nice line in tough and clever little girls who can outdo and outwit their brothers, but it doesn't, so far, carry into adult portrayals. It's *very hard* to write a convincing memorable Mum, for instance. Mothers are the dramatic downfalls of most plays in which they appear. The audience is waiting for them to get off the stage so the action can get going again.

But in being aware of the responsibilities we face in the images we are presenting, we mustn't over-analyse ourselves into creative extinction. A recent play I wrote had, I thought, a very strong adult female figure: a career-oriented computer expert obsessed by bits and bytes but still capable of participating in the problems of the life around her. Much of the time during the first two weeks of rehearsal was taken up by the actress, director and sometimes me, deliberating on where this character came from. She couldn't be American because that implied only American women could be successes; she definitely couldn't be middle class, preferably not Cockney. We went through every regional accent the actress could and sometimes couldn't quite do before settling on Glaswegian. I'm not suggesting that these questions are not important, but I think they were diversionary from the main intention which was that this character should be admirable, very funny, and *shine* on the stage. There was a point at which I felt that the indecision was bringing the actress very close to not being able to do the part at all. Meanwhile the other members of the cast – two of them men

– were getting on with solidifying their characters and their routines. When we finally broke through the actress had a lot of catching up to do.

In another context – and dealing with a play for more adult audiences – I remember reading reviews of the Women's Playhouse Trust's production of Aphra Behn's *The Lucky Chance,* and wondering why the men were getting all the good notices. When I saw the production I understood. Aphra Behn was a far-sighted and progressive woman but she did *not* live in the late twentieth century and she *was* writing a restoration comedy where almost by definition everyone, except the innocent young lovers, is venal. The men in this production ponced about, were extravagant, ridiculous, grotesque, outrageous, funny. The women were located mentally in the 'enlightened' 1980s, and regardless of the very nice touches of intelligence and female friendship (for those of us who were looking), they were not outrageous, they were not funny, so they did *not* shine.

We need to be free to explore, to discover what women can do and be on the stage. We need creative brilliance for women every bit as much as we need correct political analysis. It's dangerous. We can get it wrong. But it's important to try.

Writing plays is a voyage of discovery, not only of what we think ourselves but of what other people – our characters – think as well. If all our characters reflected our own concerns and points of view, there would be no conflict and little drama or tension. So we have to think ourselves into the minds and souls of a wide variety of characters, some of whom may say and do things that are anathema to what we believe in and struggle for.

However, we usually have an overriding theme or point of view – let's call it an intellectual framework for the play: a well-thought-out thesis for *why* these characters, this story, these actions.

But sometimes these analyses can head us in the wrong direction. When I was writing the first draft of *The Pear is Ripe,* my intellectual intention was that the main character, Suzanne Voilquin (based on a real nineteenth-century Frenchwoman), would be totally brought down when her faith in a Utopian woman-centred new religion was destroyed by the manipulation and self-interest of the men who were still in control. But this woman would not lie down and die, no matter how many times and in how many different ways I tried to make her. What I eventually discovered, by accepting what Suzanne was telling me and therefore putting her in the forefront of the play, was that the theme of the play about this character was somewhat different. In some part it was about the nature of benevolent patriarchy, and how women have grown and developed within it, but eventually have been betrayed and been forced to step outside it.

Stepping outside the traditional patriarchal structure of theatre has only worked for women in a small way so far. Many women have been stimulated, supported and creatively inspired by working with other women outside traditional structures. But such companies have remained under-funded and small. There has been no equivalent of Virago or The Women's Press. So, because of the need for resources and wages and challenges, many women are still trying to make their way within the traditional structures.

There are small triumphs. There is an increasing awareness in small-scale and community theatres of the role that women can play. Some artistic directors will go to considerable trouble to find a woman director for a particular play and encourage writers to explore themes in a non-sexist way, but such people are still on the periphery. More women artistic directors are being appointed. Still not nearly enough – but more. The two major theatres in Liverpool are now being run by women, for example. But Liverpool is one of the most financially and industrially depressed of the major urban centres and these two theatres were treated most meagrely and unfairly in the Arts Council of Great Britain's much touted division of extra funds to the region. Their job will not be easy. In the mainstream of theatre generally, the status quo persists: very few major outlets for women dramatists, and distorted and outmoded portrayals of women – if they are not excluded altogether.

In the end we may have to look to our daughters to force the changes. Last year I took my two children to the Tricycle to see the second half of the Black Theatre Co-operative's production of Sam Shepard's *Tooth of Crime*. The centre piece of the act is the brilliant musical duel fought out between Hoss and Crow. In the middle of it my then ten-year-old daughter, obviously troubled about something, turned to me and said, not quietly, 'Mum, *why* is there only one girl in this show?' And I realised something important. She's *used* to seeing herself and her interests and concerns as an involved participating female reflected on the stage. When that is absent, she notices, and she doesn't like it. And she's not very good at keeping her mouth shut when she doesn't like something. I see it in her often now – in little things – an unwillingness to accept slights or second best when it can be put right if you assert yourself. *If* she is at all typical of her generation and *if* she and countless others can continue to have positive theatrical experiences during the crucial early teens, then there should be brewing a large and vocal objection to the exclusion of women and their point of view from the stage. If we can push hard from both ends – creator and audience – we might just break through.

Women's theatre is one area where – as Shirley discusses – some change, at least, is becoming noticeable. Certain traditions have for long been closely associated with women – like painting, weaving, story-telling, singing – in contrast to all those playwrights, film directors, architects, composers and so on who have been men. We know it is neither accident nor an a priori truth that male-dominated arts should on the whole enjoy higher status than what is seen as women's work. That there are economic, not aesthetic nor biological, reasons for this has been sufficiently amplified by feminist theory; and the growth in large-scale work, as women achieve greater economic independence – installations like The Dinner Party *or performance experiments like* Magdalena 86, *an international women's theatre spectacle – as well as in smaller-scale work in hi-tech areas, both of which require capital and maintenance funding, is the practical demonstration. As women make and fill these metropolitan spaces, the question of 'what for?' becomes more pressing. On the one hand, the traditional conservative community has virtually disappeared as inspiration, context and venue for creative work; while on the other, 'self-expression' is inadequate as either description or justification for what many women are doing.*

So 'what for?' uncovers a trail of further questions. One of these is to do with 'professionalism'. In industrial society, women typically have to choose between career and family. Lisa Kopper – a visual artist, like Viv Quillin and Gabriela Müller, but with different priorities from either of theirs – suggests here that the same 'choice' is no less stark for women as artists. Her concern then extends to the dilemma facing any artist who, having chosen that vocation, lacks a social role in the modern world.

No More Picassos

Lisa Kopper

It's a late night and another deadline looms. I'm sitting with my nose glued to a drawing board and I am thinking – is this what creativity is? I find it odd to be sitting here at all seeing as I was brought up by my mother to be a great painter. She suffered from the starving artist romance. But Mammon called to her daughter and the split between what I am doing and what I feel I should be doing continues to dominate my life. My quandary isn't so much about the practical problems of doing two things as about the meaning of what I do and how I use my talent.

I am a children's book illustrator. I earn well and my work is in demand. I am lucky to have an interesting job which I enjoy. It hasn't happened without some personal sacrifice. Rumour has it that a woman can have everything these days. I don't think this is true. I believe we can have a lot, but not everything – there are choices that have to be made. My parents knew they had a gifted child and did much to encourage and develop my talent. I always have felt that the buck stops here. I have to do something with this. What is the point of my having children – encouraging their abilities and not doing something with my own? It would be such a waste of what has been given to me. So art has always come first. Illustration is a part of it – a practical application. I would like to find a way of integrating painting and illustration so they were not so separate from each other.

But this is not so easy. Making a living has always been hard for artists and compromises have to be made. Today, the role of artists in society is dubious. When I illustrate, I know what it is for. Books are not élitist – they travel, unlike canvases. I feel I'm contributing to the quality of children's lives in my own way.

But who are paintings for? And is this important?

Friends often say, 'Paint for yourself.' But it isn't enough and it isn't so simple. Painters who consider themselves to be 'professionals' need and want a place within their society the same as any other working person. You wouldn't say to a doctor, 'Practise for yourself.' I don't believe it's good for art to go on in isolation from the world – this encourages élite personality cults and creates a circle of greater isolation.

But ah – the mysterious cult of the artist. Artists live for their art in bohemian squalor, in poverty and oblivion, but justice is done to their reputation in the end – usually after their death. We were all nurtured on these stories, we were all going to be Van Goghs or Picassos. We have been brought up and trained for it – for a world that doesn't exist. I can't think of any artists – even dead ones – who have had any great impact on anything recently. Yet art schools continue to perpetuate the myth that genius will bring you fame and influence – you could be The One. And students leave college confused about their role in society, unprepared for the real art world which is actually cynical big business. Who makes it, or doesn't, is of interest only to the few people in the gallery scene. It is no wonder that so much talent turns to the commercial world where motives are, if nothing else, clear.

This has its own pitfalls. I started illustrating, like so many people, to support what I wanted to do, to paint. But if you are successful enough to achieve this, you are well and truly on a merry-go-round. The means to the end become all-consuming; time and thought for anything else are almost non-existent. Britain in particular is difficult for painters because there is no tradition of buying art; there is little choice but to join the media. Perhaps commercial art is the real art of today.

But art wasn't always divided into specialities. Once upon a time there was no division between fine art and commercial art. The artist did it all. Some old masters virtually had factories to produce their work. The humble artist's purpose was clear and it was a job. If you couldn't draw – no job. The rich, then as now, dictated taste. Then it was individual or family patronage; now it's companies, corporations and governments who control the media.

It was the photo that changed the artist's role. Suddenly there was liberation – artists could 'express' themselves. The time was right – it was a visual revolution. And it had a real impact on the society in which it happened. You'd be hard pressed to find a headline about what artists are up to these days.

Recently I ran an illustrators' workshop in Zimbabwe. The illustrations I saw were undeveloped but art is much more integrated into life there than in the West. There was decoration on poor accommodation; children carved wonderful toys; beautiful fabrics were in abundance. And it wasn't just for the tourists, it was daily life. Perhaps not for much longer but it was still there and a joy to see.

I do believe art is important; it seeps through and enriches life. Artists should have a place in the world. The ethos of 'self-expression' doesn't mean what it did 80 years ago – it's a con and attracts con people. The 'art scene' reveals that again and again. Public respect continues to diminish. I don't know what the answers are – if I did there wouldn't be a conflict for me. I once had a professor who said, 'I have so many paintings in my head but I've only done numbers two and 11. Why should I paint them if no one sees them? I get all the pleasure out of thinking them.' And he asked us if we would still paint if we were on a desert island. I think we are.

I'd better get back to my drawing board. Maybe tomorrow I'll put the questions aside and do some painting – sod what it's for!

P.S. I did.

Well, what is *art for? Lisa has criticised a current emphasis on self-expression as purpose (rather than merely as impetus). The expectation that the self is both interesting and subversive is, as she suggests, historically traceable – the Expressionists and Surrealists had formulated the idea between them by the second decade of the century. The 'self' has been formally constituted as something other than the conscious ego of the artist since the appearance of European Romanticism: it has meant, variously, the unconscious or the automatic or the unrepressed aspects of the person and has been a favourite subject of art. Liberating as this undoubtedly has been and continues to be for the individual – and it has had its brilliant moments as both an artistic and a political pretext – it has now become, by one of history's appalling ironies, quite compatible with the individualism of the eighties as offered to us by Thatcherism. It is feminism's responsibility to interrogate itself as well as others about this.*

For, now revolution is no longer on the agenda, you can buy books by the armful, attend workshops every week, on how to become more 'creative'. The means are varied but whether they are convincing or cranky, the bottom-line is the same. This is the familiar double-bind of late consumer capitalism, that total resistance to incorporation into the establishment can only be 'achieved' by dropping out of the bottom of the heap; in the effort to get an income or other kind of funding, recognition, publicity – all strategems which feminists can endorse from the point of view of 'out from under' – we immediately collide with other and serious considerations. Very likely our creativity is to some extent commodified. We sell our work – if we're lucky – in the form of product or labour, we compromise between what we want and what we can do, we see enterprising projects stitched up by bureaucracy, subsidised by capitalists and philistines, or competing for increasingly curtailed Arts Council grants. We know that those who can pay us for what we do probably have less need for what we are offering than those who can't. We find ourselves rationalising all this, too.

'Choice' is apparently everywhere but is offered within an invariable structure (ten kinds of washing powder in the supermarket, all vying to appeal to individual preferences and all ecologically harmful). Personal autonomy is sloganised by right and left, with no agreed paradigm of exercising it. Beliefs are rendered as personal style to be chosen, rather than moral system to be argued. The pleasure industry thrives on our discovered 'needs' – capitalism isn't

troubled as to whether those needs are constructed by advertising or unearthed in primal therapy, so long as we spend money fulfilling them.

In this social environment, the images – and existence – of art are immediately overtaken by their context. Commitment is passé, *high purpose naïve. The market-led demand for style and novelty has indeed made them so. Various head-in-the-sand postures have taken the place of the clenched fist, the steady gaze. Manoeuvring elegantly in the interstices of life, these experiments have led predictably enough not to a series of self-transcendent moments but to a theory and practice of the insignificant; a politics of quiescence. However, feminists, black activists and socialists have, on the whole, a more optimistic relationship with meaning than that, too conscious of the way it has been systematically denied to them to acquiesce in the implication that meaning is a game with arbitrary rules played by equals.*

One less involuted and politically impoverished alternative has been the attempt to harness cultural practice to a party political agenda; energetic instances have materialised in the last five years, notably around the Labour Party in opposition (see Bibliography), the Socialist Workers' Party and the Communist Party. But there is somehow a tendency for the whole to appear less than the sum of its parts, for some potential to remain unrealised.

Without claiming to avoid the impact of Thatcherite recession on ideals and identity, feminism – or a feminist practice of cultural expression – has produced a different response: one that is certainly preferable to a total abdication of responsibility but open to artistic evolution in the sense of not being tied to a party line. It is arguably a sort of politically-skewed Romanticism. Feminists have been concerned with uncovering, or constructing, a notion of 'self' that was not privatised and ultimately trivial, that could speak purposively to and for others of its kind. In simultaneously allying themselves to the imagination and a vivid female iconography, and identifying themselves with the vastness of physical landscape and organic form, many feminists have found – or invented – a form of expression that manages to be genuinely collective. It also manages neither to deny nor to idolise self.

I asked the contributors in their questionnaires to name their source of inspiration. In their replies appeared the Goddess, the Sybilla, faeries and elfpeople, the wildcats, the Shekhinah, Africa and her diaspora. I don't want to imply an ideological unity which doesn't exist, but I think these personages and anthropomorphs have precisely that mythopoeic, collective quality in common. More introverted formulations – experiences associated with psychotropic drugs, for instance, or daemonic possession – were conspicuous by their absence. The search is not, apparently, for altered states of private consciousness, but, however indirectly, for altered relations with society.

In contrast with party political art, the whole often seems greater than the sum of its parts in this other disposition. It becomes hard to make a clear division between art, politics and everyday living: the question 'what for?' is answered in the activity. One fulfilment of this tendency or mood was in the art of the women at Greenham Common. Their work – in posters, leaflets, banners, chants; in the web-weaving, the fire dragon, the dance on the silos, the decoration of the perimeter fence with emblems of female sexuality – was almost completely transitory in terms of saleable artefact (there were some beautiful photo-postcards), but far-reaching in its emotional and social impact. It was instantaneous, interactive, collective, continual and non-consumable. It was playful rather than solemn; agitprop as well as mythopoeic. It could not be reproduced outside its context. This is a practice of art as regenerative and transformative; the artistic process and the political programme were the same thing. The material and the purpose were human life, of which women were now perceived – by a growing number of men as well as many women – as the primary guardians. The link between the meanings of creativity – creation of the world, creation of human life, creation of art and meaning – was re-established and re-experienced.

This tendency has passed its peak. Life in the Greenham camp is once more a matter of day-to-day survival as police and local authority tactics become increasingly brutal and militaristic; and the national media, losing interest, have several times consigned the camp to oblivion. But the images and direction of feminist art since then testify to its power as a model. Since it did not, like situationist art, degenerate into rampant sensationalist individualism, the problem it has given feminist artists now is both inspiring and intractable, being precisely the one to which Greenham art was in a sense the solution: how do we relate this model – whereby womanspace was actually located in the wilderness – to our urban and privatised lives, our male-defined, state-bounded, consumer-oriented society? Is it a question of bringing a flourishing wilderness inside the margins of the dominant but dying culture? Or is it that the true wilderness which is human society in its characteristic brutality needs to be domesticated by womanist cultivation? In either case, how are we to counteract the susceptibility of all such art to the tiresomely characteristic loss and invisibility of women's work?

The following article by Frankie Armstrong describes and explores one form of 'untutored' expression, an area we might call the fruitful wilderness. There are many similar projects in other media, in which the participants are called upon to trust aspects of their being not normally valued or visible. Such approaches often also depend on a view of women as the traditional and legitimate exponents of culture, and on the efficacy of cultural expression to heal, personally and collectively. Creativity in these terms touches on ritual and therapy, and draws its meaning from that relationship.

The Voice is the Muscle of the Soul

Frankie Armstrong

There is little that touches, stirs, excites or moves me like the human voice raised in melody. Especially the voice bare, unaccompanied by orchestra or band, piano or guitar. I do not necessarily expect you to share these feelings, but would like you to listen with me while I explain why it is so for me, and why it touches on areas of experience which go beyond what are usually considered the boundaries of 'singing'. This may turn into a plea for a widening of those boundaries and hence a realisation of the power and possibilities within the voice.

Having said this, I have to confess the impossibility of the task I've taken on. I'd need to be a poet to conjure up the voice by using words on paper. When I say that the voice can move me like little else, 'move' means literally that. The central nervous system resonates: my stomach turns, my spine chills, my eyes water. My feet dance, my mouth smiles or laughs spontaneously: some part of me literally moves. A lot of music does this to me – some classical, some jazz, occasional pieces of commercial pop (my prejudices are showing early!), and much ethnic or 'folk' music. I listen both to live performances and to a largeish collection of records and tapes. But for the last ten years, my greatest thrills have come from the sounds produced in voice workshops by so-called 'ordinary people'. Many of these participants, if asked, 'Can you sing?' would respond with one of a variety of anecdotes on the theme of 'My parents/teachers/friends have all said what a horrible/tuneless/loud/flat voice I've got.' And yet, given permission and a few helpful hints, these same people may well excite me both aesthetically and emotionally more than most of the 'professional' singers I hear. To explain why and how this can be will take us into realms touching on psychology, theology, physiology, history and sexual politics. 'Ah, at last,' you will say, 'some hint of what this has to do with women.' For me it is profoundly tied up with women, with the 'feminine' in its archetypal sense as well as the fact that it has overwhelmingly been women who have been the majority of workshop participants.

The use of the word 'feminine' is fraught with difficulties. I employ it here as a convenient, if not altogether satisfactory, shorthand to denote the ability to experience and express the emotional, intuitive and sensual qualities of existence. I do not see these attributes as being biologically determined, the property only of biological females. Historically, they have usually been attributed to women and denigrated as inferior in some way to so-called masculine qualities. But we do not have to accept men's location or evaluation of them.

Because my relationship with the voice calls upon so many ingredients, I find it hard to know where to begin. Perhaps I should start by telling you a little about voice workshops, how they came about and how they grew to become central to my life and learning at present.

In July 1975, in a scruffy upstairs pub-room, I ran my first voice workshop. I had been singing professionally for over ten years by then, though I had also been working as a social worker. What formal training I have had has been in social and group work; I have had none in voice. I based this first session on the work of a woman I had come to know and work with in the States, called Ethel Raim. Ethel taught Balkan singing and I had become as fascinated and enamoured of her 'warm-ups' as I was with the glorious Eastern European songs she taught. My starting-point for that first workshop, then as now, was Ethel's basic warm-up exercises. I sat in a circle of 20 or so people, mostly women (with a tape-recorder with Ethel on it, in case I dried up), and simply called. Everyone called back. I twiddled the calls about a bit and everyone sang back. We laughed, made daft sounds to relax the throat, yippied, yodelled, and generally had a good time. 'Can we do the same next week?' The room was free and available, so the following Thursday there we were again. These Thursday evening sessions were still happening three years later. They were free and immense fun. By 1977, friends and I had run a weekend to 'train' and encourage others to run workshops themselves. Some of the attenders at that weekend are still running workshops today.

Requests came in for me to lead them at folk festivals, women's conferences, youth clubs, women's centres, occupational and psychotherapy courses, psychiatric day centres, and theatres and dance companies. The number and size of the workshops grew. I learnt on the job, using what worked best, incorporating all the wonderful creative suggestions that participants made and, far from finding them boring as the years went by, I found them more stimulating and challenging. The voice has turned into a great teacher.

So what do these workshops do? Obviously, they do different things for different people and for some they do nothing at all. After a workshop, people often say things like, 'I have such a sense of well-being,' 'I somehow feel connected up,' 'I feel so powerful,' 'I had no idea I could make such a loud noise!' People variously laugh and cry and – importantly to me – produce melodic sequences and sounds of great beauty, skill and musicality. There inside each one of us is this voice of power, depth, expressiveness, if we can trust, open up and let it out. In so-called 'primitive' communities, people don't need a special place and permission to do this; it is as natural as breathing. But somehow most of us have been robbed of our voices. So many of us take on board negative judgements about our voices as very small children. Young girls, especially, find themselves admonished for being 'too loud', 'too shrill', 'not ladylike', and as teenagers our lusty playground voices are often squeezed into being sweet sopranos and, if we can't or won't go along with this, we are deemed not to have 'good' voices. But the negation robs us of much more than just the opportunity to sing in the choir. As one woman said to me, 'When I was told at the age of seven that I had a horrible voice, I didn't feel it just as a criticism of my voice. My voice was part of me, so in some way I must be horrible too.' Not only this but so many feel they must be unmusical because they fail to reproduce notes or scales from a piano. How is a five or ten year old who hasn't got a piano at home to translate its tonal quality into the sounds inside her head? These are only two examples among many of how our self-confidence and our musicality have been reduced and stolen from us. I don't want here to go into my ideas as to how this happened historically, I want to explore more of the sexual- and psycho-politics of the voice.

I have given you a brief outline of the how and why of the voice workshops. Now I'd like to explore a few of my current ideas and feelings. I said that the voice has been a great teacher. This has only been dawning on me recently. I have realised that all the words, images, symbols and metaphors that I use in the workshops hold for life as a whole. If I can reflect, contain and hold together the apparent contradictions and paradoxes, I may find a new balance inside myself. A balance of the 'feminine' and 'masculine', the inner and outer, the soul and spirit. The capacity to feel fully rooted in my own body and also to feel in communion with others in a way that can transcend the usual ego boundaries. Yet I know that I am reluctant to put these experiences into words, especially as many of you will never have been to a workshop. The words can sound pretentious and one of my main commitments is to demystifying the voice and to making workshops accessible to everyone. I keep advertisements for them as simple as I can: 'These workshops are for singers and non-singers alike. In fact, their whole aim is to do away with this distinction. They are based on the open-throated type of singing found in all cultures that sing out of doors . . .' I make no promises. I cannot predict what freeing and exploring the voice will do for you. I try to make the process enjoyable and unthreatening, so that each participant can experience as fully as she is able. The descriptions, the meaning, the interpretations are up to her. But, having agreed to write this chapter words are what I have to use, although I often feel that the fewer words we use in relation to such experiences, the better. So I'm only talking for myself, not wishing to impose my experience, or imply that this is what the voice and/or voice workshops should do for anyone else. I therefore ask the reader to be aware that these words are not the experience itself, but just an inadequate attempt to capture and communicate it. Now, back to the voice as teacher!

How can it be that something as simple as opening one's mouth and letting unexpurgated sound out can lead to these global ponderings? I'd like you to think of the various ways we make contact with the world. Seeing, hearing, smelling, tasting and touching. And in addition to these five senses which bring the world *into* us in various ways, is the voice, which comes from inside us and reaches *out* into the space outside. Sound is the one thing which comes from within us and makes a bridge to the outside. It can reach much further than our physical touch. I'd hazard a guess that learning to distinguish our own sounds *as* our own is a crucial part of separating ourselves from the parent figure. It is also by calling and crying that the baby brings carers who are out of her sight or out of the room. The power to summon people up, or the fear and isolation of not being heard or responded to, must be some of the most potent early experiences. Watch and listen to babies and children: their voices are truly 'full-bodied' in the sense that their whole bodies are involved in the production of the sound much more clearly than is the case with most western adults. Their movements, feelings and vocal expression are all of a piece, are organic in a way that we rarely recapture later in life. We tend to think of the baby's display as 'primitive', in the same way as we refer to cultures who still have no separation between art, religion, magic, and social and cultural structures. Gods and Goddesses often literally make themselves heard through the mouths of shamans, and spirits sound through those they possess. In workshops, people often say, 'It didn't feel as if it was me making that sound, it seemed to come through me' or 'The sound seemed to come from somewhere else.' 'Primitive' and 'primordial' are words I'm happy to use and hear used.

There are still tribal and rural communities where songs and ritual chants connected with the spirits are common, but the same vocal styles and mechanisms can also be found wherever people have not been 'educated' out of their more earthy, raw sounds by the influence of Western classical vocal technique or by homogenised commercial technology. The waulking songs and Gaelic psalms from the Hebrides are local examples of this. The sound produced by village women in Eastern Europe, particularly in Bulgaria, has a power and edge to make your hair stand on end. One of the greatest compliments my singing has ever received was from a friend who described it as 'scary', with a smile of delight on his face.

Why have we for the most part lost this power and edge to our adult voices? I have no definitive answer to this. I'll simply throw out a few thoughts on why certain sounds, particularly from women, have been discouraged and others encouraged. To do this, I need to talk a little about physiology. To produce this strong sinewy tone the sound really has to be thought of as originating from deep inside (those who use Eastern descriptions of how the body works would say from the *Kundalini chakra*). The throat needs to be wide open and the diaphragm firm. The sound is not produced *with* the throat, but rather *through* the throat. To do this you have to feel solid, rooted, grounded. My favourite description of this was from a Chilean giving a talk on Chilean folk music:

'Even when reaching up into the heavens, the folkloric voice always keeps its roots in the earth.' To create sound and song this way is to create a sense of power and energy. It did not surprise me to hear on the news recently, during the reprisals for the black rebellions in South Africa, that whistling and singing in the cells were punishable offences. They are a people finding their voice: it is suppressed in the literal and metaphorical sense by those who think they are bound to lose by the others' gain.

Let me now take you back to somewhere that may seem totally unconnected with South African jails and of course is, in many profound ways. Think of the sounds you were allowed to make in your school choir. High and sweet for the most part, I would guess. Now I have nothing against good girls' and women's choirs; I have nothing against good sopranos, but that is only *one* way of using the voice, one that came about very recently in historical terms and one that, ironically, came about through imitating men. The high parts in early European church and court music were sung by boys and *castrati*, and so, when women became acceptable in choirs, courts and opera houses, they were trained to pitch their voices unnaturally high to imitate the boys and *castrati*. Then, somehow, this fact was forgotten and we are persuaded that this is how we naturally *should* sing. What irony! I was recently told a story from another culture which parallels the process of 300 years in Western Europe – in a matter of 20 years or so in India. Apparently, that high, nasal vocal style that we have become accustomed to from Indian women singers, particularly from film music, came about with the rise of the film industry. Before this, women traditionally sang with a fuller, lower sound. It is the romantic heroine of myriad boy-meets-girl films that has made for that high whine. It's axiomatic that, with few exceptions, those who wrote the music, set the pitches, decided who was to take what part, taught voice in musical academies, and directly or indirectly set the criteria for what was good and correct, were men.

Another example from the present day: a friend tells me that in her school choir those who 'could sing' were allotted the soprano parts and those who 'couldn't' were left to be altos!

My guess is that what is deemed 'scary' by my aware and sympathetic man friend, is experienced as threatening by many men. Furthermore, I surmise that their reaction has to do with how in touch they are with the 'feminine' aspects of themselves. The less they can acknowledge and accept these aspects, the more threatened they may be by that primordial sound rooted in the dark earth. Of course, men can make this sound too, and often do. It would also be naïve to postulate that wherever women use their voices in this way they are liberated. This is clearly not the case, but I would imagine that where women sing together while working, or for ritual purposes, some part of their identity as women is left more intact and some individual and collective strength is still felt to be 'theirs'.

Turning to the commercial music of Europe and North America, what strikes me is that where women have kept their powerful, raunchy voices, the music business has used certain strategies to limit the effect. The most obvious area in which white women singers have 'taken back their voices' has been in country music. Listening to often immensely gutsy voices, it's sometimes difficult to remember that their owners are most likely wearing flounced dresses, have tiny waists, big busts, and ribbons in their hair. Neutralised. Black singers have mounted a more spirited resistance, but there too the remorseless male pressures of the commercial machine can be seen at work.

What this means is that, as young women growing up in our culture, we have a limited number of models handed to us. Of course this has always been true, and perhaps in purely quantitative terms we now have more than we would have had in the past. But my contention is that, consciously or unconsciously, most of those readily available to us through the media are in part muzzled. They do not encourage us to find the voice from the deepest part of ourselves, the voice that must have been used throughout millenia for calling up and on the spirits and goddesses, the voice that howled at funerals, shrieked at births, chanted at rituals and initiations. The sound, the singing, can be strong and gentle, strong and savage, strong and joyous, strong and despairing. It can be of exquisite beauty and subtlety. But strong.

Not all of us were born to be singers. The great singer of whatever style has gifts to do with imagination, nuance of musical and verbal phrase, ability to communicate story or feeling, to take people on a journey. These are not gifts given to everyone, nor would everyone want them. I do, however, believe that we were all born to *sing,* to express our full humanity by using the amazing instrument we all carry inside us. It can gather up and make containable all of human life. Before consumerism gave us desires for the durable, singing must have been one of the things that made life worthwhile and, in periods of hardship, bearable. The threats that face us now, at least in the west, do not come from failed crops, epidemics or marauding enemies, but if our 'primitive' ancestors kept their spirits up by song and dance, we may need this even more. In those days it wasn't the whole planet that was under threat. Our world is out of balance, we as part of it are out of balance. The only place we can start to counter this imbalance is inside ourselves and from that centre to act in the world.

This brings me back full circle. Using the voice is obviously not the only way to work on this 'inner marriage'. There are many paths, but singing is free and available to everyone if we can repossess it. At its best, it gives us power, beauty, a vehicle for individual expression and collective communion. Through us it goes from earth to sky, relates soul to spirit, brings back the repressed feminine. But only if we let it through, if we open up and let it out. This may feel risky at times, but in my experience the risk is worth it.

Calling, keening, chanting "Old and strong, she goes on and on and on, you can't kill the spirit", outside the U.S. base which had become a symbol of intimate and global destructiveness, was thrilling, revolutionising.

Juxtaposing the horrific and the lovely or the intensely vulnerable was part of the iconography of Greenham; not only in order to jar people's perceptions out of the complacency encouraged by a government committed to a nuclear defence policy, but to go beyond polarities and pose the idea of a reconciliation of opposites. The appeal to a sense of responsibility – for oneself, society and the entire planet – retains a robustness among 'green' feminists not yet weakened by post-modern sensibilities. The main difficulty is with that recurrent notion of 'feminine' or 'female'; how do we carry on both kinds of work, the preservative and the deconstructive, simultaneously? For it seems to me we must.

And in this knot lies a clue, perhaps, to one of the central meanings of this book. The focus of feminist concern is a double one: the intimate and the public agendas are not separable. Even though some contributors' purposes are explicitly political, their explication of them is conjugated in the personal voice. And those who seem to be articulating the most private fears and desires do this in the justified expectation that these are communicable and highly consequential. No single contribution makes total sense by itself; it shouldn't be expected to do so.

Working in groups, sharing dances and diaries, arms round each other or in pain and anger, plumbing depths of difference, has extended consciousness-raising into the making of art. (I had hoped to include at least one account of a group process, but due to circumstances rather than design, this wasn't possible.) To break through into something richer and truer, to create together our mothers of invention, our freed imaginations, this is the light glimpsed by each contributor.

Coming full circle now, going back to the beginning. Finding the fear and silence. The moment of birth and death. The multiple self, fragmented, visionary. Losing control, risking dissolution of sense and style in order to let in something new, glimpsing chaos and disaster. Finding the limits of choice. Hoping for transition and a regaining of order. Anticipating the loss that comes with each creative act achieved.

The making of art is supposedly and traditionally a hedge against the oblivion of death, a thrust towards immortality. What is the role for, indeed the meaning of, any art if human existence now seems provisional, posterity a useless word? What should we be composing – consolation, polemic, lament? What is the significance of individual creativity in this apparently unprecedented context? Is it possible genuinely to express anything other than selfish meanings about survival?

I went looking for connections, anything to connect me, us, indissolubly, with a universe that might outlast us; found them, when I'd stopped looking, in loving and in being loved. But the erotic is a focus of inauthenticity for women, trapping and domesticating their energy, preventing them from exercising what freedom they do have; doing them violence. It betrays us into losing, in a few seconds, the boundaries we had struggled long and hard to establish. It has become a danger-zone in art, full of abysses, dividing women into censors or libertarians, often against their own judgement and certainly in defiance of anything that can move us on. Physical love is what connects my woman's body and heart with the atom and the cosmos; love and death embrace each other and hold me whole between them; but love is just another word, to be used of ice-cream and automobiles. And death is in the air we breathe.

In Praise of Death

Lesley Saunders

Dear friend,

Once again the blank page. What did I want to tell you?

My hands, pressing the keys, are wrinkled; their nails are split and ridged, knuckles somewhat enlarged and stiff. Outside it is spring again, hailstorms and thunder; the sky is multi-coloured – sepia, turquoise, copper, blond – restless and huge as thought. The garden needs weeding. Today I have not got dressed nor done the washing up. Dust gathers like thistledown on all my surfaces. I am feeling old. Not old as the hills, old as Methuselah, just old like stale buns or flat beer. Chemical changes, gases leaking, something breaking down. I can taste it, almost.

Out of this I have set myself to write to you because, you scold, my unexplained silence has disappointed you. Something out of nothing, it will have to be.

1.

An hour or two go by, unrecorded by clock's tick, by conversation or itinerary, by conclusion of task or consummation of pleasure; only the changing sky and a straying narrative, of which these words are both purpose and product, have moved things on. Are you still with me?

It occurs to me – now I'm in an experimental mood – that I might spend the whole of the rest of my life sitting in contemplation and diminishing surprise here at this table with the drooping daffodils and half-empty cereal boxes and the typewriter and blue plastic tablecloth. I suppose I might find a way of continuing to procure food and shelter without compromising too many ideals, and of eventually inhabiting, not this familiar mild anxiety, but a state (often, as you know, recommended by sages in times of trouble) of single-minded repose. Being would be enough. The distracting dilemmas of consciousness would wither like hot-house blooms. But I'd still, one day, die. Wondering, not for the first time, how to justify having taken up space and other scarce resources in a haggard world.

So much for private nirvana. I stick with the anxiety. Pulling out tufts of moulting certainties over the years, I see I have left myself with few distinguishing features. The project of creating character, a recognisable self with which to engage the world, finds me wanting.

When we were girls, 14 or 15, we used to sit about on the radiators at school and make each other shriek with our notions of what sex would be like. It was a major feat of guess-work but the one thing we were sure of was that it would happen and then we'd be women. How would such a transfiguration come to pass? A boy's penis in your vagina, that's how. Delicious? Horrible? I don't think I felt capable of deciding – the idea was simultaneously bizarre and quite unquestionable. Having sex would change me into someone else so the me I was then literally couldn't imagine it. But I kept trying to.

Now I'm obsessed with death. Sex and death. You'd think I'd see them coming, so to speak, get equipped with some response. I try to think about dying. Terror, fascination – I weep, get angry. Then a full stop, can't get any further. I seemed to have been living up to now not despite death, in death's teeth, but as if death (my real inevitable death) either didn't exist or didn't matter. I'm treading on eggshells. Death is the only certainty, the only possibility that doesn't shrink. Do you understand? No, not quite. *Mea culpa,* my neurosis.

Last summer I wrote, 'Yesterday we went to a concert in the stadium, packed in on narrow trestles to hear Stephane Grapelli. I knew my father would have loved it. And suddenly I was struck down by the little tunes and the irreducible pain of *would have*. Why is he not here now? Life is shockingly short. What a multitude of sweetnesses, horrors, pains, boredoms, resentments, indiscriminately crammed like knick-knacks into a tiny room. And it's all we have – an effervescence, a sparkle on the water. Here and gone.' I know – you've heard it all before, so have I, but I'm no nearer understanding. Doesn't my real inevitable death make a mockery of my life? My lover has grown a beard again; this time there's white in it.

I slipped and fell on the path a week ago and still feel the shock waves rattling my bones. Small things, small things. My breasts spill on the bed like empty purses. What have I spent myself on? Is it good, is it useful? How should I tell? Half my life. Half-life.

I started writing this yesterday, now it is tomorrow. I, like you, go on as if there was a purpose, a hidden reality. The interlocking details of a particular life, not to mention what one reads with terror and fascination in the newspapers, make it look as if there must be a significance here somewhere. One thing leads to another so plausibly. But what is the purpose, what is the unifying moment, of it all? Well, well. Please be patient, I'm sure I can get somewhere. Let's find a beginning.

2.

Once upon a time it was morning. On the horizon of the middle-distant hills glimmering with a foxy light the sun was at that moment treading. As it slowly rose the sun became obscured, black. A shepherd, busy with a lamb, was the first to notice. Getting to her feet in the bracken she held the raw-looking lamb in one hand, smearing her eyes with the heel of her other. Bending quickly, she wiped the shreds of caul from the animal's hind-quarters and gave him back to the weary dam. Then the shepherd ran in the uncertain light down the steep track, in the direction of the village.

I'm writing this when I could be spring-cleaning. Spring was late this year, we were clearing snow on All Fools' day and many lambs were lost. Freak hailstorms hammered leaf-buds from the trees. The shepherd's eyes were watering and her face brilliant by the time she reached the first house in the village. She rapped on the back door; lights were on upstairs. Next she heard the bolt being drawn back and a voice saying, 'Who is it?'

The street was soon roused; the early shift-workers for the textile factory were the first out, some in parkas pushing bikes, some with sleepy children in their arms to take to a childminder, others cupping hands round fags, drawing deep. Their curiosity was bleak to begin with – there were a few comments about the bloody climate and didn't the scientists predict another ice age; someone suggested it was a government tactic to divert attention from the unemployment figures, but no one laughed. They begin to drift up the road towards the churchyard, the highest point in the village. The clock is striking seven. In the kitchen of the school caretaker's house the radio is on, softly so as not to waken the elderly man sleeping on a put-u-up in the dining room. *'The government will be issuing hourly bulletins about this latest phenomenon. In the meanwhile, there is absolutely no cause for alarm, say senior officials at the Department of the Environment.'* No one is listening. My daughter, ignored, has fallen asleep on a pile of cushions, thumb in mouth. She whimpers and snores.

The old man's daughter comes into the kitchen, waits for the kettle, pours boiling water into a brown teapot. She pulls her dressing gown round her and rocks from one bare foot to the other. She can feel her body losing the night's warmth, the last dream escaping on a trail of vivid colour. A smell of sex rises from inside the dressing gown; she takes a cup of tea to the bathroom with her, gulps it while washing. Two more cups of tea are poured for the old man and the one upstairs, whose face she had guided between her thighs in the night, whose mouth she had fastened on her nipples to draw on them till they were as long as a nanny goat's. Pulling the heavy curtains – he must have total darkness for sleep – she sees the strange light of dawn. There's mist on the windows. 'Hey, wake up. Tea's there.' She goes next to wake her daughter, brushing the hair from the damp cheeks, getting pleasure from touching this flesh of her flesh. I drink another cup of tea, not really tasting it. I am cold sitting here writing. The light is strange – a coming storm? *'We are advising people not to spend prolonged periods out of doors without some protective clothing, such as thick coats, hats and sunglasses. The government stresses that this is merely a precautionary measure. There is no reason to contemplate further action at this stage. No ill-effects attributable to the secondary atmospheric changes have been reported. Government scientists are working on the theory that fall-out will be minimal and in any case be diverted away from the British Isles by climatic shifts. There is still no indication of the causes of the catastrophe. However, in Parliament today views were being advanced that some change in the pathway of US intelligence satellites has been urgently authorised. No reaction from Moscow has been received.'*

The next day's newspapers carried reports that flocks of birds were being found dead along the beaches. A week later, leaf-buds on exposed trees shrivelled; the shepherd buried six lambs. Some of the villagers formed a protest group; the caretaker's wife ran from door to door, shouting for people to come and join them; they are lining up along the road to the factory. The air is still; no birds sing. Half a dozen uniformed policemen appear from a side road. I am frightened. I feel I am doing the wrong thing. I am frightened for my children – what shall I tell them? What words come? 'They have taught us to be afraid, to live every day with fear of death in our throats; and then to despise our own fear'? 'Imagine a world where the only living things are blind white spiders on the floors of caves and snakes that cry in the dark'? 'They try to make us believe our enemies live elsewhere, with other names, other tongues; they try to set us against each other, and too often they succeed'? The school has been temporarily closed down; the caretaker spends the days polishing the wood-block floors, washing the walls, so as to have the building spick for the returning children. No date has been given for re-opening. Most children are being kept indoors. They look pale, serious. I do not know how to end this. Shall I start from the beginning again?

3.

Once upon a time it was morning. On the horizon of the middle-distant hills glimmering with a foxy light the sun was at that moment treading. As it slowly rose, the sun became obscured, black. A shepherd, busy with a lamb, was the first to notice. Getting to her feet in the bracken she held the raw-looking lamb in one hand, smearing her eyes with the heel of her other. Bending quickly, she wiped the shreds of caul from the animal's hind-quarters and gave him back to the weary dam. Then the shepherd ran in the uncertain light down the steep track, in the direction of the village. Spring was late this year, they were clearing snow on All Fools' Day and many lambs were lost. Freak hailstorms hammered leaf-buds from the trees. The shepherd's eyes were watering and her face brilliant by the time she reached the first house in the village. She rapped on the back door; lights were already lit and she heard the bolt being drawn back. 'Who is it?'

The village was soon roused. The nuns were the first out, tucking up their skirts after the saying of lauds and seizing mattocks or shovels. Then the fields began to fill with people hurrying up to the priory. The bell strikes seven. Two postulants grip hands for comfort, not looking at each other. The light is changing every minute. The abbess spreads her hands on the table. 'It may indeed, as I think you fear, be God's judgement upon us, not indeed for individual transgressions – those He will judge severally and on their respective gravity – but for our wholly and irremediably flawed condition. St John the Divine has poetically (but piously, of course) explicated what we may expect. We should then beseech Him for the blessed kiss of His compassion as well as the necessary bruise of His judgement. On the other hand, as your own devotions, far more learned than mine, will have already assured you, it may be a sign to us who perceive primarily through the gross and precarious senses rather than in the grace of a refined and stable spirit that through God's infinite capacity for redemption of matter even the most majestic of the celestial bodies, the eye and soul of the universe, can sustain this physical mortification while retaining, still uncorrupted, its original substance. Permit me to venture that we may derive great consolation for our troubled minds and guilty hearts from such a revelation of His invincible – and inscrutable – charity.' The abbess smiled at the men facing her, though her gaze was neutral. They did not reply but rose together and gave her the curtest of bows in acknowledgement; the interview was mutually ended. She took a large book from the pile of liturgical volumes on her desk and followed the men into the field beyond the priory wall. It was land which, as a result of a boundary demarcation energetically and astutely contested by the abbess, had passed over to the priory for cultivation in perpetuity; though this morning's quota of turf lay unbreached, whitened by frost.

After compline and quite against conventual regulations, the two young women lay on a single pallet, on their backs, hands linked. The younger said, 'Isn't this a sin? We shall be punished, don't you think?' No reply. So she lay still, thinking she had offended. Then the elder one said, 'We live with images of terrible portent, we are marked out for judgement and putrefaction simply because we exist, are human. Skulls stare at us from the roof, the flames of hell threaten to lick our bare feet. We live with the fear of pestilence, corruption of the body and desecration of the soul. We know we as women constitute a threat to men's salvation because of our voluptuous bodies and our weakness of mind; we may stand accused of witchcraft tomorrow. No doubt there are people who at the minute believe our personal wickedness is responsible for the present darkening of the sun's eye. How can what we are doing make that any worse?' Her voice was angry. 'I came here because I'd seen hundreds of women and men burnt, blinded, maimed. I wanted some peace, some kind of explanation for what I'd seen. When the pestilence came to our town, men with shovels and pickaxes battered the doors of Jewish houses, murdered entire families because the Jews, they said, had poisoned our wells. Two years ago, the earthquake in Rome killed hundreds of people, and the magistrates ordered the killing of scores of others, mainly foreigners and beggars, for bringing the wrath of God on a holy city. But it is no better here. We know that whenever and however death comes to us, the salvation of our souls can be granted only through the painful purging of our inherited sins. They teach us to be afraid; but tell us there is no need for fear: God loves us. The end of the world is promised, the Antichrist will triumph here on earth – but the priests and magistrates alike tell us it must happen like this, it is God's will. It is not for us to question, to ask why!'

Her companion put her hand over the speaker's mouth. 'Do not talk so loud. You scare me. I try not to think of the demons lying in wait in the dark for my weak soul. I am so frightened – my mind cannot make sense of what you are saying.' They lay in silence for some time, till the livid sky grew dim. Then they turned and touched each other's bodies with passion, trying to stifle their voices, wiping their tears on the mattress. Salvation is promised to them through terror. One could go mad dreaming of it. The elder fell ill and died that summer; the younger was burnt as a heretic and a witch ten years later. She left behind a daughter. Eventually someone noticed that the sun was looking brighter; but that was many years afterwards and memories were unreliable. Wars, plague and economic collapse had stolen people's children and trust, robbed them of their livelihood and their ability to make sense of the world. Their souls, when they looked, did not seem to belong to them. The sun moved; the earth moved also, and nothing was ever the same. The daughter lived on into her old age; she understood and did not understand the things that had happened; she did not know with certainty what to tell her children and so without words she held them close in her withered arms as her breath and all that was familiar to her fled out through the soles of her feet.

4.

Hell-fire and nuclear catastrophe are visions of Apocalypse, tearing the heart and reason out of us, fashioned out of nightmare for our moral subjugation. But though one is myth, the other seems real and near. My friend, if your patience has stayed with me in this fragile making of something out of nothing (which I undertook more in consciousness of duty than in confidence of success), I have something – not small – to ask of you. Every departure into passion, even though I land safely, weeping with relief, brings me closer to the edge. One day I will not come back. One day I shall be irreversibly dispersed, my soft morsels will be furnishing the gut-lining of larvae, my brain will be turning to ooze and my skull will be grinning in the rubble like all skulls do. I do not seek your comfort for my private fantasies. The house of sex is the house of death and also of secrets. What I need from you now is a reminder that there are, must continue to be, images of death as personal and quirky as images of life and as numberless as the leaf-buds on trees or the words in stories – alternatives to the index of mass destruction dictated and controlled by an economy of concentration camps, nuclear fall-out shelters and war-heads. Please remind me that my knowledge of the fear of death (which is the knowledge cells have from their moment of birth) is what somehow makes passion or poetry even possible; as passion or poetry make death imaginable. Help me to resist their usurpation by terror.

With love,

The appearance of a book, we know, is in an odd way a lie. It suggests that what is contained between its covers is more remarkable than what has been left out. It suggests also a self-sufficiency, a dissociation from the insecure childminding arrangements, the private insanities, the lack of a desk or the departure of a lover, of each of its contributors. It implies, uniform print on uniform paper, that what you're reading now has had a smooth transition into being. No amount of authorial disclaimer can quite undo that impression.

No use protesting overmuch; this is one of the points at which writers choose to make a connection with the world as it is constituted. While we cannot in good faith deny the fact of the commodification of our creativity, we can try to strengthen the insights and practices which will assist other, imaginable futures to slip through a narrowing gap into actuality.

Epilogue

'The imagination imitates. It is the critical spirit that creates.'
Oscar Wilde, *Intentions,* 1891

It was integral to this project that the connections and divergences between the articles be somehow brought to the surface. Critique as well as celebration, analysis as well as shareable experience, were required. The outcome is neither tidy nor conclusive. But the main contours can be signposted.

Perhaps the most important of these is the question: should a communality between women be based on our oppression (which, to say the least, is structurally and historically complex, traceable by a maze of mechanisms to the prior facts of class and race as well as gender) or on our gender itself (upon examination no less complex a concept in definition and implication)? Are the politics of identity more, or less, effective in energising creative potential than the appeal to a kind of class struggle or than policies of resistance on specific issues? What happens when two identities, sexual and ethnic, claim equal cogency – collision or collusion?

The socio-biological argument for feminism is, crudely put, that women have something more, and more positive, than our oppressed history in common. But this skirts perilously near biological essentialism whose grave difficulty for feminists is that it upsets, intentionally or no, the principles on which social change can be predicated. Scrutinising that means being sceptical about the primacy of the organic idiom that seems to have become annexed to one kind of feminist discourse. In particular, the expropriation of the forces of 'Nature' to stand for political power – as in a matriarchalist narrative – does not, I think, guarantee the right denouement for either personal or social transformation. The discussion of both ethics and creativity needs to be delivered, at least temporarily, from Her embrace. There is a sleight of hand in that matching of human actions and non-human processes which relies for its effect on the close fit of 'Nature' with our emotional and aesthetic habits. Though of course contemplating a severance invites the corollary question: with what comparable symbolism can it be replaced?

Also up for interrogation is the belief that subjectivity and self-expression constitute the key virtues of the creative process. Lately, 'creativity' has been assimilated to the articulation of needs and rights, which has suppressed the currency of effort and excellence. Feminists have, in exemplary fashion, debunked the universalising pretensions of art which puts itself outside the apparatus of opportunity, wealth and power. 'Self-expression' has been a powerful antidote to cultural oppression. But it is clear that an overriding commitment to self-expression can be an impediment to 'honouring the subject'; can raise the distracting spectre of the 'true self'; can, in a higher gear, repudiate social as well as artistic responsibilities.

Feminists have brilliantly deconstructed the political theory (of left and right) which was based on a detached, bodiless rationalism; feminists also helped to expose bourgeois appeals to artistic decorum and self-evident truths as rationalisations of a power structure. Feminists proposed instead that experience – the constellation of first-hand, uncensored, fluid data – was a valid mode of acquiring knowledge, a defensible basis for instigating action and making art. They also, on the whole, protested an inescapable ethical dimension to that experience; and took that moral meaning, subversive of the dominant moralistic consensus, into their poetry, music, painting, theatre. Feminist art has been integral to modern feminist politics: it is hard to imagine the one without the other. Feminism is unique among political movements in this respect.

Precisely because feminists have continued to insist on the connection between creativity and morality, it is important that the feminist myths, metaphors and loyalties which are intended to supplant ubiquitous forms of oppression should not, under the pressure of recession, be melted down into mere emotional allegiance or into a 'reflex of power and desire' (in Terry Eagleton's words*), however sophisticated. Parsing society into (powerful) individuals – or alliances of individuals – belongs to the grammar of so-called liberalism, itself the language of anti-community. The rhetoric of personal liberation does not logically or historically precede the extension of democratic practice and accountability.

Yet there is no room for doubt but that feminism is still supplying some of the most energetic understandings, the most spirited expressions of art in a time of political recession. I was never tempted, in the course of compiling this book, to fold up its umbrella in favour of one – gaudier maybe but dubiously weather-proof – marked Post-Something or Other.

Lesley Saunders
Slough
November 1986

*In 'The Poetry of Radical Republicanism', *New Left review* no. 158.

Bibliographies

A. Contributors' Choice of Books

Diana Scott

Emily Brontë, the artist as a free woman, Stevie Davies, Carcanet, 1983.
Cassandra, a novel and four essays, Christa Wolf, Virago Press, 1984.
The Wild Girl, Michèle Roberts, Methuen, 1984.
Three Guineas, Virginia Woolf, Penguin Books, 1977.
Virgin Territory, Sara Maitland, Pavanne, 1984.

Alix Pirani

The White Hotel, D. M. Thomas, Penguin Books, 1981.
'You're too hot to handle', D. M. Thomas, in *Cosmopolitan*, March 1984.
Reclaim the Earth: an Eco-Feminist Anthology, Leonie Caldecott and Stephanie Leland, The Women's Press, 1983.
'The Metaphysical Poets' in *Selected Essays*, T. S. Eliot, Faber and Faber, 1932.
'Against Interpretation', Susan Sontag, in *Evergreen Review*, 1964.
The Wise Wound, Penelope Shuttle and Peter Redgrove, Paladin, 1986.
The Spirit of the Valley, Sukie Colegrave, Virago Press, 1979.
Your Body Speaks its Mind, Stanley Keleman, Simon and Schuster (USA), 1975.

Helen McNeil

Silences, Tillie Olsen, Virago Press, 1980.
How to Suppress Women's Writing, Joanna Russ, The Women's Press, 1984.

Monica Sjöö

Some books that have kept me from going crazy during many long nights of despair:
Silbury Treasure: The Goat Goddess Rediscovered, Michael Dawes, Thames and Hudson, 1976.
The Swan at Evening, Rosamund Lehmann, Virago Press, 1982.
Survival? Body, Mind and Death in the Light of Psychic Experience, David Lorimar, Routledge and Kegan Paul, 1984.
Return from Death: An Exploration of Near-Death Experience, Margot Grey, Routledge and Kegan Paul, 1985.
Life after Life and *Reflections on Life after Life,* Dr Raymond A. Moody, Bantam Books, 1975, 1979.
Seth Speaks and *The Seth Material,* Jane Roberts, Bantam Books, 1972.
The Tao of Physics, Fritjof Capra, Wildwood House, 1975.
PSI – Psychic Discoveries behind The Iron Curtain, Sheila Ostrander and Lynn Schroeder, Abacus, 1973.
Life in the World Unseen, Anthony Borgia, Psychic Press, 1984.
The *Don Juan* books, Carlos Castaneda, Penguin Books, 1970, 1973, 1974.
The Way of the Wyrd, Brian Bates, Century Publishing, 1983.
Shaman, the Wounded Healer and *Shamanic Voices,* Joan Halifax, Penguin Books, 1982, 1980.
Women of Wisdom, Tsultrim Allione, Routledge and Kegan Paul, 1984.
The Body Electric, Thelma Moss, Granada, 1981.

Catherine Itzin

These books have widened my vision:
Woman on the Edge of Time, Marge Piercy, The Women's Press, 1979, 1987.
Gyn/Ecology, Mary Daly, The Women's Press, 1979.
Of Woman Born: Motherhood as Experience and Institution, Adrienne Rich, Virago Press, 1977.

Man Made Language, Dale Spender, Routledge and Kegan Paul, 1980.
Women: Their Present Situation in the World, the Need for the Liberation of All Women, the Difficulties and the Opportunities, Detailed Proposals for Policies and Actions, Diane Balser, Rational Island Publishers, PO Box 2081, Main Office Station, Seattle, Washington 98111, USA, 1985.

Amrita Mohan

Three books I have always loved and always will:
The Story of my Experiments with Truth, Mahatma Gandhi, Phoenix House, 1949.
Discovery of India, Pandit Jawahar Lal Nehru, Asia Publishing House, 1961.
My Life with Martin Luther King Jr, Coretta King, Hodder & Stoughton, 1970.

Maud Sulter

The Black Unicorn: poems, Audre Lorde, Norton, 1978.
Movement in Black, Pat Parker, The Crossing Press, 1983.
The Color Purple, Alice Walker, The Women's Press, 1983.
Also these novels:
Native Son by Richard Wright; *Notes of a Native Son* by James Baldwin; *Uncle Tom's Cabin* by Harriet Beecher Stowe.

Nadine Otway

Che Guevara Speaks: Selected Speeches and Writings, George Lavan (ed), Pathfinder Press, 1968.
The Heart of the Matter, Graham Greene, Bodley Head, 1948.
Sex and Destiny: The Politics of Human Fertility, Germaine Greer, Pan Books, 1984.
The Black Jacobins: Toussaint l'Ouverture and the San Domingo Revolution, C. L. R. James, Allison and Busby, 1980.

Sandi Russell

The Story of Jazz, Marshall Stearns, Oxford Press (NY),1956.
Blues People, Leroi Jones (Amiri Baraka), William Morrow (NY), 1963.
Bessie, Chris Albertson, Stein and Day (NY), 1974.

Jazzwomen 1900 to the Present, Sally Placksin, Pluto Press, 1985.
Stormy Weather – the Music and Lives of a Century of Jazz Women, Linda Dahl, Pantheon Books (NY), 1984.
American Singers, Whitney Balliet, Oxford Press (NY), 1979.
Billie's Blues: A Survey of Billie Holiday's Career 1933–1959, John Chilton, Stein and Day (NY), 1975.
Lady Sings the Blues, Billie Holiday with William Duffy, Double-day and Co. (NY), 1956.
In Search of Our Mothers' Gardens: Womanist Prose, Alice Walker, The Women's Press, 1984.
Sister Outsider, Audre Lorde, The Crossing Press (NY), 1984.
Recordings – any of the following:
Bessie Smith; Billie Holiday; Ida Cox; Alberta Hunter; Ella Fitzgerald (preferably with big bands or trios); Sarah Vaughan; Mahalia Jackson; Lambert, Hendricks and Ross; Ivie Anderson; Nina Simone; Abbey Lincoln (Aminata Moseka); Betty Carter; Carmen McRae; Flora Purim; Adelaide Hall (with the Duke Ellington Orchestra).

Shirley Barrie

The Status of Women in the British Theatre, Sue Parrish and the Conference of Women Theatre Directors and Administrators, 1984.
Women and Theatre: Calling the Shots, Sue Todd (ed), Faber and Faber, 1984.

Lesley Saunders

Look Me In The Eye: Old Women, Aging and Ageism, Barbara Macdonald with Cynthia Rich, The Women's Press, 1984.
The White Bird, John Berger, Chatto and Windus, 1985.
And our faces, my heart, brief as photos, John Berger, Writers and Readers, 1984.

B. Books Referred to in the Editorial Passages

1.

Of Woman Born: Motherhood as Experience and Institution,

Adrienne Rich, Virago Press, 1977.
'The Theory and Function of the Duende', Federico Garcia Lorca, in *Selected Poems*, J. L. Gili (ed), Penguin Books, 1960.
Fantasia of the Unconscious, D. H. Lawrence, William Heinemann Ltd, 1923; Penguin Books, 1971.
Women Artists, Karen Petersen and J. J. Wilson, The Women's Press, 1979.
State Of The Art: Ideas and Images in the 1980s Channel 4 January 1987. Also a touring exhibition; and a book, published by Chatto and Windus, 1987.
The Dinner Party: A Symbol of Our Heritage, Judy Chicago, Anchor Press/Doubleday, 1979.
Women Writers and Poetic Identity, Margaret Homans, Princeton University Press, 1980.

2.

Women and Leisure, Margaret Talbot, The Sports Council and Social Science Research Council, 1979.
'Thatcherism and Women: After Seven Years', Elizabeth Wilson, in *The Socialist Register 1987*, Merlin Press, 1987.
Black and White Britain: The Third PSI Survey, Colin Brown, Policy Studies Institute, 1984.
Racial Discrimination: 17 Years after the Act, Colin Brown and Pat Gay, Policy Studies Institute, 1985.

3.

No I'm Not Afraid, Irina Ratushinskaya, Bloodaxe Books, 1986.
The Color Purple, Alice Walker, The Women's Press, 1983.
Voices from Arts for Labour, Nicki Jackowska (ed), Pluto Press, 1985.
Women's Work: Two Years in the Life of a Women Artists' Group, Women's Work Collective, Brixton Art Gallery, 1986.

C. Some Other Useful Books

Through the Flower: My Struggle as a Woman Artist, Judy Chicago, The Women's Press, 1982.
Women Artists: A Graphic Guide, Frances Borzello and Natacha

Ledwidge, Camden Press, 1986.

Feminist Aesthetics, Gisela Ecker (ed), The Women's Press, 1985.

The Heart of the Race, Beverley Bryan, Stella Dadzie and Suzanne Scafe (eds), Virago Press, 1985.

Black Women Writers, Mari Evans (ed), Pluto Press, 1985.

On Not Being Able To Paint, Marion Milner, Heinemann Educational Books Ltd, 1971.

Descent to the Goddess, Sylvia Brinton Pereira, Inner City Books (Canada), 1981.

The New Feminist Criticism, Elaine Showalter, Virago Press, 1986: contains an excellent bibliography.

Feminist Review 18: Cultural Politics, Winter 1984.

'The Woman Poet: Her Dilemma', Eavan Boland in *Stand* magazine, Winter 1986-7.

Editorial introductions in *The World Split Open: Women Poets 1552 – 1950,* Louise Bernikow (ed), The Women's Press, 1979.

Bread and Roses, Diana Scott (ed), Virago Press, 1982.

The Bloodaxe Book of Contemporary Women Poets, Jeni Couzyn (ed), Bloodaxe Books, 1985.

See also:

Facts About The Arts 2, John Myerscough, Policy Studies Institute, 1986.

The Shock of the New: Art and the Century of Change, Robert Hughes, BBC Publications, 1980.

The Hornsey Affair, Students and Staff of Hornsey College of Art, Penguin, 1969 (o/p).

The Country and the City, Raymond Williams, The Hogarth Press, 1985.

The Act of Creation, Arthur Koestler, Pan Books, 1975.

Notes on the Contributors

Liz Hood: I don't know what to tell you that might put me 'in a nutshell'. My life has been marked by extremes of aloneness, feeling of utter disconnection, and terror; yet, looking now, I see that the threads I have woven from my belly, though few, are strong. A bit like Genesis – 'and she saw that it was good'! My journey in some significant way has not yet begun. I have spent up until now trying, with long periods of wandering, to find the way into my 'magical' self, which I dare to presume is my birthright. I think my work in *this* life is perhaps to grow to want to choose life against a huge sense of opposition.

Ruth Noble: is involved in movement and performance art, including environmental dance/theatre work. She is a practising psychotherapist and healer working with groups and individuals.

Diana Scott: Forty in 1987, looking for who I am and what's true about me – mother of a daughter just ending childhood and beginning life as a young woman – feminist poet, humorist and seeker, too often now at a loss for words. Right now (Christmas 1986) I'm helping to run a neighbourhood community centre in Leeds . . . I'd really like life to be predictable, but relish the unexpected which turns up in my life. I love the lights and sounds of the rainy city at night, the sharp colours and scents of the northern countryside. I'm still looking for the poetic language that will take that variety of experience in. How can I tell the truth in a way that isn't simply the product of political perspectives, random points of view or the influence of other writers? How can I write in a way that serves and supports my readers, my friends?
   Publications:
Bread and Roses (ed), Virago Press, 1982.

'Six Poems for Hospital Workers' [mentioned in Diana's article] in *One Foot on the Mountain*, Lilian Mohin (ed), Onlywomen Press, 1979.
Yesterday Today Tomorrow, ILEA, 1985.

Alix Pirani: writes poetry, plays and fiction; also material relating to her work as a therapist and leader of workshops in creativity and women's spirituality. Her less documented assets are four admirable children, an irreverent sense of humour and a passion for colour, music and massage.
   Publications:
The Absent Father and the Crisis of Creativity, Routledge and Kegan Paul *(forthcoming)*.

Helen McNeil: I have been living in England for 14 years now, a fact I find startling. My daily life involves addressing the contradictions between (on the one hand) personal energy and a sense of life-long creative potential and (on the other hand) a deep, despairing involvement with a declining profession (academia, University of East Anglia) in a declining economy. I'm married to the sculptor Graham Ashton and I have two wonderful children, Liberty and Gabriel, from a previous marriage. Last year I wrote a book about Emily Dickinson. I only wish it had been longer. 'Of Bliss the Codes are few –' Dickinson wrote. But that language exists when we use our strength and speak it.
   Publications include:
Emily Dickinson, Virago Press, 1986.

Monica Sjöö: I was born in the north of Sweden in 1938 (the year the atom was split) but have lived most of my adult life in Bristol and Wales. Between 1965 and 1967 I lived in Stockholm again, working with the Vietnam anti-imperialist movement. Since 1969 I've been active in the present women's liberation movement, in grassroots campaigns like Women's Abortion and Contraception Campaign, Wages for Housework, Bristol Gay Women's Group and the Unsupported Mothers Group in Bristol Claimants' Union. Recently I've been involved in working with feminist artists in the UK and abroad, with the Matriarchy Network, Women for Life on Earth, Radical Pagans and the Fishguard CND.
   Publications:
Women are the real left – Wider We: towards an anarchist politics,

with Keith Motherson, Matriarchy Publications, 1978.
The Ancient Religion of the Great Cosmic Mother of All, with Barbara Mor, Rainbow Press, Norway, 1981; published by Harper and Row as *The Great Cosmic Mother*, 1987.
Spiral Journey, Stages of Initiation into Her Mysteries (in preparation).
WomanMagic – Celebrating the Goddess Within Us (an exhibition); also numerous postcards and articles.

Joan Blaney: I was born Joan Marie Smith in Kingston, Jamaica, on 16 May 1957. My father died when I was six years old and a year later I was 'sent for' by my mother to join her in England with her husband and their four children. I found it difficult to adjust for I was a child in a strange land living in a house full of strangers. I missed my father and often cried myself to sleep. The happy memories of Jamaica and the hostile and oppressive attitudes I faced in England reinforced my independent spirit. At 16 I left home, a lot more ready than most black teenagers to face a hostile world. I survived and have my own family now, a wonderful and supportive husband and a beautiful daughter. I am a keen sportswoman with a strong interest in black art, the dance, drama and music of Africa. I take each day as it comes and refuse to allow prejudices within this society to affect my basic happiness with life.

Ange Grunsell: All my life I've written about everything I saw, did and felt; but until very recently I maintained a clear division between 'public' educational writing and 'private' personal writing. After two decades of frantic activity on various fronts, I am now – in my forty-first year – finding that writing is an increasingly urgent part of my life, and facing the challenge of change. I am the mother of two children, Leila 13 and Jonah 9. I've lived and worked in education, in and around Holloway in London since 1969 with my husband, apart from a year in the Sudan. I currently work in Oxfam's education department.

Catherine Itzin: Whether my creativity has been channelled into mothering (now two teenage young people), counselling, writing (non-fiction primarily) or research, women's liberation – including and especially my own – has been its motivating force. In the 1970s as drama critic for *Tribune*, editor of *Theatre Quarterly* and author of a book on alternative theatre (1), I have campaigned on issues of women and employment (2), the position of single parents (3), and education (4). In recent years I have chosen to work in the field of ageing. This has included a research project on elderly people for the NHS (5) and articles/chapters on ageism and sexism (6). Work in progress includes a PhD on race, gender, social class and ageing, and a book on ageism and sexism. As an Equal Opportunities consultant I do group work on issues of ageism, sexism, classism, racism and disability. I am 42.

Publications:
(1) *Stages in the Revolution,* Methuen, 1980.
(2) *Tax Law and Childcare: The Case for Reform,* with The National Council for One Parent Families, 1980.
(3) *Splitting Up,* Virago Press, 1980.
(4) *How to Choose a School,* Methuen, 1985.
(5) *Elderly People in the Community: Screening, Support and Services,* with Newham Health Authority, 1986.
(6) 'Media Images of Women: The Social Construction of Ageism and Sexism', in *Feminist Social Psychology,* S. Wilkinson (ed), Open University Press, 1980.

'Margaret Thatcher is my Sister: Counselling on Divisions Between Women', in *Women's Studies International Forum Vol.8 No.1, pp.73-83, 1985.*

'Ageism Awareness Training: A Model for Group Work', in *Dependency and Interdependency in Old Age,* Chris Phillipson, Miriam Bernard, Patricia Strang (eds), Croom Helm, 1986.

Amrita Mohan: I was born in India in 1939 and educated there (an MA in English and a bachelor's degree in teaching). I taught in a college for five years before coming to England. After I arrived, I worked in a factory and then the post office. Then I taught in the language centre attached to a first school in Slough; and am now teaching in the main school.

Publications:
Poems and articles in various Indian magazines, including appraisals of the dowry system and its impact on women.

Gabriela Müller: I was born, raised and miseducated in Mannheim, West Germany. I have long been working with visual media: painting, sculpture, film and video. I trained as an art therapist in 1980; I have done work for the Women's Therapy Centre and som⌐ community projects, mainly women's groups. I am working now iɪ a therapeutic community. I am committed to finding ways in which politics, art and therapy can be synthesised.

Anna Wilson: After some years working in expectation of the changing of the world, she has currently retired to American graduate school, an experiment in passive resistance. She remains a radical feminist and committed to the idea that writing may articulate possibilities for change.
   Publications:
Cactus, Onlywomen Press, 1980.
Altogether Elsewhere, Onlywomen Press, 1985.
'The Reach' and 'Movement of Pawns', in *The Reach and Other Stories,* Onlywomen Press, 1984.
Poems in *One Foot on the Mountain,* Onlywomen Press, 1979.

Maud Sulter: was born in Glasgow, Scotland, in 1960. She is a writer and a visual artist. Currently living in London, she works in/around blackwomen's creativity.
   Publications:
As A Blackwoman, Akira Press, 1985.

Nadine Otway: I was born in British-ruled Jamaica and left when I was 18 to be married and live in St Lucia. My father-in-law was deputy Prime Minister of the West Indies Federation and this further stimulated my interest in politics – although it eventually disillusioned me totally as to what will be achieved by politicians in terms of improving the lot of the people they are supposed to serve. I returned to Jamaica and saw the general election of 1972 bring in the socialist party of Michael Manley, with all the hopes for a better standard of living for the poor. I also witnessed the political violence orchestrated by right-wing thugs and the attempts at destabilisation by the CIA. I left Jamaica when I was expecting my fourth child and lived in Canada for five years, after which I was so bored by the bland Canadian lifestyle that I returned to St Lucia and worked for the Tourist Board. I met my second husband, an Englishman, there and in 1981 we all moved to England.
   Publications:
Short of a few thousand tourist brochures written in the usual over-the-top style, my only success has been a short story in the magazine *Damocles.* I am now preparing a collection of short stories to be called *Mary Ann Street.*

Sandi Russell: Born in Harlem, New York City, USA. Trained classically in voice. Now a jazz singer, journalist and writer residing in Durham, England. Left New York because I was choking on the 'Big Apple'. I am working on a series of short stories.

In preparation:
Black American Women Writers: A Graphic Guide, Camden Press.

Viv Quillin: was born in Derbyshire and moved to London at 17 to experience the delights of kids, housework and earning a living (mostly at the same time). She's produced five books so far and her work has been exhibited at The Everyman Gallery, The People's Gallery and travelling exhibitions in England and Europe. Her cartoons have cropped up in most of the women's mags, particularly a feminist frog called Lily Leaf who regularly appears in *Spare Rib;* there's also a newspaper strip in the *News on Sunday.* She runs occasional cartoon workshops and also produces children's illustrations and, recently, stories for kids. She aims to cure the human condition (particularly her own) and learn to spel propur.

Publications:
Taking the Lid off Kids, Pan Books, 1983.
The Pick Up Book, Blond and Briggs, 1984.
Women's Work, Elmtree Books, 1984.
When The Chips Are Down, Who Cooks The Fish? Elmtree Books, 1985.
The Opposite Sex, Grafton *(forthcoming).*

Shirley Barrie: I was born in a small town in south-western Ontario, Canada, and was very slow in figuring out what I wanted to do with my life. For someone who is drawn towards stability, I seem to be continually making changes. I started out as a teacher of English but left both the job and the country in order to spend a year in England. That year somehow turned into 14, during which time I started a theatre company, Wakefield Tricycle Company, with Ken Chubb (in which I fulfilled every possible function – except acting – at some point or other); decided to write plays (ten produced for theatre, two broadcast on radio), had two children and opened a theatre – the Tricycle in Kilburn, London. Then I gave up the hurly-burly and daily crises of running a theatre to concentrate on writing. In 1985 I sold up much, packed up little and returned to Canada with my family. Things haven't quite come full circle. I'm not teaching English. I'm still writing.

Stage Plays:
The Adventures of Supergranny and the Kid, 1978.
Bully For You, 1979.
One Jump Ahead, 1980.
Now you see it . . ., 1981.
Rising Dump, 1981.
Riders of the Sea, 1982.
Jack Sheppard's Back, 1982.
Shusha and the Story Snatcher, 1984.
Sawdust, 1984.
Topsy Turvy, 1985.
Work Play, 1985.
The Pear is Ripe, 1985.
Carrying the Calf, 1986.
The Challenge, 1986.
Radio Plays:
When Wings Have Roots (BBC Radio), 1979.
The Unofficial Guide (BBC Radio), 1986.
The Devil's Land (commissioned by CBC Radio).

Lisa Kopper: I was born in Chicago in 1950. I studied painting and sculpture at Carnegie Mellon University, Pittsburg. I came to England in 1970 and have been working here ever since. I had nine one-woman exhibitions before the age of 24, in the USA, Canada, Britain and Switzerland – since then I've stopped exhibiting! I illustrated my first book in 1979 and have had about 50 books published.
Publications include:
Jafta Family series with Hugh Lewin, Evans, 1981.
Arjuna Family series with Peter Bonnici, Evans, 1984.
Small World series with Leila Berg, Methuen, 1983.
Coming Home, with Ted Harriott, Gollancz, 1985.
Amber's Other Grandparents, with Peter Bonnici, Bodley Head, 1985.
An Elephant Came to Swim, with Hugh Lewin, Hamish Hamilton, 1985.
What's That? series, Franklin Watts, 1986.
Frankie Armstrong: I have been singing publicly since the mid-fifties but until recent years I've also plied my trade as a social worker. Songs of women's lives and experiences, old and new, became important to me in the late sixties and, as my repertoire

includes many old songs as well as contemporary ones, I'm hoping to capture some sense of my and women's history through the voice in these songs. In 1975 I began running voice workshops and my enthusiasm for song and sound grows with each workshop and each opportunity to encourage and hear all those amazing voices too often kept locked up inside. I now earn my living both singing and running workshops and spend about half the year touring abroad.

Publications and recordings:
My Song is My Own, with Kathy Henderson and Sandra Kerr, Pluto Press, 1979.
Lovely On The Water; Songs and Ballads; Out of Love, Hope and Suffering; And the Music Plays So Grand; My Song is My Own, with Alison McMorland; and numerous recordings with other artists.

Frankie performs in a wide range of venues, and for anti-nuclear and women's groups. For bookings contact 8 Abbeville Road, London SW4 9NJ.

Lesley Saunders: I was born in 1946. I have two children. I have been a teacher (infant, secondary, adult), a researcher (into anything from electronic typewriters in Saudi Arabia to women's participation in sport), an administrator, a poet, unemployed. I live in Slough; I write and perform with The Bloody Poets. I like chocolates and brandy and long hot baths; as an aid to inspiration, I find them best taken together.

Publications:
Motley; I prefer contemplating future publications to rereading previous ones. I am pleased to have had poems and fiction in various magazines and journals, including *Everywoman, Spare Rib, Women's Review, Writing Women;* also in the following anthologies:
One Foot on the Mountain, Onlywomen Press, 1979.
Why Children? The Women's Press, 1980.
Bread and Roses, Virago Press, 1982.

I have co-written these books:
Intercontinental Ballistic Poems, with Gabriel Chanan, Windsor Arts Centre, 1985.
Room to Write: an anthology of writing by unwaged women (ed), Slough Unemployed Centre and the WEA, 1985.